ENCYCLOPAEDIA OF INDIA, PAKISTAN AND BANGLADESH

ENCYCLOPAEDIA OF INDIA, PAKISTAN AND BANGLADESH

(In 9 Volumes)

(Volume 9)

OM GUPTA

ISHA

ISHA BOOKS

Delhi-110033

Encyclopaedia of India, Pakistan and Bangladesh
(In 9 Volumes)

ISBN : 81-8205-389-7 (Set)
ISBN : 81-8205-398-6 (Vol. 9)

Rs. 6300 (Set)

Published in 2006 in India by
Isha Books
D-43, Prithviraj Road,
Adarsh Nagar, Delhi - 110033
e-mail : ishabooks@hotmail.com

Laser Typesetting : Vinayak Printers, Delhi
Printed at : Salasar Imaging Systam, Delhi

Preface

According to Oxford dictionary Encyclopaedia is a book or aset of books that gives information on many subjects or many aspect of one subject. This encyclopaedia does that on India, Pakistan and Bangladesh. It is the first work of its kind. There have been anthologies on India but there is no compendium of information in an alphabetical order. Even Britannica could go as far as four-volume encyclopaedia on Indian history.

Encyclcpaedia is an extension of a dictionary. The latter gives you meanings of words while the former gives facts about people, places and events. No one can claim to compile all the facts and that of a sub-continent called India. But then it is the prerogative of the editor to pick up his entries that he considers would be useful to his reader. Generally we soon find our comfort levels in a language. And rarely consults a dictionary and lesser an encyclopaedia. But those who dare, find the experience worth it. It can be easily compared to a human body. In our daily life we tend to be our own quacks and medicate on the basis of common sense. If we refer to a doctor we come to know the actual cause of the symptom and get relieved on knowing the gravity of the situation or the absence of it. One would realize that encyclopaedia reveals the fundamentals of any situation, person or the event and we feel at home with that information.

A dictionary and an encyclopaedia can easily enlarge the process of learning even to an uninitiated person. It is truer in case of humanities. Popular myth about encyclopaedia is that it is meant to be referred to in a library only. The librarians, the world over keep encyclopaedia in such zealously guarded protection that the generally refrain from asking for it. Since the advent of internet in our life, the bulkiness of encyclopaedias has disappeared. That is why we have divided this enterprise in nine volumes. Encyclopaedias are generally global in its expanse. Even subject-related encyclopaedias give the global perspective.That is why country-specific encylopaedias have never been seriousy attempted. We hope that this effort will fill that volume. Traditionally encyclopaedias don't deal with factual data e.g. Indian exports, population figures, GDP. That is the job of annual reference books. They are also different from alamans in as much as that they don't give dated entries. That will become texts on history. Encyclopaedias need to be updated. A country is alive and kicking. People and events continue to play role in various aspects of life. Hence they need to be added. That is why either annual supplements or updation needs to be done in encyclopaedias. We would strive for that.

Regarding its contents only those entries have been included that continue to influence the life of a nation. There are historical figures who might have played a significant role in their times but if those deeds have no relevance to the present they have been excluded. Another example is literary awards. They always create controversies because their selection at times is subjective. Hence only universally accepted meritorious work has found place in these volumes. In this context a debatable point need to be stated. Who is more important book or the author. Conventionally work is an end product and only that is a measure of the author's importance but then a prolic writer might have produced a large body of creations. Hence to save space the author is entered with all his important work.That is also an international practice.

Lastly, why India, Pakistan and Bangladesh have been clubbed together. Before India's independence they were one nation. They share a common heritage and composite culture. Their post-independence history is different but 22their foundation is undivided. In order to appreciate the historical context better it is necessary to cross-refer and that was possible when they are juxtaposed.

Om Gupta

T

Tabaqat-i-Nasiri : Tabaqat-i-Nasiri is a medieval text by Minhaj-i-Siraj. It is an important source book for the reconstruction of the history of foundation of Muslim rule in Bengal. The history of the first fifty years of Muslim rule in Bengal is found only in this text.

Tabla : Tabla is one of the most famous instruments of India. It is said that drums appeared early as 6-7th century AD. Drums are seen in the Pushkaras depictions in the Ajanta sculptures. The most interesting part of Indian drum is the loading of the leather surfaces, the right face carries a permanent loading.

The tabla consists of two drums the 'bayan' played with the left hand and the 'dayan' played with the right hand. Bayan is made either of clay or copper while dayan is usually hollowed out of a block of wood. Both are covered with the skin fastened to leather hoops which are stretched over the body of the drum by means of leather braces. Cylindrical block of wood are wedged between the braces and the wall of the tabla. Wedges can be pushed up or down to lower or raise the pitch. The application of a mixture of flour and water to the left head of the dayan lowers the pitch and gives the dull bass sound. This plaster is always scraped off after use. In bayan, the plaster is mixed with iron fillings and it is applied once for all.

Tabla has a light and sweet sound. Therefore it is well suited for accompanying kheyal, thumri and other soft instruments like sitar and sarod. Dayan can be tuned accurately, but bayan has an infinite pitch. It can be tuned accurately to an octave lower than tabla. The drums are kept erect on the ground and played with the fingers. Sound is produced by striking the center with full hand or the tip of fingers and press the bass of the palm towards simultaneously sliding it over the drum head. Tabla has a highly developed technique of playing. This instrument is capable of producing almost all the patterns of rhythms that a musician can conceive of Artists such as Ustad Zakir Hussain have well known this instrument around the world.

Tablighi Jamaat : Tablighi Jamaat is a movement founded in the late 1920s by the great Deobandi Islamic scholar Muhammad Ilyas in the Mewat province of India. Tabligh in Arabic means "to deliver (the message)" and Tablighi Jamaat claims to revive this duty which they consider as a primary duty of Muslims. They usually limit their activities within Muslims itself and their main aim being to bring spiritual awakening to the world's Muslims.

Tabo : Tabo is a small town in the district of Lahaul and Spiti on the banks of the Spiti river in Himachal Pradesh, India. The town lies on the road between Reckong Peo and Kaja, the sub-divisional headquarters of Spiti. The town surrounds a Buddhist monastery which, according to legend, is said to be over a thousand years old. His Holiness the Dalai Lama has expressed his desire to retire to Tabo, since he maintains that the monastery at Tabo is one of the holiest.In 1996,HH the Dalai Lama conducted the Kaal chakra initiation ceremony in Tabo,which coincided with the millenium anniversary celebrations of the Tabo monastery.The ceremony was attended by thousands of Buddhists from across the world.

Tabu : Tabu was born in Hyderabad, Andhra Pradesh as Tabassum Hashmi on November 4, 1972. Largely considered one of the Indian film industry's best actresses working today, Tabu has won the coveted National Film Award for Best Actress two times - once for Maachis (1996) and most recently for Chandni Bar (2001). She has also won three statuettes in the Filmfare Critics Award for Best Performance category for Virasat (1997), Hu Tu Tu (1999), and Astitva (2000) respectively and in 1995 she was awarded with the Filmfare Sensational Debut Award

Despite a few exceptions, Tabu "Tabassum Hashmi" is known best for her willingness to play characters in artistic, low-budget films that go on to garner more critical appreciation than they do substantial box office figures.

Tadoba National Park : This park was set up in 1955 in Chandrpur district and is spread over an area of 116.55sq.km. The nearest town is Chandrapur which is 45km from the park and also serves as the rail head. The airport nearest to this park is Sonegaon, Nagpur 208km from the park. The park is covered with deciduous forests featuring teak around Tadoba lake. The fauna consists of leopard, leopard cat, pangolin, tiger, panther, sloth bear, gaur, sambar, cheetah, nilgai, chinkara, crocodile, Python and Bengal monitor lizard. A motorable road goes round the artificial Tadoba lake. It has few rest houses. The best months for visiting the park are November to June.

Taj Mahal : The Taj Mahal is a monument located in Agra in India, constructed between 1631 and 1653 by a workforce of more than twenty thousand. The Mughal Emperor Shah Jahan commissioned its construction as a mausoleum for his favorite wife, Arjumand Banu Begum, who was known as Mumtaz Mahal.

The Taj (as it is often called) is generally considered the finest example of Mughal architecture, a style that combines elements of Hindu and Islamic architectures. The Taj has achieved special note because of the romance of its inspiration. While the white domed marble mausoleum is the most familiar part of the monument, the Taj is actually a complex of elements.

Tajuddin Ahmad : Tajuddin Ahmad(1925 - November 3, 1975) Was a Bangladeshi lawyer, politician, and the first Prime Minister of Bangladesh. Tajuddin Ahmed was born in 1925 at village Dardaria in Kapasia thana of Gazipur District. He obtained Matriculation in 1942, I.A in 1948, and B.A (Hons) in Economics from Dhaka University in 1953. He obtained a law degree in 1964. He was the first Prime Minister of Bangladesh from April 11, 1971 until January 13, 1972. While Sheikh Mujibur Rahman was the charismatic leader of the Bengali movement, Ahmed was the thinker, the organizer, and the planner. He was Mujib's friend and comrade of arms for more than thirty years, his companion in politics and comrade in struggle until their relationship deteriorated after the liberation of Bangladesh.

On the night of March 25, 1971 the Pakistani Army attacked the civilian Bengalis in what was then East Pakistan. The leader of Awami League, Sheikh Mujibur Rahman, was arrested and taken to West Pakistan. The independence of Bangladesh was declared and the liberation war started. On April 17, in a mango orchard of Meherpur, the government of Bangladesh was sworn in with Sheikh Mujibur Rahman as the president, Nazrul Islam as the acting president in the absence of Sheikh Mujib and Tajuddin as its prime minister. The government kept functioning from Kolkata, India until Bangladesh became independent on December 16, 1971. In liberated Bangladesh, Tajuddin became the victim of Awami League's infighting and lost Mujib's trust, despite the fact that he led the country and the war in exile in Mujib's name. Shortly after Mujib was released from prison in January 1972, he forced Ahmad to resign as prime minister and appointed himself to that position. Sheikh Mujib was assassinated in a military coup in August 1975. Many of his main aides including Tajuddin and Nazrul Islam were arrested. On 3 November 1975, Tajuddin Ahmed and Nazrul Islam were assassinated in the prison with two other colleagues.

Taj-Ul-Masjid : Believed to be the largest mosque in the country, this pink towering mosque was commenced by Shah Jahan Begum, (1868-1901) Bhopal's eighth ruler. The work of the mosque was incomplete on her death and the construction could only resume in 1971 cause of lack of funds. The credit for Bhopal's postal system, railways and waterworks goes to this queen. The most striking features of the mosque are the impressive main hall with its inter-arched roof, the three white domes and the two white domed massive minarets. Its broad façade, spacious courtyard and smooth marble floors are impressive. A three-day 'Ijtima', a congregation of Muslims in India, held here annually, draws people from all over the country.

Taka : The Taka is the official currency of Bangladesh. Also, in neighboring India, speakers of Bengali and Assamese use the term taka to refer to the Indian Rupee. Taka is subdivided into 100 paise. The term taka is derived from Sanskrit 'Tanka' which was in ancient, and even in medieval times, a denomination of silver coin of four masha weight. The term Taka was widely used in different parts of India but, of course, with different meaning.

In north India, Taka was a copper coin equal to two paisa and in the south, it was an aggregate of four paisa or one anna. It was only in Bengal where Taka was taken as a sliver rupee. However, in all areas of India, Taka was used laxly for money in general. But Bengal was the stronghold of Taka.

Takerghat Hillocks : Takerghat Hillocks are small low hills in Bangladesh. The Takerghat Hillocks are situated in the Sunamganj district and have a maximum elevation of about 22m above mean sea level. They consist of Palaeogene sediments belonging to the Tura and Sylhet Limestone formations. Although the sandstone of the Tura forms four small hills in the Takerghat area the top of the formation lies buried under the Alluvium.

Alternating white, pink and brown, fine to coarse grained extensively crossbedded sandstones, light-grey, ash-grey shales, mudstones and streaks of carbonaceous matter make up the Tura Formation in that area. Outcrops of the Sylhet limestone in Bangladesh are confined to the narrow strip of the E-W aligned Dauki Fault zone along the southern spur of the Shillong Massif. The exposed limestone occurrences are located at the bank of the Dauki Nala, in the Takerghat-Lalghat-Bhangerghat area and near Bagali Bazar, all in the Sylhet district.

Takht Bhai : Takht Bhai (or Takht-i-Bahai or Takht-i-Bahi) is a site of historical importance in the Mardan District of the North-West Frontier Province of Pakistan. It contains the remains of a famous Buddhist monastery and is listed as a World Heritage Site. Takht means "throne" and bhai means "water". The Takht Bhai was a Buddhist place in ancient time. It was called Takht Bhai because the Buddhist monastery was on the top of a mountain, and on the mountain there was a stream. Now there is a small spring at the place of the stream which can be found at the bottom of the mountain. Takht Bhai is the most fertile tehsile in the Mardan Division, There are many crops grown in the Takht Bhai Tehsile, some of which are tobacco, wheat and sugar cane. Asia's first sugar mill was built here by the British Government near the Buddhist monastery

Takht-i Sulaiman : The legend of the Sulaiman mountain range is east of Quetta, overlooking the plain of the Indus river. The highest peak (11,295 feet) is called Takht-i Sulaiman, Solomon's Throne; Ibn Battuta names it Koh-i Sulaiman. Of this it is related, that the Prophet of God, Hazrat Sulaiman (peace be upon him) climbed this mountain and looked out over the land of South Asia, which was then covered with darkness - but he turned back without descending into this new frontier, and left only the mountain which is named after him.

Takht-i-Bahi : The Buddhist monastic complex of Takht-i-Bahi (Throne of Origins) was founded in the early 1st century. It is located about 80 kms from Peshawar and 16 kms northwest of the city of Mardan. Its position on the crest of a high hill, helped it to escape successive invasions and is still exceptionally well preserved. Nearby are the ruins of Sahr-i-Bahlol, a small fortified city of nearly the same period. The ruins of an ancient Buddhist monastery are situated on the top of a 500 feet high hill. This site has produced fragmentary sculptures in stone and stucco that indicate the highly developed sculptural sense of their creators. The design and arrangement of the range of small shrines, which surrounds the main stupa-court, is most remarkable. The group of buildings unearthed after archeological excavations at Takht-i-Bahi include; the court of many Stupas, the monastery, the main stupa, the assembly hall, the low-level chambers, the courtyard, the court of three stupas, the wall of colossi and the secular building.

Tal Chhapar Sanctuary : Tal Chhapar Sanctuary is situated in the Churu district of Northwestern Rajasthan in the Shekhawati region of India. It is 210 km from Jaipur and situated on road from Ratangarh to Sujangarh. It is known for black bucks but it is also home of variety of birds. It is named after the village Chhapar that is located at 27°-50' North and 74°-25' East. It is a flat saline depression locally known as "Tal" that has a unique ecosystem in the heart of the Thar Desert.

It lies on the way of the passage of many migratory birds such as harriers. These birds pass through this area during September. Birds commonly seen in the sanctuary are harriers, Eastern Imperial Eagle, Tawny Eagle, Short-toed Eagle, sparrow, and Little Green Bee-eaters, Black Ibis and Demoiselle Cranes, which stay there till March. Whereas skylark, crested lark, Ring Dove, brown dove and blue jay are seen throughout the year.

In the Tal Chhapar Sanctuary one very special type of grass is found. This grass locally is called Mothiya. The word mothiya comes come from the word Moti or from the English word for Pearl. The shape of the seed of this grass is like very fine round shaped pearls. Mothiya has a very sweet taste. People enjoy eating it, but and it is found in very small quantities -production is only few kilograms every season. This grass and Mothiya is also food for Black bucks and other birds who dig it from earth with their starks.

Tala : In Indian classical music, Tala (tal (Hindi), tala (anglicised from talam; in Sanskrit), literally a "clap", is a rhythmical pattern that determines the rhythmical structure of a composition. Each composition is set to a tala, and as a composition is rendered by the main artist(s), the percussion artist(s) play the pattern repeatedly, marking time as well as enhancing the appeal of the performance.

The most common instrument for keeping rhythm in Hindustani music is the tabla. In Carnatic music, the Mridangam is a stock feature in vocal, violin, Veena and flute concerts, with the Ghatam, the Khanjira and the Morsing also featuring at times. In Nadhaswaram concerts, the Thavil takes the place of the Mridangam.

Talakaveri : Talakaveri situated in the Brahmagiri hills in Kodagu district, Karnataka, is the place where the River Kaveri originates. The river begins here as a small perennial spring, but flows underground again to emerge a short distance away. It is situated at a height of 4187 feet (1,276 m), and is 7 km away from and Bhagamandala, 48 km from Madikeri. Apart from a major pilgrimage center it is also an important tourist spot in Karnataka. On Tulasankramana day (October 17) thousands of pilgrims flock to the river's birthplace to witness the miraculous rise of the fountainhead, when water gushes up from the spring at a predetermined moment.

Talat Aziz : Talat Aziz (born May 14, 1955) in Hyderabad, India is a famous Indian ghazal singer. His real name is Talat Abdul Aziz Khan. Amongst many successful albums and concerts, his album Dhuan was particularly very popular. His wife's name is Bina.

Talat Mahmood : Padma Bhushan Talat Mahmood (February 24, 1924—May 9, 1998) was one of the most popular playback singers of Indian films in his time. Born in Lucknow, Talat was known as the King of Ghazals. He was one amongst six children. His father Manzoor Mahmood owned an electrical curio store. Talat showed his musical leanings from a very young age and would enjoy sitting through all-night music soiree's listening patiently to some of the biggest names in Indian classical music. Later, for a very short period of time Talat studied music at Marris Music College, before people began noticing his natural singing talent and offers to sing began to pour in. Talat began his singing career at an age of 16 on All India Radio singing ghazals.

Talimeran Ao : Dr. Talimeran Ao, first captain of independent India's Olympic football team, died at Kohima, Nagaland at the age of 80 years in September

1998. In 2002 The Mohun Bagan Ratna award went to Dr. Talimeran Ao - an Assamese footballer. Born in 1919 in the Naga village of Chanki (Mokuchong district) Dr. Ao started his football career in the Maharana Athletic Club in Gwahati.

Talish : Talish was a leading character actor of the Pakistani cinema. On January 5, 1962 Shaheed was released, his biggest hit.

A film on the relevant theme of Palestine with a script by Riaz Shahid and music by Rasheed Attre; it was produced and directed by Khalil Qaiser. The highlight was the instant hit Uss bewafa ka shehr by renowned poet Muneer Niazi.

Talpur : Talpur is a Baloch tribe that conquered and ruled Sindh, and other parts of present-day Pakistan, from 1783 to 1843 AD. Talpur army defeated Kalhora dynasty in the Battle of Halani in 1783 to became rulers of Sindh. The Talpur dynasty was defeated by the British invaders in 1843 in the Battle of Miani.

Tambura : The tambura is a type of string instrument found in different versions in different places around the world; most are plucked lutes.

A tambura (South India) or tanpura (North India) is a long-necked Indian lute, unfretted and round-bodied. It has four or five (rarely, six) wire strings, which are plucked one after another to make a drone sound.

Hindustani classical music tanpuras come in different sizes: bigger "males" and smaller "females". Male singers pitch their tonic note (Sa) to C#, female singers usually a fifth higher. The male instrument has an open string length of one metre, the female is sized down to 3/4. The standard tuning is 5881 sol do' do' do or in Indian sargam: PA sa sa SA, the last SA low. With a five-string instrument, the seventh or NI (natural minor or major 7th) is added: PA NI sa sa SA, the last SA low again. Both the instrument and how it is played look very simple, though in fact it takes a lot of experience and a very good ear to tune and play the tanpura.

Tamil : Tamil is a classical language and one of the major languages of the Dravidian language family. Spoken predominantly by Tamils in India, Sri Lanka, Malaysia, and Singapore, it has smaller communities of speakers in many other countries. As of 1996, it was the eighteenth most spoken language, with over 74 million speakers worldwide.

Tamil is one of the few living classical languages and has an unbroken literary tradition of over two millennia. The written language has changed little during this period, with the result that classical literature is as much a part of everyday Tamil as modern literature. Tamil schoolchildren, for example, are still taught the alphabet using the átticúdi, an alphabet rhyme written around the first century A.D.

Tamil Nadu : Tamil Nadu is a state at the southern tip of India. The bordering states/territories are Pondicherry, Kerala, Karnataka and Andhra Pradesh. The island nation of Sri Lanka, which has a significant Tamil minority, lies off the southeast coast. Tamil Nadu is the second most industrialized state in India. Unlike most other parts of the country, Tamil Nadu gets its rainfall largely from the "North-East monsoon" in the months of October-December. There is a long standing dispute with Karnataka over the matter of water from the Kaveri River. The river flows south from Karnataka to Tamil Nadu, and both regions draw on water from the river, prompting concerns over whether the upper riparian Karnataka has released its fair share of river water to the lower riparian Tamil Nadu.

Tamil People : The Tamil people are an ethnic group from South Asia with a recorded history going back more than two millennia. The oldest Tamil communities are those of southern India and northeastern Sri Lanka. There are also a number of Tamil emigrant communities scattered around the world, especially in Malaysia, Singapore, Fiji, Mauritius, and South Africa, with more recent emigrants also found in Australia, Canada, and parts of Europe.

Tamluk: Tamluk is an ancient city of West Bengal state in India, near the Rupnarayan River. Tamluk is the headquarters of Midnapore East district. It was home of many great leaders during independence movement. Kolaghat is another town on the bank of Rupnarayan River and famous for Hilsa (Ilish) fishes. Archaeological remains show continuous settlement from about 3rd century BC; it was known as Tamralipta or Tamalitti, and was a seaport, now buried under river silt.

Tamor Pingla Wildlife Sanctuary : Tamor Pingla Wildlife Sanctuary is located in Surajpur tehsil of Surguja District, Chhattisgarh. It is named after the Tamor hill and Pingla nalla, the old and prominent features of the area. Comprising Sal, mixed and bamboo forests, the area is under Ghui and Biharpur ranges of the South Surguja Forest Division. Spread over 608 sq km, the sanctuary supports tiger, panther, bear, sambar deer, blue bull, chital, bison, four-horned antelope, chinkara, barking deer, wild bear, wild dog, wolves, jackals, striped hyena, hare, cobra, nag, python, red jungle fowl, brown jungle fowl and green pigeon. The sanctuary is aroudn 35 km west of Ambikapur. Anuppur Junction Railway Station is the major railhead nearby. Bishrampur Railway Station is the nearest railhead.

Tana Mana : This is a custom designed to stop the spread of epidemics in a village and is prevalent in the villages along the Indo-Tibetan border. When anyone in these areas contracts a contagious disease and is critically ill, a locally available boulder of white stone is put at his door steps at a spot where any one may see it and know that some one within the house is lying ill with a contagious disease. Due to the taboos this custom enforces, in order to isolate the patient, even the doctors are not allowed into the patients rooms. The entrance to each village in the area is guarded to check the entry of some one suffering from the disease. Between the villages of Raja and Kibbar, each person that enters the area has to be checked by the Lama against contagious diseases.

Tandoor : A tandoor is a cylindrical clay oven used in Punjab northern India and Pakistan in which food is cooked over a hot charcoal fire. Temperatures in a tandoor can approach 480°C (900°F). It is common for tandoor ovens to remain lit for long periods of time to maintain the high cooking temperature.

The word tandoor comes from the Urdu words tandur and tannur; these derive from the Persian tanur, which comes from the Arabic word tannur, from which Turkish word Tandir (which has the same meaning as explained in the article) originates. It is used for cooking certain types of Indian and Pakistani food, such as tandoori chicken and bread varieties like tandoori roti and naan. (The word tandoori is the adjective form.) Some modern day tandoors use electricity or gas instead of charcoal. It is also known as a tonir in Armenian which is a widely used method of cooking barbeque and lavash bread.

Tandoori Chicken : Tandoori Chicken is a chicken dish dating back to the time of the Mughal Empire in Central and Southern Asia, it is still popular throughout that area. It has gained popularity even among people whose religion forbids the consumption of meat (Hinduism/Sikhism) in India. The chicken is marinated in a yogurt seasoned with garam masala—garlic, ginger, cumin, cayenne pepper, and other spices depending on the recipe. It is traditionally quite hot. Cayenne, red chili powder, or other spices give it its red color. Turmeric produces a yellow-orange color. In some modern versions red and yellow food coloring is used instead. It is traditionally cooked at high temperatures in an earthen oven (i.e. tandoor), but can also be prepared on a traditional grill.

Tangon River : Tangon river is also known as the Tongon River. The river was named after the name of Zamindar Tankonath of Ranisankail upazila in Thakurgaon district. It enters Bangladesh from the Indian state of West Bengal through the western border of Panchagarh district (which lies in the northwestern corner of the country). It passes through Ruhia, Pirganj and Bochaganj. It again enters West Bengal through Biral upazila of Dinajpur. It returns to Bangladesh when it meets with the Punarbhaba near Rohanpur of Naogaon district. It becomes dry during winter and navigable in the rainy season. In 1989, a five-vent Barrage was built over this river 10 km west of Boda. About 5,000 ha of land including 1,000 to 1,500 ha of wheat fields get gravity irrigation in the dry season.

Tangsa : The Tangsa tribe, also known as the Tase, lives in the Tirap and Changlang district of Arunachal Pradesh. Ethnically related to the Naga, they are well-built and of medium-stature. Traditionally, the Tangsa kept long hair in both sexes, which is tied into a bun and covered with a piece of cloth, known as the Khu-phak. The menfolk wear a green lungi, which is lined with yellow, red and white yarns, and accompanied with a sleeveless shirt. On the other hand, the costume of the womenfolk include an artistically woven petticoat, which acts as the lower garment, and a linen blouse.

As an united tribe, the Tangsa believed in a joint family system, and property is equally divided between all family members. A tribal council, known as Khaphua, is administered by a Lungwang chief, who sees to the daily affairs of the Tangsa tribe. Followers of the Donyi-Polo religion, the Tangsa believed in a supreme being that crated their existence, locally known as Rangfrah, although belief in other deities and spirits is maintained as well.

Tanguturi Prakasam Pantulu : Tanguturi Prakasam Pantulu (23 August 1872 - 20 May 1957) was an Indian freedom fighter and the first Chief Minister of the state of Andhra. He was widely revered as Andhra Kesari (literally, Lion of Andhra).

After completing the barrister course with a certificate of honour in London, Prakasam relocated to Madras high court. He was the first prominent Telugu barrister to be successful; until then, most of the successful lawyers were either Europeans or Tamilians. He started attending the Congress Party sessions regularly after the Lucknow pact and signed the Satyagraha pledge in October 1921. He gave up his lucrative law practice.

He was arrested for more than three years for participating in the Quit India movement of 1942. After his release in 1945, he toured South India to get back in touch with the masses. In 1946, congress party again contested and won in the Madras Presidency. This time, Prakasam became the chief minister as he and Kamaraj, a Tamil leader, were against Rajaji—the choice of leaders such as Gandhi and Nehru—becoming the chief minister. However, the government lasted for only 11 months, as it was felt that Prakasam was not accommodating enough to various varying interests. He was not gracious in losing power and levelled corruption charges against the new ministry.

Tanjore Painting : Tanjore painting is an important form of classical South Indian painting native to the town of Tanjore in Tamil Nadu. The art form dates back to the early 9th Century, a period dominated by the Chola rulers, who encouraged art and literature. These paintings are known for their elegance, rich colours, and attention to detail. The themes for most of these paintings are Hindu Gods and Goddesses and scenes from Hindu mythology. In modern times, these paintings have become a much sought after souvenir during festive occasions in South India.

The process of making a Tanjore painting involves many stages. The first stage involves the making of the preliminary sketch of the image on the base. The base consists of a cloth pasted over a wooden base. Then chalk powder or zinc oxide is mixed with water-soluble adhesive and applied on the base. To make the base smoother, a mild abrasive is sometimes used. After the drawing is made, decoration of the jewellery and the apparels in the image is done with semi-precious stones. Laces or threads are also used to decorate the jewellery. On top of this, the gold foils are pasted. Finally, dyes are used to add colors to the figures in the paintings.

Tansen : Tansen, the legendary musician was born in Gwalior in 1506. It was only after the age of 5 that Tansen showed any musical talent. It was his Guru Hari Dasa who recognised his hidden talents as a musician. Tansen was one among the nine gems in the court of Emperor Akbar. He was also a poet, who composed many couplets. When Tansen was in the court of Akbar, he started to compose new ragas or melodies based on classical Indian music. He is believed to be the father of Hindustani Music. His 'Sangeeta Sara' and 'Rajmala' are important documents on music. He popularised the 'Drupad' style of music.

He was such a great artist that he became a legend in his own times. His talent was recognised early and it was the ruler of Gwalior who conferred upon the maestro the honorific title 'Tansen'. He died in 1589, and was buried according to his wishes near the grave of his mentor, Ghaus. A national music festival known as 'Tansen Sangeet Sammelon' is held every year in December, near the tomb of Tansen at Behat as a mark of respect to his memory.

Tansen Music Festival : The Tansen Sangeeth Sammelan or Music festival is held in Gwalior in memory of the great musician Tansen. Tansen one of the nine gems in the court of Emperor Akbar is believed to be the father of Hindustani Music especially the 'Drupad style'. One of the most well known and the oldest Gharana of Hindustani classical music is the Gwalior Gharana. Gwalior has retained its strong musical tradition. The festival is held, near the tomb of Tansen at Behat, Gwalior in the month of November/ December every year. The tomb build in the early Mughal architectural style is a part of Gwalior's cultural heritage. Renowned classical singers from the country gather and perform for five night-long sessions. The venue resounds with the various ragas.

Tantya Tope : Tantya Tope(1814-1859) also known as Ram Chandra Pandurang was born in 1814 at village Gola in Maharashtra. His father, Pandurang Rao Tope was an important noble at the court of the Maratha Peshwa Baji Rao II. He shifted his family with the ill-fated Peshwa to Bithur where his son became the most intimate friend of the Peshwa's adopted son, Nana Dhondu Pant, known as Nana Sahib and Maharaja Madhav Singhji.

In 1851, when Lord Dalhousie deprived Nana Sahib of his father's pension, Tantya Tope also became a sworn enemy of the British. In May 1857, when the political storm was gaining momentum, he won over the Indian troops of the East India Company, stationed at Kanpur (Cawnpore), established Nana Sahib's authority and became the Commander-in-Chief of his forces. After the reoccupation of Kanpur and separation from Nana Sahib,

Tantya Tope shifted his headquarters to Kalpi to join hands with the Rani Lakshmi Bai and led a revolt in Bundelkhand. He was routed at Betwa, Koonch, and Kalpi, but reached Gwalior and declared Nana Sahib as Peshwa with the support of the Gwalior contingent. Before he could consolidate his position he was defeated by General Rose in a memorable battle in which Rani Lakshmi Bai was killed leading her forces against the British assault on Gwailor.

After losing Gwalior to the British, he launched a successful guerrilla campaign in the Sagar and Narmada regions and in Khandesh and Rajasthan. The British forces failed to subdue him for over a year. He was, however, betrayed into the hands of the British by his trusted friend Man Singh, Chief of Narwar, while asleep in his camp in the Paron forest. He was captured and taken to Shivpuri where he was tried by a military court and executed at the gallows on April 18, 1859. There is a statue of Tantya Tope at the site of his execution near present collectorat in Shivpuri town in Madhya Pradesh.

Tanzeem-e-Islami : Tanzeem-e-Islami is an Islamist organization based in Lahore, Pakistan, headed by Dr Israr Ahmed. It was founded by Dr Ahmed in 1975 as an offshoot of the Jamaat-e-Islami.

Tapash Baisya : Tapash Baisya (born 25 December 1982 in Sylhet) is a Bangladeshi cricketer. Tapash Baisya is one of Bangladesh's best pace bowlers to date, having taken 36 Test wickets, although they have come at a bowling average of nearly 60. Nevertheless, he has taken the second-most wickets of any Bangladeshi fast bowler, behind Mashrafe Mortaza. Baisya has, however, only taken four wickets in a Test innings once - he took four for 72 against West Indies on their 2002-03 tour of Bangladesh. However, two of those wickets were Daren Powell and Jermaine Lawson, batting at nine and eleven respectively.

Tapovan : In contrast to the hustle and bustle of the city, Tapovan—16 kms. from Joshimath—is a peaceful place known for its hot springs that are believed to possess healing powers.

Tapper Mats : Tapper mats are made on a large scale in Palamau district, Bihar. Tapper is rather like jute, taken out of the sun hemp plant. The usual method of soaking and using pressure is used to extract the fibre which is then spun into yarn and used for making tapper. This is said do be more durable than jute fibre. The yarn is dyed generally in indigenous colours which used to transport grain on any heavy stuff. Today a number of article, of modern use are made like travel kit and hand bags, some of them quite, stylish looking. Hazaribagh and Purnea also produce tapper.

Tappeta Gundlu : Tappeta gundlu is a folk dance confined to the coastal districts of Srikakulam, Vijayanagaram and Vishakhapatnam. This was originally performed by cowherds and shepherds as a ritualistic dance propitiating the rain god and their favourite deity Gangamma. While dancing they sing devotional songs on Sri Krishna, Dasavataras and on goddess Gangamma besides other folk songs and narratives. Tappeta or gundlu is a small percussion instrument in the shape of a drum hanging on the chest and tied to the sides and neck of the players. A troupe consisting of eight to sixteen artistes sing and dance in circles beating with their hands the drums tied to their chests. The players tie jingling bells to their ankles. They put on tight knickers stitched with jingling bells all over. They tie colourful clothes around their waists and long loin clothes hanging up to their feet in front as well as at the back resembling two tails.

Tapti River : The Tapti River (also Tapi River) is a river of central India. It is one of the major rivers of peninsular India with a lenth of around 724 km. It is one of three rivers, with the Narmada River and the Mahi River that run from east to west. The river rises in the eastern Satpura Range of southern Madhya Pradesh state, and flows westward, draining Madhya Pradesh's Nimar region, Maharashtra's Kandesh and east Vidarbha regions in the northwest corner of the Deccan Plateau and South Gujarat before emptying into the Gulf of Cambay of the Arabian Sea, in the State of Gujarat. The Western Ghats or Sahyadri range starts south of the Tapti River near the border of Gujarat and Maharashtra.

Taramon Bibi : Taramon Bibi is the one of the two decorated female freedom fighters in Bangladesh, and the only one of them to have engaged in direct combat. She fought for the Mukti Bahini (Liberation Army) which was a guerilla force that fought against the Pakistan military in during Bangladesh War of Independence in 1971. She fought in her village home in Shankar Madhabpur, Kurigram District. She was in Sector 11 under the leadership of Sector commander Abu Taher. After the war, she was awarded honored with the title Bir Protik (Symbol of Valor) by the Bangladesh government. But her whereabouts were unknown and the award was never handed over to her. She herself remained unaware of this until 1995, when a researcher from Mymensingh discovered her. She was finally given her award by the Prime Minister of Bangladesh on December 19, 1995.

Tarashankar Bandopadhyaya : Tarashankar Bandopadhyaya, one of the three great Bandopadhyaya of post-Tagore era of Bengali literature was born in 1898.

He wrote 65 novels, 53 story-books, 12 plays, 4 essay-books, 4 autobiographies and 2 travel stories. A notable man of wisdom, he was awarded Rabindra Purashkar, Sahitya Akademi award, Jnanpith Award, and Padma Bhushan. No writer, except Rabindranath Tagore, in Bengali literature, won such honours in our days as him.

Tarbela Dam: Tarbela Dam is a dam on the Indus River in Pakistan. It is one of the largest earth filled dams in the world and it produces much of Pakistan's hydroelectricity. Construction began in 1968, and continued until completion in 1976. The dam has a volume of 138,600,000 cubic yards. With a reservoir capacity of 11,098,000 acre-feet, the dam is 469 feet (143 m) high and 8,997 feet (2,743 m) wide at its crest. It helps to maintain the Indus River's flow during seasonal fluctuations.

Tareen : Tareen is a Pashtun tribe living in Pakistan and Afghanistan. Tareen are settled in Pishin, Harnai, Dukhi, and Gulistan districts in Balochistan and the Hazara Division of the North-West Frontier Province of Pakistan. They are also present in sizeable proportions in the areas near Kandahar in Afghanistan. They played a very important role in Sultan Mohammad Ghori's army and showed great bravery. The Tareens of Hazara Division migrated from Kandahar in the 17th century CE under the leadership of Sher Khan Tareen.

Taren Taran : It is an important Sikh tank about 25km south of Amritsar. There's a temple, which predates Amritsar, and a tower on the east side of the tank, which was also constructed by Ranjit Singh. It's said that any leper who can swim across the tank will be miraculously cured.

Tareq Masud : Tareq Masud is a Bangladeshi film director. Along with his wife, Catherine Masud, he directed several movies and documentaries of international fame. He won the International Critic's Award in the Cannes film festival in 2002 for his semi-autobiographical movie, Matir Moyna (The Clay Bird).

Tariq Ali : Tariq Ali (born October 21, 1943) is an author, filmmaker, and historian. He is also a long-time member of the editorial committee of New Left Review, and regularly contributes to The Guardian, Counterpunch and the London Review of Books. Ali was born and grew up in Lahore, now part of Pakistan, into a communist family. While studying at the Punjab University, he organized demonstrations against Pakistan's military dictatorship. His parents sent him to England to study at Oxford, because they feared for his safety due to his connections to radical movements. There he quickly became a leader, being elected President of the Oxford Union.

Tariq Saeed Saigol : Tariq Saeed Saigol is the head of the Kohinoor Maple Leaf Group. The Saigol family is a very old and respected family in Pakistan. They come from Lahore, and their primary business concerns are Khinoor Textiles and Maple Leaf Cement. The Saigols also used to own the United Bank Limited, which was nationalised by the government in the 1970s, and has now been bought by the Bestway group.

Tarkhan Dynasty : Tarkhan Dynasty or Turkhan was established by Turkic Tarkhan and they ruled Sindh, Pakistan, from 1554 to 1591 AD. General Mirza Isa Beg founded the Tarkhan Dynasty in Sindh after the death of Shah Hassan Arghun of the Arghun Dynasty. Mughal emperor Akbar annexed Sindh after defeating the last Tarkhan ruler.

Tarnetar : At this exceedingly colourful gathering of most handsome rural men and women, there is a heady mixture of Gujarati folk dance and music and a riot of lovely handcrafted umbrellas for 2 days in September every year. Just 3 hours from Ahmedabad.

Tarpha Nach or Pavri Nach : This dance is typical of the Kokna tribals found in the hilly regions of the Northwest. The dance is accompanied by the tarpha or pavri, a wind instrument made of dried gourd.

Taslima Nasrin : Taslima Nasrin, also known as Taslima Nasreen, (born 25 August 1962 in Mymensingh, Bangladesh) is a Bengali Bangladeshi physician, writer, radical feminist, human rights activist and secular humanist. She was awarded the Sakharov Prize for Freedom of Thought in 1994, and a Humanist Award (from the International Humanist and Ethical Union) in 1996.

Taslima Nasrin was born in Mymensingh. Her father was a physician and a professor at the government medical college. She studied at Mymensingh Medical College. She initially gained fame as a poet and columnist. In her autobiography, she said that she was raped by her uncles at a very early age. Critics say that these incidents along with other horrible experiences may caused her deep rooted prejudice against some groups.

Nasrin has spoken out in favour of equal rights for women and has expressed opposition to the oppression of non-Islamic minorities in Islamic societies, such as in her home country Bangladesh. In 1993, sparked by a series of newspaper columns in which she was critical of the treatment of women under Islam, Islamic fundamentalists pronounced a fatwa against her and offered a bounty for her death. Later, the government banned her book Lajja, (a Bangla word meaning shame), which drew attention to the torture of Hindu minorities in Bangladesh. Again there were calls for her death and her passport was confiscated by the government.

In 1994, organised groups identified with religious fundamentalists demanded her execution by hanging after she was quoted in the The Statesman stating that "...the Koran should be revised thoroughly." The government of the day, whilst not taking action against those who had issued threats, filed a court case against Nasrin on the charges of hurting the religious feeling of people and an arrest warrant was issued. Although she anticipated that she may have faced a jail term of up to two years, Nasrin felt it was very likely that she would have been murdered in jail; she went into hiding. After two months she was granted bail and left the country.

In the same year she received the Sakharov Prize for Freedom of Thought from the European Parliament and other awards. Nasrin is an Honorary Associate of the National Secular Society. Her books have been translated into twenty different languages. Nasrin's four autobiographical books are banned in Bangladesh. The government has claimed that they "contain anti-Islam sentiments and statements that could destroy the religious harmony of Bangladesh". Nasrin has been living in exile for more than 10 years. Still a citizen of Bangladesh, the government has not been seen to have taken the necessary steps to ensure her safe return.

Tata Consultancy Services Limited (TCS) : Tata Consultancy Services Limited (TCS) is an Indian information technology, consulting, services and business-process outsourcing organization which commenced operations in 1968. It is currently Asia's largest IT services firm with revenues of US $2.28 Billion for Financial Year 2004-2005. As of 2005 it has the largest number of employees among all the Indian IT companies (over 50,000). It has posted a net profit of Rs. 2,052 crore (approximately US$ 450 million) for the Financial Year 2004-2005. Ever since its inception, TCS has pioneered the offshore delivery model for IT services.

TCS is part of one of Asia's largest conglomerates - the Tata Group - which has interests in Energy, Telecommunications, Financial Services, Chemicals, Engineering & Materials to name a few. TCS was conferred the best IT employer award by Hewitt Associates and best place to work award by Dataquest. CEO Ramadorai got the Businessman of the Year award from Business India in 2004. He has also been conferred the prestigious Padma Bhushan by the Government of India recently. Maitree is the social service wing of TCS.

Tata Engineering and Locomotive Company (TELCO) : The Tata Engineering and Locomotive Company (TELCO) is a heavy engineering company based in India and is a part of the Tata Group of companies. The automobile division of TELCO is now known as Tata Motors.

Tata Group : Tata is one of the oldest and best-known groups of companies in India. The group takes the name of its founder, Sir Jamshedji Tata, a member of whose family has almost invariably been the chairman of the group. The present chairman is Ratan Tata, who took over from the justly renowned J.R.D. Tata in the 1990s. TISCO is now renamed as Tata Steel Limited while TELCO has become Tata Motors Limited. Tata group of enterprises comprises 93 companies in seven business sectors

Tatanagar : Tatanagar is the station name for the city of Jamshedpur located in the state of Jharkhand. Previously, it belonged to the state of Bihar before a portion of south Bihar came to be incorporated into the new state of Jharkhand. It is known for TISCO (Tata Steel) and TELCO (TATA Engineering and Locomotive Company).

Tatar Khan: Tatar Khan was the governor of sonargaon under the Tughlaqs and entitled Khan-i-Azam Bahram Khan. Tatar Khan claimed himself to be the son of a king of Khurasan. Adopted by Sultan ghiyasuddin tughlaq, he was appointed governor of satgaon in 1324 and of Sonargaon in 1328. He died in 1337. A great patron of learning he, with the assistance of some scholars, produced a commentary on the Quran entitled Tafsir-i-Tatarkhani and compiled a law book called Fatwa-i-Tatarkhani.

Taufiq Rafat : Taufiq Rafat (1927-1998) was an English language Pakistani poet born in Sialkot, India in 1927. Educated in Dehra Dun, Aligarh and Lahore, Rafat and his family returned to Sialkot (now in Pakistan) following Partition in 1947. After graduating from the Hailey College of Commerce, Lahore, Rafat became a company executive and married his wife Rehana, who was a social worker and women's rights activist from the local Kashmiri community.

Tava : A tava (sometimes also tawa) is a large, flat or slightly concave disc-shaped griddle, made from cast iron, steel or aluminium. It is used in Indian cuisine to prepare several kinds of roti or Indian breads, including chapatis and parathas, chaap, pao bhaaji, chaat, tava parathas, etc. It is also used for a class of foods known as tava fry or tava masala.

Tawang : Tawang the headquarters of the Tawang district located on the Western tip of the state on a mountain side at 12000 ft above sea level, is the land of the Monpa tribes and a major centre of the Mahayana Buddhists. Tawang is famous for its 400 year old Buddhist monastery which overlooks the wide Tawang Valley. The best season to visit is from April to October. The nearest airport is Tezpur which is 345 km from Tawang and the nearest Railhead is Bhalukpong at 280 kms. Buses and Taxi ply regularly from Bomdilla to Tawang which is 180 km and takes 10 hrs. Tawang is also ideal for trekking and hiking. On the way to Tawang lies the World's second highest pass, the Sela Pass through a high altitude lake of crystal blue water. Both sides of the lake are decked with miles of Rhodendrons. There is also a Orchidarium at Tipi near the banks of the Kameng River in the West Kameng District, Enroute Tawang.

Tawang District : The Tawang district is located at the north-west of the state of Arunachal Pradesh in India.

The sixth Dalai Lama, Tsangyang Gyatso, was born in Tawang. Tawang borders the Line of Actual Control between India and China on disputed Indian-administered territory, as part of Arunachal Pradesh. From China's point of view it is considered as part of the Cona County of the Tibet Autonomous Region. It also shares another international border with Bhutan, and a district border with West Kameng.

It roughly lies between the latitude 27 ° 45′ N and the longitude 90° 15′ E on the Northwest extremity of Arunachal Pradesh. Elevations range between 6,000 to 22,000 feet, and inhabitants are found in lower altitude, where they enjoy a cool temperate climate. The district is administer by the current MP, Shri Jorbom Gamlin. Tawang district is further sub-divided into the Lumla, Jang and Tawang sub-dividsions. The district itself has 3 principal monasteries as well.

Taxila : Taxila is an archaeological site, located in the Punjab province of Pakistan, west of the Islamabad Capital Territory and Rawalpindi, on the border of the Punjab and North West Frontier Province and just off the Grand Trunk Road. Its coordinates are 33.76° N 72.84° E. Taxila (then called taksh-shila) was an ancient Hindu and Buddhist seat of learning, connected across the Khunjerab pass to the Silk Road, attracting students from all over the world. Ancient Takshashila was renowned all over the Buddhist world as home to the world's first university (Takshashila University). It flourished during the first-fifth centuries AD. Located at the junction of three major trade routes, it was of considerable economic and strategic importance. Taxila has been listed by the UNESCO as one of the World Heritage Sites.

T Balasaraswati : T.Balasaraswati (1918-1984) was born in a family that has been a repository of the Carnatic tradition of music. Her formal training started at the age of four under the late Guru Kandappa Pillai. Balasaraswati's debut took place in her seventh year at Kancheepuram at the Amanakshi Amman temple. Soon she was in great demand for public performances. No dancer captured the public imagination as Balasaraswati did in the thirties and forties.

Balasaraswati made the public aware of Bharata Natyam by the beauty and the eloquence of her dancing. She is the recipient of several honours and awards, which include the Sangeet Natak Akademi Award, Padma Bhushan and an honorary doctorate from the Rabindra Bharati University.

Tea Gardens : The tea industry is the backbone of Sonitpur's economy. There are 55 tea gardens in this district of Assam. For his livelihood, every fifth person is dependent on the industry in one way or another. The tea gardens are efficiently managed self contained units that produce the best tea in the world. The recreational clubs of the planters boast of the best tennis courts, golfing greens, squash courts and billiard tables. The well maintained luxurious bunglows with their manicured lawns and gardens are well worth a visit.

Technopark, Kerala: Technopark Kerala, located at Trivandrum, India, is India's first industrial park dedicated to electronics, software, and IT ventures. Started 1990, the 180 acres (728,000 m^2) campus is now home to over 60 companies from numerous countries. Technopark was promoted by the Government of the State of Kerala in India. The policy of economic liberalisation initiated by the Government of India in 1991 and the rapid growth of the global software industry during the 1990s has substantially contributed to the growth of Technopark.

Teej : Teej festival is celebrated in various parts of Rajasthan by girls/ married women during monsoon season.They worship Godess Parvati.A day before this festival is celebrated as Sinjara wherein girls/ladies put on mehandi on their hands and eat ghewar/feeni and other sweets. On Teej, Married women pray to Godess Parvati for well being of their husbands. Idols of goddess Parvati are decorated and parades in the streets accompanied by singing, music, and dancing.

Teesta Bazaar : Teesta Bazaar is a junction on National Highway 31A on the Siliguri-Gangtok highway in the state of West Bengal, India. Teesta Bazaar is on the right bank of Teesta River. Continuing upriver on the right bank from Siliguri, the road leads to Darjeeling. The river is crossed here over the Teesta Suspension Bridge. A junction, three kilometres ahead on the same highway, splits from the main route towards Kalimpong. Teesta Bazaar is located four kilometres downstream from the industrial town of Melli.

Teesta Bazaar is situated at an elevation of 90 m above mean sea level. River rafting can be undertaken at this point. It is also at the point where the river Teesta flows into West Bengal. Most of the area around Teesta is patrolled by the Indian Army as it comes under a sensitive border area.

Teesta River : The River Teesta, said to be the lifeline of the Indian state of Sikkim, flows for almost the entire length of the state; carving out verdant Himalayan temperate and tropical river valleys. The emerald coloured river then forms the border between Sikkim and West Bengal before joining the Brahmaputra as a tributary in Bangladesh. The river originates in the mysterious Cho Lhamu Lake at an elevation of 5,330 m (17,500 feet) above sea level in the mighty Himalayas. This lake lies to the north of the Donkia Pass near Shetschen, where the summit of the pass is about eight kilometres north-east of Darjeeling as the crow flies.

Teeyan : *Teeyan, a festival of the rainy season,* is celebrated on the 3rd of the bright fortnight of Sawan (July-August). The four months from Harh (June-July) to the first half of Assu (September) are called Chaumasa. During this period the sky generally remains overcast and the weather shifts between sultriness and rainfall. Rains bring the longed-for relief to the heat-stricken Punjabis, and the rhythm of the little and big drops of rain instills in them the enthusiasm which must seek expression in fun and frolic. A newly-married girl looks forward to the rainy days when a brother or some other male relative from the parental home may come to escort her to her father's place. This reversal from bride hood to being just a daughter again is such a liberating and thrilling experience that it cannot be put into words. One day before the Teeyan, girls apply henna to their hands and feet, and on the day of the festival they put on their best clothes and go out to the fair. The fair resounds with the songs of love and the rhythm of dance. The songs are known as Teeyan songs. The Giddha dance has become a regular and most enchanting feature of this festival. At home women make kheer, a dish specially associated with Sawan.

Tehri : Tehri is a town in Uttaranchal state of northern India. It is the administrative seat of Tehri Garhwal District. The old town of Tehri lies at the confluence of the Bhagirathi and Bhilangna rivers, the site of the Tehri dam. The town of Tehri was emptied to make space for the Tehri dam, and the population has been shifted to the town of New Tehri. The town is famous as the site of protests against the dam by Sundarlal Bahuguna and his followers.

Tehri was the capital of the princely state of Tehri Garhwal in British India, which had an area of 4180 square miles, and a population of 268,885 in 1901. It adjoined the district of Garhwal, and its topographical features are similar. It contained the sources of both the Ganges and the Yamuna, which are visited by thousands of Hindu pilgrims.

Tej Bahadur Sapru : Sir Tej Bahadur Sapru (1875–1949) was an eminent lawyer, political and social leader in India during the British Raj. He was knighted in 1922. Tej Bahadur Sapru was born on December 8th, 1875 in Aligarh, in what is now the state of Uttar Pradesh. He was born in a Kashmiri Hindu family. He was educated at the Agra College. Sapru worked in the Allahabad High Court as a lawyer where Purushottam Das Tandon worked as his junior. Sapru was a jurist and leader of the Indian Liberal Party. He favoured a dialogue with the British Empire and sought self-government reforms, but not independence from the Empire.

Sapru and others like M.S. Jayakar favored discussions and dialogue with the British, and were regular participants in the provincial and central legislatures that most Indians thought were rubber-stamps of the Viceroy. He carried forward the moderate policies of Gopal Krishna Gokhale in the radicalized post-Amritsar Massacre period after World War I. Sapru criticized Mahatma Gandhi's leadership, as well as the Non-Cooperation Movement and the Salt Satyagraha.

However, he often acted as a mediator which helped him to broker the Gandhi-Irwin Pact, bringing the Salt Satyagraha to an end; and the Poona Pact, striking an agreement between Gandhi, B.R. Ambedkar and the British government. However, in the polarized atmosphere of the time, his Liberal Party remained an intellectual talking shop with little popular backing—it was less than the sum of its distinguished leadership.

Sapru strongly supported Britain and the inclusion of British India in World War II. However, Sapru was one of the most important lawyers engaged to defend captured soldiers of the Indian National Army, led by Subhas Chandra Bose. Although regarded with respect in independent India, Sapru was very unpopular amongst common people due to his pro-British opposition to the Indian National Congress and leaders like Mahatma Gandhi. He died shortly after India's independence, on January 20, 1949 in Allahabad.

Teknaf : Teknaf is a upazila or sub-district of Cox's Bazar District in South-eastern Bangladesh. It forms the southernmost point in mainland Bangladesh (St. Martin's Island is the southernmost point). The name of the region comes from the Naf River which forms the eastern boundary of the upazila.

Telangana : Telangana or Telingana is an unofficial region in the Indian state of Andhra Pradesh. It includes the northwestern interior districts of Khammam, Mahbubnagar, Nalgonda, Rangareddi, Warangal, Karimnagar, Nizamabad, Adilabad, Medak, and the state capital, Hyderabad. The region lies on the Deccan plateau to the west of the Eastern Ghats range. The Krishna and Godavari rivers flow through the region from west to east.

Unlike as in the rest of Andhra Pradesh Telangana has a fair sized Hindi/Urdu speaking population. This region is primarily agricultural producing rice and wheat as major crops and sugarcane, vegetables etc to a lesser extent. The region was ruled by the Hindu Satavahana dynasty in the 3rd century and Kakatiya kings of Warangal in the 12th-14th centuries, and afterward by a succession of Muslim rulers: the Bahmani sultans, the Adil Shahi sultans of Golconda, the Mughals, and finally the Nizams of Hyderabad. Warangal is famous for 1000 pillars and Kakatiya temple which was constructed during the Satavahana dynasty.

Telangana was formerly part of Hyderabad State and was added to Andhra Pradesh in 1956 on linguistic grounds following the States Reorganization Act. There is an active political movement in Telangana that is seeking to secede from Andhra Pradesh to form a separate state, arguing that the underdevelopment of Telangana results from Andhra Pradesh being too big a state to govern effectively. In addition, they argue that the state government focuses on the more prosperous region of Coastal Andhra to the east. The Telangana Rashtra Samithi, a political party which advocates for a separate Telangana state, became part of the ruling coalition of Andhra Pradesh after the 2004 state legislative elections.

Telangana Rashtra Samithi (TRS) : Telangana Rashtra Samithi (TRS)is a regional political party in the southern Indian state of Andhra Pradesh. Its main agenda is the creation of a separate state of Telangana from Andhra Pradesh. The founder and party chief is K. Chandrashekar Rao who is a member of the United Progressive Alliance (Coalition Government led by Indian National Congress). He is the Minister of Labour in Dr. Manmohan Singh's cabinet.

Telugu : Telugu belongs to the Dravidian language family and is the official language of the state of Andhra Pradesh, India. It is the second largest spoken language in India after Hindi, and one of the 24 official national languages of India. 19th century Englishmen called it the Italian of the East as all words in Telugu end with a vowel sound.

Telugu Desam Party : Telugu Desam Party (Party for Telugu Land) or TDP is a regional political party in India's Andhra Pradesh state. It was founded by former Telugu film star N.T. Rama Rao on March 29, 1982. Rama Rao wanted an alternative to the ruling Congress Party in the state. After establishing his party, he embraced Sanyasa (or renunciation) and vowed to dedicate himself to the Telugu people and to rejuvenate Telugu pride. In the 13th Lok Sabha (1999-2004), it was the fourth largest party with 29 members.

Rama Rao toured Andhra extensively in what was called Chaitanya Ratham (literally—a Chariot which spreads energy), his "election vehicle", and made use of the immense popularity of his on-screen movie image to win the next election. The party was voted to power in a record nine months after its establishment. TDP also won more than 35 (out of 40) Lok Sabha seats in the 1984 Indian elections. This made TDP the largest opposition party in the Lok Sabha as Congress won more than 400 (out of about 500) seats in that election. The TDP was voted out of power in the state in 1988. During his first tenure, Rama Rao introduced many populist measures like selling a kilogram of rice for Rs.2.

Between 1988 and 1993, N.T. Rama Rao gave up his sanyasa and married a part-time journalist and student of political history, Lakshmi Parvati. In this period he also played a significant role in national politics by pledging support to the then prime Ministers V.P. Singh and Chandra Shekhar (who formed coalition governments in the absence of absolute majority for their respective parties). TDP returned to power in 1993. Rama Rao was elected to be the Chief Minister for the second time. But his governing cabinet and his family suffered from what many political observers saw, as "unconstitutional interference in affairs" by his new wife. In 1995, Nara Chandrababu Naidu, finance minister and the son-in-law of NTR (who is married to NTR's daughter through his first wife) overthrew Rama Rao's government by gathering a majority of the MLAs. The overwhelming consensus against his party led the Election Commission to recognize a break-away faction under the party's original name. NTR, the founder of the party, had to rename what was left of the party as "NTR TDP". He vowed to go to the people, seeking a fresh mandate after this humiliation. However, within a year, he died of natural causes.

After the demise of N.T. Rama Rao in 1996, his widow split the minority party again in the face of other opponents who were claiming to inherit his legacy. However, the infighting, fragmentation and the lack of a charismatic leader, led them to political oblivion in the subsequent elections. Chandrababu Naidu remained the leader of the majority faction, now recognised as the official Telugu Desam. Naidu has expressed a goal of establishing Hyderabad and the state as a center for information technology. He wants to make Andhra Pradesh what he calls Swarnaandhra Pradesh (literally Golden Andhra Pradesh).

Temple Festivals : There are thousands of centres, religious or secular where weekly, monthly or annual fairs are held. Every village and town in Andhra has some kind of temple or place of worship where religious festivals are held accompanied by fairs. Some of them are of local importance, others have a wider significance. Amaravati Srisailam, Tripurantakam, Kaleswaram, Daksharamam, Kalahasti Vemulavada and Inavole are the most important Saiva Kshetras and Srikurmam, Simhachalam, Nellore, Tirupati, Ahobilam, Srikakulam Yadagiri, Bhadrachalam and Mamgalagiri are the most important Vaishnava Kshetras. Warangal, Mandapaka, Alampuram, Secundrabad, Bejawada, Sulurpeta and Donakonda are important Sakti Kshetras. These places attract millions of devotees throughout the year, and the rituals observed here are traditional, in accordance with the Agamas.

Temple of Kamakhya : Temple of Kamakhya on the Nilachal Hill near Gauhati has been a part and parcel of Assamese life and culture from ancient times. It is around this temple that the Tantric form of Hinduism evolved. The stone images and other relics found around the temple have been dated by archaeologists to the eighth century onwards. It is 8 Km north west of Guwahati by bus or taxi. The temple is dedicated to the goddess Kamakshya. The temple is in the shape of beehive and it has the nymph motifs and the long turtle back hall. Non-Hindus are not allowed to enter the sanctum. Kamakhya Temple on Nilachal Hill, eight km west of the city is believed to be an ancient 'Khasi' sacrificial site. The temple dedicated to the Goddess Kamakshya is one of the oldest and most sacred centre for Shakti worship and Tantric Hinduism. The original 10th century temple was destroyed by Muslim converts but was rebuilt in 1665 by King Naranarayana of Koch Bihar.

The Sikhara or spire is in the shape of a beehive and it has the nymph motifs and the long turtle back hall. The stone images and other relics found around the temple have been dated by archaeologists to the eighth century onwards. It attracts pilgrims from all over India, especially during the Ambubachi Festival which usually falls around July. The ponds here are home to some giant turtles. There is a majestic view of the city and the Brahmaputra river from the hill top.

Ten Degree Channel : The Ten Degree Channel is a channel (strait) that separates the Andaman Islands from the Nicobar Islands in the Bay of Bengal. The two sets of islands together form the Indian Union Territory (UT) of Andaman and Nicobar Islands. The Channel is approximately 150 km wide, running essentially along an east-west orientation. It is so named as it lies on the 10-degree line of Latitude, north of the equator.

Tenzing Norgay : Tenzing was the first Indian to scale the highest peak of the world, the Mount Everest (height 8,848 metres) on 29, March 1953. He achieved this mountaineering feat together with Sir Edmund Hillary the well known adventurist of New Zealand.

Tenzing was born in Nepal in a poor family. Tenzing was a follower of Buddhism and had acquired the Indian citizenship in 1933.The childhood name of Tenzing was Namgyal Wagundi. He was also called Khumjung Bhutia.

The Government of India conferred the title of 'Padma Bhushan' on Tenzing in 1959. Tenzing was also awarded the George Medal in recognition of his excellent service in the field of mountaineering. For imparting training in mountaineering the Government of India established the 'Himalayan Mountaineering Institute' at Darjeeling in West Bengal In1954 and Tenzing was appointed Director (training) in this Institute. Tenzing Norgay was nick named as 'Tiger of Snows'.

Tera Taali or Terahtal : Tera Taali or Terathal is performed by the Kamar community of Pokhran and Deedwana in honour of their local deity, Baba Ramdeo. This dance is especially performed during the Ramdevra Festival, which is held in August of September at the small village of Ramdevra, near Pokaran in Western Rajasthan. It is a rather unusual performance where the men play a four-stringed instrument called a chau-tara and the women sit with dozens of manjeeras, or cymbals, tied on all over their bodies and strike them with the ones they hold in their hands.

Terai : The Terai or Tarai ("moist land") is a belt of marshy grasslands, savannas, and forests at the base of the Himalaya range in India, Nepal, and Bhutan, from the Yamuna River in the west to the Brahmaputra River in the east. Above the Terai belt lies the Bhabhar, a forested belt of rock, gravel, and soil eroded from the Himalayas, where the water table lies from 5 to 37 meters deep. The

Terai zone lies below the Bhabhar, and is composed of alternate layers of clay and sand, with a high water table that creates many springs and wetlands. The Terai zone is inundated yearly by the monsoon-swollen rivers of the Himalaya. Below the Terai lies the great alluvial plain of the Yamuna, Ganges, Brahmaputra, and their tributaries.

Terai-Duar Savanna and Grasslands : The Terai-Duar savanna and grasslands is an ecoregion that stretches across the middle of the Terai belt, from Uttaranchal state through southern Nepal to northern West Bengal. The Terai-Duar savanna and wetlands are a mosaic of tall grasslands, savannas and evergreen and deciduous forests. The grasslands are among the tallest in the world, and are maintained by silt deposited by the yearly monsoon floods. Important grasses include Kans grass (Saccharum spontaneum) and Baruwa grass (Saccharum benghalensis). The ecoregion is home to the endangered Indian Rhinoceros (Rhinoceros unicornis), as well as elephants, tigers, bears, leopards and other wild animals. Much of the ecoregion has been converted to farmland, although Royal Chitwan National Park and Royal Bardia National Park preserve significant sections of habitat, and are home to some of the greatest concentrations of rhinoceros and tiger remaining in South Asia.

Tezpur : Tezpur has always been the cultural centre of Assam. It has plenty of urban delights besides being a place of historical significance. Hailed as the city of eternal Romance, Tezpur has been the seat of legendary love of Usha and Aniruddha. Agnigarh or the rampart with a 'Moat' of fire still preserves the memory of the young lovers. Legend has it that Princess usha, the only daughter of the Demon King Bana was kept in Agnigarh. The ruins are on a hillock facing the Brahmaputra and offers a panoramic view. The ruins of the portals of the Da-Parbatia temple and the carvings and sculptures in the temple complex are a delight to the archaeologist and the devout. Tezpur and its outskirts offer other equally interesting, fascinating and even challenging places to visit.

There is an imposing stone inscription of the Ahom General Kalia Bhomora Phukan who had planned to build a bridge across the Brahmaputra two centuries ago. His dream has become a reality because the present 3.05 km bridge at the same site is named after that intrepid and imaginative Ahom General. Cole park, with a pond, also shelters the cultural remains and ruins of the famous Bamuni hill. Hazara Pukhuri, a 70 acre 19th century tank and the Maha Bhairab temple are the other significant destinations in Tezpur.

Thakazhi Sivasankara Pillai : Thakazhi Sivasankara Pillai (17 April 1912—10 April 1999) was a novelist and short story writer of Malayalam literature. He focused on the oppressed classes as the subject of his works, which are known for their attention to historic detail. He has written several novels and over 600 short stories. His most famous works are Kayar (the Rope, 1978) and Chemmeen (Shrimps, 1956; film adaptation, 1965). He was awarded the Indian government's highest literary award, the Jnanpith in 1984.

Thakurgaon : Thakurgaon is a district (Rajshahi division) with an area of 1809.52 sq km, is bounded by Panchagarh district on the north, West Bengal of India on the west and south, Panchagarh and Dinajpur districts on the east. Annual average temperature: maximum 33.5 C, minimum 10.5 C; annual rainfall 2536 mm. Main rivers are Tangon, Punarbhaba, Nagar, Pathari, Talma, Kulic, Dhepa. Thakurgaon subdivision was established in 1860 and was turned into a district in 1984. The district consists of 2 municipalities, 18 wards, 32 mahallas, 5 upazilas, 51 union parishads, 643 mouzas and 643 villages. The upazilas are

Baliadangi, Haripur, Pirganj, Ranisankail and Thakurgaon Sadar; municipalities are Thakurgaon Sadar and Pirganj.

Thandiani Hills : Thandiani hills (Thandiani - 'Very Cold'), the part of west Himalayas, is located in the Abbottabad District of Pakistan. There are boosters of many TV channels, including PTV, Channel 3 and PTV World. There is a rest house and a hotel for tourists. The hills are 9,000 feet (2,750 m) above sea level. The winters are very harsh and in winters the temperature drops to -20 degrees Celsius. There is also heavy snowfall (about 120 inches or 3 m) every winter which makes it difficult for transportation. The area and its surrounding villages were damaged by 2005 Kashmir Earthquake.

Thane : Thane (formerly Thana) is a city in Maharashtra, India, part of the Mumbai Conurbation, northeast of Mumbai at the head of the Thane Creek. It is the administrative headquarters of Thane District. The city of Thane is situated on the western banks of Thane creek with Parsik hills on the east and Yeour hills on the west. The creek not only provides a natural protection to the place but has also facilitated transport of big and small ships since ancient times. This has also acted as an impetus for the development of local and international trade since the pre-historic times. Besides being the stamping ground of the pre-historic tribes, Thane city has a rich cultural heritage, mythological background, and has been home to many events of historical importance.

Thanedar Wala : Thanedar Wala wetland site is located 15 km east of Lakki, Bannu District, North-West Frontier Province, Pakistan. It comprises the Kurram River from its confluence with the Gambila River downstream almost to the border with Punjab province. Thanedar Wala is a good characteristic example of a river floodplain wetland in Pakistan. It hosts the globally threatened ferruginous duck Aythya nyroca. The site is an important wintering place for herons, Anatidae and shorebirds. The wetland consists of a 10 km stretch of the Kurram River and its associated floodplains. Most of the area consists of a few braided river channels and sandy or muddy islands with a maximum width of 4 km, and some permanent and seasonal fresh to brackish marshes and ponds.

Thanesar : Thanesar is an old and historic town on the banks of the Ghaggar river in Haryana state of northern India. It is located in Kurukshetra District, approximately 160 km northwest of Delhi. Thanesar was an obscure village until the 1950's. After the partition of India, a large refugee camp was set up here, which became the nucleus of a bustling commercial city. It grew so much that in 1973, a new district named "Kurukshetra" was created, of which Thanesar was the main town. People now tend, erroneously, to refer to Thanesar town as "Kurukshetra".

The new district was named Kurukshetra in order to capitalize on the purported mythological significance of the area. "Kurukshetra" is in fact the name of a mythological battlefield, where the Mahabharata war was waged, the actual location of which is impossible to confirm. Local hearsay identifies the legendary "Kurukshetra" with a nearby obscure hamlet, and with the active abetment of the state government, Thanesar is presently experiencing a tourist boom. Historians are also trying for a long time to somehow establish this city's link with the Indus Civilisation. They are also trying to prove somehow that the Ghaggar river is actually the famous Saraswati river of the vedas.

Thanesar derives its name from the words "Sthaneshwar" which means "Deity of the Place". The Sthaneshwar Mahadev Temple, whose presiding deity is Lord Shiva, is believed to be the oldest temple in the vicinity. Other religious sites include the Brahma Sarovar, the Sannihit Sarovar, Gurdwara 6th Patashahi and the Devi Bhadrakali temple, which is counted among the 51 Shakti Peethas. The bathing-fair held here on the occurrence of a solar eclipse is said to be attended by half a million pilgrims. Thanesar was sacked and many of its temples were destroyed by Mahmud of Ghazni.

The modern city of Thanesar is an important educational center; it is home to Kurukshetra University, the National Institute of Technology, Kurukshetra (Formarly Regional Engineering College) and the Shri Krishna Government Ayurvedic College.

Thang-ta : This is one of the most thrilling dances of Manipur and is performed by young men with swords and shields. *Yumsarol, Pae-S-Jogoi, Lai Haroba* and *Ras Lila* are the other important dance forms of Manipur.

Thanjavur : Thanjavur, formerly known as Tanjore, is a city in Tamil Nadu, in southeastern India. The city lies on the south bank of the Kaveri River, 200 miles south of Chennai. Thanjavur is also the capital of the Thanjavur District. Tanjore is also the name of Air India One, the special aircraft of the President of India and the Prime Minister of India.

Thanjavur derives its name from Tanjan-an asura (demon) who according to local legend caused devastation and was killed by Sri Anandavalli Amman and Sri Neelam-egapperumal. Tanjan's last request that the city might be named after him was granted.

Thanjavur is famous for the Brihadeeswara Temple built by Rajaraja Chola, the first sailor king of India. The Brihadeeswara Temple also known as the Big Temple is one of the UNESCO World Heritage Sites. The temple is enclosed in two courts, surmounted by a lofty tower and including the exquisitely decorated shrine of Subrahmanya. Among the other historic buildings is the Vijayanagara fort, which contains a palace that was expanded by the Maratha raja Sarfoji with an armoury, a Bell Tower and the Saraswathi Mahal Library, which contains over 30,000 Indian and European manuscripts written on palm leaf and paper.

Thar Desert : The Thar Desert, also known as the Great Indian Desert, is a desert located in western India and southeastern Pakistan. It lies mostly in the Indian state of Rajasthan, and extends into the southern portion of Haryana and Punjab states and into northern Gujarat state. In Pakistan, the desert covers eastern Sind province and the southeastern portion of Pakistan's Punjab province. In Pakistan's Punjab province it is known as the Cholistan Desert. The Thar Desert is bounded on the northwest by the Sutlej River, on the east by the Aravalli Range, on the south by the salt marsh known as the Rann of Kutch (parts of which are sometimes included in the Thar), and on the west by the Indus River. Its boundary to the large thorny steppe to the north is ill-defined. Depending on what areas are included or excluded, the nominal size of the Thar can vary significantly.

According to the WWF definition, the desert proper has 92,200 square miles (238,700 km^2). Another source gives the area of the Thar Desert as 446,000 km^2 extending 805 km (about 500 mi) long and about 485 km (about 300 mi) wide, with 208,110 square kilometres in India. Of the Indian portion, 61% falls in Rajasthan, 20% in Gujarat and 9% in Punjab and Haryana combined. The greater portion lies in Rajasthan, covering about three-fifths of the total geographical area.

Thar Express : Thar Express is the cross country train that connects Karachi in Pakistan to Jodhpur in India. Six kilométres apart, Munabaó and and Khokrophar are the two last railway stations of India and Pakistan border respectively. The train link has been revived after a period of 41 years. The link was distroyed during the Indo-Pakistani War of 1965.

Tharparkar : Tharparkar is a town located in the [[Tharparkar District], which is one of 22 districts located in the Sindh province in Pakistan.

Tharu : Tharu are indigenious people living in the Terai plains of South Nepal and India. According to Nepal's 2001 census, there are 1,533,879 ethnic Tharu (6.75% of Nepal's total population) of which 1,331,546 speak one of the seven Tharu dialects as a mother tongue. Tharu living in Nepal are concentrated in the jungles of the southern Terai lowlands of Nepal in Bardia, Kailali, Kanchanpur, Morang, Saptari and Jhapa districts, as well as in the inner Terai valleys of Chitwan, Dang, Deukhuri Surkhet and Udaipur. Tharu living in India live near the Nepali border, mainly in Naini Tal in Uttaranchal, Kheri and Gonda Districts of Uttar Pradesh State and Champaran district of Bihar State. The Tharu population in Nepal is estimated to be at 1.2 million.

Thatto : Thatto, or Thatta is a historic town of 22,000 inhabitants in the Sindh province of Pakistan. Its major monuments are listed among the World Heritage Sites. The city, formerly commanding the delta of the Indus, was the capital of Lower Sindh from the 14th century. Since 1592, it was governed in the name of the Mughal emperors of Delhi. After the province was ceded to Nadir Shah of Persia in 1739, Thatta has fallen into neglect.

Thatta's monuments include the Jama Mosque, built by Shah Jahan in 1647-49 and lined with glazed tiles. There are also the tombs of Jam Nizamuddin (reigned in 1461-1509), several Tarkhan rulers and Mughal officials. A vast old necropolis with thousands of graves may be found at the nearby Makli Hills.

Thavil : The thavil is a barrel shaped percussion instrument from South India. It is used in folk music and Carnatic music, often accompanying the nadaswaram. The thavil and the nadaswaram are essential ingredients of traditional festivals and ceremonies in South India.

The thavil consists of a cylindrical shell hollowed out of a solid block of wood. Layers of animal skin are stretched across the two sides of the shell using hemp hoops attached to the shell. The right face of the instrument has a larger diameter than the left side. The instrument is hung by a leather strap from the shoulder of the player. The right head is played with the right hand, wrist and fingers. The player usually wears thumb caps on all the fingers of the right hand. The left head is played with a stick made from the wood of the portia tree. It is not uncommon for left-handed players to use the opposite hands, and some nadaswaram groups feature both a right- and a left-handed thavil player.

Thayambaka : Thayambaka is a solo Chenda (drum) performance that are unique to Kerala state of south India, where the performer uses one stick and the other hand to play the instrument (Chenda) instead of the usual two sticks. Thayambaka is generally performed by a lead drummer surrounded by about 3-4 assistant drummers(Veekku Chenda), and 3-4 Elathalam players. It is a concert like performance of percussion instruments alone lasting approximately 90-120 minutes.

Thayir Sadam : Thayir sadam (also called yogurt rice, yoghurt rice, or curd rice) is a dish originating with the Tamil culture of South India. It is most popular in the Indian states of Tamil Nadu, Kerala, Andhra Pradesh, and Karnataka. To prepare the dish, rice is boiled so that it breaks down, becoming almost like a paste (kuzhaiya saadam vadikkavum). It is then seasoned with fried finely chopped green chiles, ginger, and curry leaves, and sometimes also urad dal, mustard seeds, and asafoetida. Finally, milk, yogurt, and salt are added. Thayir sadam is often eaten accompanied by South Indian pickles, especially vadu manga (tender mango) or lime.

The Aranyakas : The Aranyakas are part of the Hindu Shruti; these religious scriptures are sometimes argued to be part of either the Brahmanas or Upanishads. The name translates to "of the forest", meaning, treatises for hermits or sadhus living in the wilderness. This contrasts with the grhyasutras, treatises intended for domestic life. Their language is early Classical Sanskrit, and together with the bulk of the Upanishads, the Aranyakas form the basis of Vedanta, roughly dating to a few centuries on either side of the beginning of the Common Era.

The Aranyakas discuss philosophy and sacrifice. They are believed to have originated with the various mystical ascetic groups that developed in post-Vedic India. The Aranyakas constitute a more philosophical and mystical interpretation of the themes presented in the Vedas, as opposed to the Brahmanas, which were primarily concerned with the proper performance of ritual. Like the Upanishads, the Aranyakas may have initially constituted a secret or hidden teaching, not in the sense of being forbidden or restricted, but rather being both a non-obvious expansion on the themes of the Vedas and a teaching that was primarily conveyed individually from teacher to student.

The Archeological Museum : Archaeological Museum at Vaishali includes terracottas, seals, coins, pottery and sculpture. Entry—free, Opens from 1000 to 1700. Closed on Fridays.

The Ashtavakra Gita : Ashtavakra Gita (Song of Ashtavakra) also known by the name Ashtavakra Samhita is an influential nondualist Hindu text traditionally said to have been written by the Sage Ashtavakra, though its authorship is not known with certainty. There is little doubt though that it is very old, probably dating back to the days of the classic Vedanta period. The Sanskrit style and the doctrine expressed would seem to warrant this assessment.

The Asian Age : The Asian Age is a newspaper sold in the Indian city of Bombay. The Asian Age has editions in five cities in the country and one in London. The newspaper was launched in February 1994, simultaneously in Delhi, Mumbai and London. At present, it has editions in Delhi, Mumbai, Kolkatta, Bangalore and London. The Asian Age brings out several trendy supplements and special sections on movies, fashion and lifestyle, education, information and technology, health and books.

The Bay of Bengal : The Bay of Bengal is a bay that forms the northeastern part of the Indian Ocean. It resembles a triangle in shape, and is bordered on the east by the Malay Peninsula, and on the west by the India. On the northern tip of the "bay" lie the Indian state of West Bengal and the country of Bangladesh, thus the name. The southern extremes reach the island country of Sri Lanka, and the Indian Union Territory Andaman and Nicobar Islands.

Many major rivers of India flow west to east into the Bay of Bengal: in the north, the Ganges River (or Ganga), Meghna and Brahmaputra rivers, and in the south Mahanadi, Godavari, Krishna and Kaveri (sometimes written as Cauvery) rivers. The Sundarbans mangrove forest is formed at the delta of the Ganga, Brahmaputra and Meghna rivers on the Bay of Bengal. The Irrawaddy River of Burma also flows into the bay.

Major Bangladeshi ports on the bay include Chittagong and Mongla. Major Indian ports on the bay include Chennai (formerly Madras), Vishakhapatnam, Kolkata (formerly Calcutta) and Pondicherry. Cox's Bazar, on the northeastern coast of the bay, is one of the longest unbroken natural beaches of the world.

The Bhagavad Gita : The Bhagavad Gita is revered as a sacred text of Hindu philosophy. The name 'Bhagavad Gita', when translated into English, literally means 'The Song of God'. Its written format is that of a poem which is 700 verses long, originating from the famous puranic epic Mahabharata. Commonly referred to as The Gita, it is a conversation between Krishna and Arjuna which takes place on a battlefield, just prior to the start of a climactic war. During the conversation, Krishna proclaims that he is God Himself (Bhagavan), and at the request of Arjuna, displays His divine form, which is described as timeless, that leaves the latter awestruck. The conversation summarizes a number of different Yogic and Vedantic philosophies, explaining the meaning and purpose of life and existence. The Bhagavad Gita refers to itself as an 'Upanishad', and is sometimes called Gitopanisad.

It is not exactly clear when the Bhagavad Gita was written. Astronomical evidence cited in the Mahabharata place the incidents upon which the Gita is based in the year 3137 BCE, while the Puranas suggest a date of c. 1924 BCE. Scholarly estimates place the actual writing of the Gita in the latter half of the 1st millennium BC (roughly 4th century BC), making it a contemporary of the older Upanishads.

The Bhrigu Rishi Temple : Bharuch in Gujarat, is an ancient town with a 2000 year history situated at the mouth of River Narmada. It is located between Vadodara and Surat and is about one hour from each place. One of the oldest seaports which flourished in the 1st century AD, Bharuch came under the rule of the Solanki rajputs much later. The city got its name 'Bhrigukachba' from the Temple of Bhrigu Rishi, the name later shortened to Bharuch. Today the city is well known for its textile mills and long staple cotton. Bharuch got its original name, 'Bhrigukachba' from this temple. The temple is situated on the east of the city, on the banks of the River Narmada.

The Bhumij Kols : The Bhumij Kols in Bihar who occupy parts of the two Singhbhum districts west and south of the Kasari river, are ethnically related to the Mundas and resemble them in physical appearance. Dark brown in complexion, they have thick noses and lips, broad chests, well developed hands and are short in stature. Since they claim to be Hindus and employ Brahman priests they are accepted as such, but their exact position in the Hindu caste hierarchy is not well defined. They do not appear to have fully assimilated the essential elements of Hinduism and completely jettisoned their tribal religion. Many among them still worship their own village deities. Their totemic exogamous clans are fast being forgotten and they have adopted the surname of 'Singh'. Their agricultural technique is not so advanced.

The Black Hole of Calcutta : The Black Hole of Calcutta was a small dungeon where Indian troops held British prisoners of war after the capture of Fort William on June 20, 1756. According to a disputed account by a survivor, 123 of 146 prisoners died of heat exhaustion in the confined conditions. Certain historians now believe the number to be at most 43.

The Bori Boot Festival—Hill Miris Festival : The Bori Boot festival is exclusively performed by the Hill-Miris. The festival usually falls in February. Bori Boot means to get together irrespective of age, sex, caste to hail the spring and successful harvest. The festival also invokes the spirit of Bori Boot to bless them with prosperity and free from diseases of any kind. The festival is performed collectively. The young members do all the work under the elders guidance. The Nibu (priest) performs Puja as well as conduct sacrifice. 'Etting' is co piously applied on one and all. The festival is of three days duration.

The Brahma Sutra : The Brahma sutra is the nyaya prasthana, the logical text that sets forth the philosophy systematically. No study of Vedanta is considered complete without a close examination of the Prasthana Traya. Brahma Sutras are also called Vedanta Sutras. Additionally, they also known by other names: Uttara Mimâmsâ-sutras, Shariraka Sutra, Sâriraka Mimâmsâ-sutras and the Bhikshu sutra. While the Upanishads and the Bhagavad-Gita are authoritative Vedanta texts, it is in the Brahma sutra that the teachings of Vedanta are set forth in a systematic and logical order. Additionally, the Brahma Sutras reconciled seemingly contradictory verses of the Upanishads and set forth its teachings in a systematic manner. The Brahma Sutra consists of 555 aphorisms or sutras, in 4 chapters, each chapter being divided into 4 sections each.

The Brahmana : The Brahmana (Sanskrit) are part of the Hindu Shruti; They are composed in Vedic Sanskrit, and the period of their composition is sometimes referred to as the Brahmanic period or age (approximately between 900 BC and 500 BC). They are essentially commentaries of the Vedas, explaining Vedic ritual. The earliest Brahmanas may have been written several centuries earlier, contemporary to the Black Yajurveda commentary prose, but they have only survived in fragments.

The Buddhist Temple : This temple which is located in Arunachal Pradesh on the top of a hill amidst gorgeous green gardens with yellow roof reflects the extensive Tibetan influence. There is a stupa erected in front of the shrine. The Dalai Lama planted a tree by the side of the shrine. The grounds of the temple afford a good view of Itanagar Town.

The Chach-Nama : The Chach-Nama is a Muslim chronicle. It is also known as the Tarikh-i Hind Wa Sindh. It was translated from the original Arabic to Persian by Muhammad Ali bin Hamid bin Abu Bakr Kufi. The book is a history of the Muslim conquest of South Asia, mostly modern Pakistan, and also contains an account of the invasion by Muhammad bin Qasim. The work describes that many of the people in Sindh were Buddhists, though later Muslim chronicles that were written after the decline and extinction of Buddhism do not mention the Buddhist monks.

The Cheros : The Cheros in Bihar who have Dravidian physiognomy and vary in colour, at one time ruled over the Gangetic provinces and claim to be Rajputs. They are divided into two sections; Barahazar and Tarahazar. The former rank as the higher and include most descendants to the former ruling families in Palamu. The social status of the Cheros was very high even in the Mughal period and they were given the rank of Mansabdars in Akbar's court. Their children were invested with the sacred thread by a Brahman priest at the time of marriage. Agriculture is their original occupation. Nowadays they keep shop, do carting, work on roads or in coal mines and collect Tasar, Lac and Catechu. They are on the whole, a proud race and have never forgotten that they were once a great people and that their descents are honourable ones. They are also found in the villages of Rohtas and in the Morang region.

The Chitrakootam : The Chitrakootam is another shrine in Tamil Nadu, situated adjacent to the Nataraja temple is dedicated to Lord Govindraja. It has five halls. The Nritta sabha, the hall of immortal dance has 56 pillars depicting dance figures. The Deva Sabha was the hall of festivals and meeting place of the administrators. The Chit sabha (Hall) houses the Akasa Lingam and Kanaka sabha houses the Nataraja image.

The City Palace : The citadel of the Kachchawah Rajput rulers of Jaipur. The palace houses a museum with a superb collection of costumes and armoury of Rajputs & Mughals. The vast complex occupies one seventh of the walled city of Jaipur and is wonderful blend of Rajput and Mughal architecture.

The Concert For Bangladesh : The Concert For Bangladesh was the event title for two benefit concerts held on the afternoon and evening of August 1, 1971, playing to a total of 40,000 people at Madison Square Garden in New York. As East Pakistan struggled to become the separate state of Bangladesh, tremendous political and military turmoil led to a massive refugee problem. This problem was compounded by torrential rains causing devastating floods and threatening a humanitarian disaster. Bengali musician Ravi Shankar consulted his friend George Harrison regarding a means of providing help to the situation. Harrison recorded the single "Bangladesh" to help raise awareness and pushed Apple Records to release Shankar's single "Joi Bangla" in a dual-pronged effort to raise funds.

Shankar also asked Harrison's advice regarding a small fund-raising concert in the United States. Instead, Harrison took over and persuaded his friends to join him at a large concert at Madison Square Garden. The event was organised within five weeks. Harrison first asked his fellow Beatles to appear. John Lennon agreed to take part in the concert, however Harrison stipulated that Lennon's wife Yoko Ono not perform with him. Lennon agreed, but left New York two days before the event following an argument with Ono regarding his and Harrison's agreement that she not participate. Paul McCartney declined because of the bad feelings caused by the Beatles' legal problems on their break-up. Ringo Starr, however, readily ageed to appear.

Shankar opened the concert with a 17-minute recital of Indian music (Bangla Dhun). Eric Clapton made his first public appearance since the end of the five-month Derek and the Dominos tour the previous December. Clapton was still in the grip of a heroin addiction, and partook of his habit, also using methadone, before going onstage. The heroin had been cut with talcum powder and Clapton collapsed on stage. A doctor was able to revive him, and Clapton continued the performance.

Musical help was also on hand from Billy Preston, Leon Russell, Klaus Voormann and Badfinger (along with Jim Horn, Carl Radle, Jesse Ed Davis, Don Preston and a host of backing singers organized by Don Nix). Bob Dylan made his first stage appearance since the Isle of Wight Festival in August 1969. Apart from sitting in for a few numbers with The Band on New Year 1972 and an unannounced appearance backing John Prine on harp at a Greenwich Village club, he did not play live again until January 1974.

The Daily Jang : The Daily Jang is the largest Urdu language newspaper of the world, published by the Jang Group simultaneously from Pakistan's main cities, Rawalpindi/Islamabad, Karachi, Lahore, Quetta and Multan, as well as from London as well for circulation throughout Europe. Mir Khalil ur Rehman was the founder of the newspaper and now his younger son Mir Shakil ur Rehman is the present owner.

The Daily Ummat : The Daily Ummat is a Karachi based Urdu conservative Islamist newspaper, which has become famous for its investigative reporting, rare in Urdu journalism.

The Discovery of India : The Discovery of India was written by India's first Prime Minister Jawaharlal Nehru during his imprisonment in 1942-1946 at Ahmednagar in the Ahmadnagar Fort. Nehru was jailed for his participation in the Quit India movement along with other Indian leaders, and he used this time to write down his thoughts and knowledge about India's history. The book is widely regarded as a classic in India since its first publication in 1946, and provides a broad view of Indian history, philosophy and culture, as viewed from the eyes of a liberal Indian fighting for the independence of his country. This book contains many stories, beginning with a reference to the Indus Valley Civilization, and then covers the country's history from the arrival of the Aryans to government under the British Empire. The effect of these various peoples on Indian culture and their incorporation into Indian society is examined. This book also analyses in depth the philosophy of Indian life. A popular serial of the same name by noted director Shyam Benegal gave a theatrical interpretation of this book.

The Doon School : The Doon School was one of India's first public schools. It owes its existence to the vision and foresight of Mr. Satish Ranjan Das, one of pre-independence India's most eminent barristers and a member of the Executive Council of the Viceroy of India. The Doon School was founded on the September 10, 1935, when seventy two boys moved into the ivy covered, red brick buildings of what had once been the Imperial Forest College and Research Institute in the Chandbagh Estate at Dehra Dun, approximately 250 km north-east of Delhi. Today the school spans 69 acres (280,000 m^2), and has approximately 500 students between grades seven and twelve. A goal of the school is to provide young Indians with a rounded education, and to instill in them a respect for the ideals of secularism, discipline and equality.

The Economic Times : The Economic Times, launched in 1961, is India's largest financial daily and the world's second largest financial daily after The Wall Street Journal. It is published by India's largest media group, Bennett, Coleman & Co Ltd, (This company along with its other group companies are more popularly known as The Times Group), which also publishes The Times of India, the Navbharat Times, the Maharashtra Times, Femina, and Filmfare.

The Four Varna System : The terms Varna and caste (Jati) are actually two distinct concepts. Varna is a supposed unification of all the Hindu castes into either four groups: Kshatriya, Brahmin, Vaishya, Shudra, or into one of several varna-sankaras. Caste is an endogamous group. Generally a sub-caste is divided into exogamus groups based on same gotras.

For the last few decades, the varna system is getting weakened but the sub-castes jatis(endogamous groups) getting strengthened and quite influential politically. In some regions, some of the jati sub-castes have 25-30% of the population, and that gives them great political clout. The caste system, although not currently officially sanctioned by their governments, is used by Hindus, particularly in India and Nepal for reasons of determining lineage and is passed down through patrilineal descent. It is based on four varnas: Brahmins, Kshatriyas, Vaishyas, Shudras.

The first three castes are seen as 'twice born'. They are allowed to study vedas. In India and Nepal the sub-castes within a Varna are called Jat or Jati (The caste is also used instead of Jat). Each Jati members are allowed to marry only with their Jati members. People are born into their Jati and it cannot be changed. Once someone is born to certain sub-caste or Jati he or she cannot be changed to another Jati. Caste is a permanent attribute among the Hindus. The occupations of the Vaishya are those connected with trade, the cultivation of the land and the breeding of cattle; while those of a Kshatriya consist in ruling and defending the people, administering justice, and the duties, of the military profession generally and ruling by Dharma. Both share with the Brahman the privilege of reading the Vedas. To the Brahman belongs the right of teaching and expounding the sacred texts vedas. Shudras were the serfs, and performed agricultural labour.

The Hindu : The Hindu is a leading English-language newspaper in India, with its largest base of circulation in south India. It is over 125 years old. Founded in 1878 by Subramanya Aiyer, it was later headed by a co-founder, Veeraraghavachariar. Kasturi Iyengar, the legal adviser of the newspaper from 1895, bought it in 1905. Since then his family has retained ownership of the paper. The two basic priciples on which the founders flagged the newspaper were fairness and justice. Headquartered at Chennai (formerly called Madras), The Hindu was published weekly since 1878 and daily since 1889. Its current net-paid circulation exceeds 1 million copies. It is said to enjoy a readership of 3 million in India and abroad and an annual turnover of around 4 billion rupees ($80 million). In 1995, The Hindu became the first Indian newspaper to offer an online edition.

The Indian Express : The Indian Express is an Indian newspaper started by Ram Nath Goenka, and is published from New Delhi. The Indian Express is owned by the Indian Express Group, which also owns the Financial Express, a newspaper focused on the Indian economy, stock markets, and fiscal policies. In 1948, Ram Nath

Goenka partnered with Lala Deshbandhu Guptato of Daily Tej Limited to publish Indian News Chronicle, an English daily, from New Delhi. After the demise of Guptato, the daily was bought by Ram Nath Goenka and renamed as The Indian Express.

During the days of the political emergency imposed by the then Indian Prime Minister, Indira Gandhi on June 25,1975, the Indian Express was utilised by Mr Goenka as a weapon to call to account the errant establishment. Goenka is revered today for his journalistic crusades to uphold democracy and as a tireless soldier who fought corruption in the highest circles.

The Indian Express purpotes to emulate the highest standards of journalism as set by Goenka, and expresses its pride through its motto: Journalism of Courage. There have been allegations, however, that The Indian Express is overtly sympathetic to the current government of India ruled by the Congress party, though this popular notion is somewhat debunked by the newspaper's equally persistent crusade against the Left, members of the present government and its policy of embarassing the establishment, something it is best known for. It is rumoured to be the first newspaper read by all government leaders in the morning.

The Kerala Model : The Kerala model refers to the economic practices developed in India's province of Kerala, which are used to assist in disadvantaged areas. For more than one reason Kerala is widely known as a special state in India and abroad. Quite often, its demographic characterstics and the achievements on the socio-economic front are highlighted as 'kerala model' and is unique among developing countries.

The Manusmriti : The Manusmriti (Sanskrit), translated "Laws of Manu" or "Institutions of Manu", is regarded as a foundational work of Hindu law and ancient Indian society, compiled and written quite late, c.200 CE in India. It is one of the eighteen Smritis of the Dharma Sastra (or "laws of righteous conduct"); Smriti means "what is remembered" and is applied in general to a Hindu text other than the Vedas, including traditional Indian epics, the Puranas, and science and grammar treatises. Unlike the Vedas which are considered to be eternal or of divine origin, the Smritis are considered to be of human origin and therefore susceptible to the flaws of humans. They contain laws, rules and codes of conduct to be applied by individuals, communities and nations. Some of these laws codify the Hindu caste system and discuss the "stages of life for a twice-born man". The book is ascribed to Manu, said to be the forefather of all human race. Manu's writings condemned the indian sub continent into the dark ages which still continue for more than 250 million people living under the hindu belief in the oppressive caste system.

The Marathas : The Marathas" is a collective term referring to an Indo Aryan group of Hindu, Marathi-speaking castes of warriors and peasants hailing mostly from the present-day state of Maharashtra, who created a substantial empire, covering a major part of India, in the late 17th and 18th centuries AD. The "Marathas" were known by that name since their native tongue was almost invariably Marathi; however, not all those whose native tongue is Marathi are Marathas. The term "Maratha" refers only to those marathi-speaking people who also belong to certain specific Hindu castes: for one available listing, refer to Maratha Clan System. Thus, the terms "Marathi people" and "Maratha people" are not interchangeable and should not be confused for each other.

The Mirror : 'The Mirror' was a popular Pakistani social magazine which ran from 1951 to 1971. It was published monthly, and its full name was 'The Mirror of the Month'. Its editor, founder and publisher was Zaib-un-Nissa Hamidullah.

The Mundas : The Mundas in Bihar are polytheists and worship numerous deities and spirits. Singbonga is their Supreme Being, he is not merely a spectator of their deeds but possess the authority to punish evil-doers, he ranks highest in their Pantheon. The spirits of their ancestors are called Orabongako-the house hold gods. Hatubongako or the village gods occupy the most significant place, they are regarded as the guardians of the village and their help is invoked in agricultural and other economic operations.

All the deities are worshipped by the village priest known as the Pahan on behalf of the entire community. The presence of the spirits of the ancestors is very real to the Mundas. The Mundas really feel that they are constantly with them in the house. A few days after a man dies, his spirits is brought from the grave by an elaborate ceremony to live in the house which was his during his life time. To the Mundas, there are gods or spirits in many natural objects such as mountain-peaks, waterfalls and trees.

The Nalanda Archaeological Museum : Opposite the entrance to the ruins of the university and houses, it has a small but beautiful collection of Buddhist and Hindu bronzes and a number of undamaged statues of the Lord Buddha that were found in the area. Two enormous terracotta Jars of the first century stand intact behind the museum in a shaded enclosure. The collection includes copper plates and stone inscriptions, coins, pottery and samples of burnt rice (12th century AD) found among the ruins here. Open during 10.00 to 17.00 hours. Closed on Friday.

The Nalanda University : The total area of the excavation of The Nalanda University in Bihar is about 14 hectares. All the edifices are of red brick and the gardens are beautiful. The buildings are divided by a central walkway that goes south to north, the monasteries or "Viharas" are east of this central alley and the temples of "Chaiyas" to the west. The Vihara-1 is perhaps the most interesting with its cells on two floors built around a central courtyard where steps lead up to what must have been a dais for the professors to address their students. A small chapel still retains a half broken statue of the Lord Buddha. The enormous pyramidal mass of the Temple No.3 is impressive and from its top commands a splendid view of the entire area. It is surrounded by smaller stupas, many of which are studded with small and big statues of the Lord Buddha in various poses or 'Mudras'.

The News International : The News International is the largest English language newspaper in Pakistan, published simultaneously from Islamabad, Karachi and Lahore. An international edition is published from London, England and plans are currently underway to start publication in New York City, USA. The News is published by the Jang Group of Newspapers, publisher of the Daily Jang the largest Urdu language newspaper in the world. Mir Khalil ur Rehman was the founder of the newspaper and now his younger son Mir Shakil ur Rehman is the present owner.

The Ogre : The Ogre or Baintha Brakk is a steep, craggy mountain, 7,285 m high, in the Karakoram range of Pakistan. It is famous for being one of the hardest peaks in the world to climb; 23 years elapsed between the first ascent in 1977 and the second in 2000. The Ogre rises above the north side of the Biafo Glacier, one of the major glaciers of the central Karakoram. It lies about 75km north of Skardu, the major town of the region, and about 30km north of the roadhead at Askole.

The Oraons : The Oraons in Bihar believe in hosts of Gods, goddesses and the spirits of their ancestors. Dharmes is the omnipotent deity to them who creates and destroys the world whenever he likes, he is not worshipped in any shrine or temple. The Oraons have a sacred grove for the worship of numerous other deities who are said to belong to ten different grades. They are worshipped offerings and sacrifices by the village priest popularly known as the Pahan on behalf of the entire village.

In olden days the Pahan used to be the sacerdotal as well as the secular headman of the village. Later the office of the secular headman grew very important and was entrusted to another member of the same class to which the Pahan belonged. Sometimes the Pahan has to perform so many varied functions that he is given an assistant called the Pujar. A large number of the Oraons believe in witchcraft and worship Hindu gods. The worship of the Devi Mai seems to be greatly in vogue in most of the Oraon settlement. The Oraons have borrowed this practice from Hindus. They have assimilated it so fully in their religion that one is apt to mistake it for an indigenous custom. They worship goddess collectively on behalf of the entire village. In many Oraon villages a small mud-built house roofed with tiles for the worship of this Hindu deity.

The Raj Mahal : It is the example of Bundela Rajput architecture. It has two rectangular courtyards around which the floors rise in tiers, typically there are cool chambers below ground and a fountain. Some of the original blue tile decoration remains on the upper outer walls. The palace has plain outer walls. Left side of the first courtyard is the Hall of Private Audience. This hall is covered with rich carpets and cushions.

The Ramayana : The Ramayana (Sanskrit:, march or journey (Ayana) of Rama) is part of the Hindu smriti, written by Valmiki. This epic of 24,000 verses in seven kands (chapters or books) tells of a Raghuvamsa (Sanskrit - "Of the Sun Dynasty") prince, Rama of Ayodhya, whose wife Sita is abducted by the Rakshasa, or demon, Ravana. The Ramayana had an important influence on later Sanskrit poetry, primarily through its establishment of the Sloka meter. But, like its epic cousin Mahabharata, the Ramayana is not just a good story. It contains the teachings of the ancient Hindu sages and presents them through allegory in narrative and the interspersion of philosophic and devotional. The characters of Rama, Sita, Lakshmana, Bharat, Hanumana and Ravana (the archvillain of the story) are all fundamental to the grander cultural consciousness of India. Just like Christians historically believe in the birth of Jesus, people of the Hindu religion believe in the birth of Rama.

The Rise of Mahatma Gandhi : Mohandas Gandhi's taking helm of INC was a turning point in its history due to his enormous following, his spiritual powers and his non-violent means of fighting. Gandhi introduced the concept of Satyagraha which appealed to the common Indians who were largely pious and religious. Woman Weaves Handspun Cotton Under Gandhi's Bust. People from all walks of life followed Gandhi's ideals. Gandhi adhered to a strictly non-violent protest. Every time a disturbing incident broke out, he suspended his actions, fasted and prayed for peace. and every time he was successful.

The Rock Fort : It is 272ft above the city on the banks of the river Cauvery in Tamil Nadu. The rock cut into 437 steps, leads to the temple. The temple is dedicated to Lord Vinayaka (the mythical half-man, half-bird Garuda who is Vishnu's Vehicle, famous in the Epic Mahabharata). Along the way to temple there are landings and shrines. There are cave temples cut into the rocks, dedicated to Ganesh (the elephant God) and Shiva. There is an excellent view of the city from the top of this fort.

The Si-Doni Festival—Tagin Festival : It is the most significant festival in Arunachal Pradesh of the Tagins and is celebrated in January. Si signifies the earth and Doni is the sun. They believe that, the sun, the moon, the earth and the natural elements around them play a vital part in their day to day functions. It is with these factors in back ground that their important festivals are performed. During the festival 'Etting', rice powder mixed with Apeng (rice-beer) is made to a paste and everyone liberally applied with it.

Everybody contributes in kind and cash. Si-Doni festival being conducted on a large scale cannot be performed individually due to huge expenditure involved. Hence it is celebrated collectively. The local youths work day and night for about a month in preparation of the festival. The elderly person who form the members of the Si-Doni committee direct the operations and the selected Nibu (priest) guides and performs the Si-Doni festival like 1) Sune-Rabo, 2) Takar, 3) Gene Koni Bakar and Hoye Penam. It is understood that by celebrating the Si-Doni festival the creators Si and Doni would not only be satisfied but also bless the people with good crops and prevent diseases. In fact Si-Doni festival is the festival for prosperity, plenty and success. During this festival boys and girls in colourful dresses and split bamboo head gears (Donger) sing and dance.

The Sikh Gurus : Sikhism was established by ten Gurus, teachers or masters, over the period 1469 to 1708.

These teachers, believed to be sent from God for the troubled people of the land, were enlightened souls whose main purpose in life was the spiritual and moral well-being of the masses, or the equivalent of Prophets & Messiahs of the other major respective monotheist religions. Each master added to and reinforced the message taught by the previous, resulting to the creation of the religion of Sikhism. Guru Nanak was the first Guru and Guru Gobind Singh the final Guru in human form. When Guru Gobind Singh left this world, he made the Guru Granth Sahib the ultimate and final Sikh Guru.

The Six Points of Sheikh Mujibur Rahman : The Six Points, or 6 Point Demand, was first announced by Sheikh Mujibur Rahman of Bangladesh on February 12, 1966 in Karachi as manifesto of general election. It was formally declared on March 23, 1966, and carried out by the Awami League and the Student's League. The Six Points are:

1. The character of the government shall be federal and parliamentary, in which the elections to the federal legislature and to the legislatures of the federating units shall be direct and on the basis of universal adult franchise. The representation in our federal legislature shall be on the basis of population.

2. The federal government shall be responsible only for the defense and foreign affairs and subject to the conditions provided in (3) below.

3. There shall be two separate currencies mutually of freely convertible in each wing for each region, or in the alternative a single currency, subject to the establishment of a federal reserve system in which there will be regional Federal Reserve banks, which shall devise measures to prevent the transfer of resources and flight of capital from one region to another.

4. Fiscal policy shall be the responsibility of the federating units. The federal government shall be provided with requisite revenue resource for meeting the requirements of defense and foreign affairs which would be automatically appropriable by the federal government in the manner provided, and on the basis of the ratio to be determined by the procedure laid down in the constitution. Such constitutional provisions would ensure that federal government's revenue requirements are not met consistently with the objective or ensuring control over fiscal policy of the governments of the federating units.

5. Constitutional provisions shall be made to enable separate accounts to be maintained of the foreign exchange earnings of each of the federating units, under the control of the respective governments of the federating units. The foreign exchange requirements of the federal government shall be met by the governments of the federating units on the basis of a ratio to be determined in accordance with the procedure laid down in the constitution. The regional governments shall have power under the constitution to negotiate foreign trade and within the framework of the foreign policy of the country which shall be the responsibility of the federal government.

6. The governments of the federating units shall be empowered to maintain militia or paramilitary force having Naval Headquarter in East Pakistan in order to contribute effectively towards national security.

The Statesman : Established in 1875, The Statesman is among the leading daily newspapers of India. It is published simultaneously in Calcutta, New Delhi, Siliguri and Bhubaneshwar. It has its headquarters at Statesman House, Chowringhee Square, Calcutta and its national editorial offices in Statesman House, Connaught Place,

New Delhi. It was incorporated and directly descended from The Englishman, which was published in Calcutta from 1811. During the British era, it was British run and managed, but after independence, its control passed to Indians.

The Story of My Experiments with Truth : The Story of My Experiments with Truth (or My Experiments with Truth) – the autobiography of Mohandas Karamchand Gandhi (or Mahatma Gandhi) covers his life from early childhood through to 1920, and is a popular and influential book. It was initiated at the instance of Swami Anand and other close co-workers of Gandhi, in his mother-tongue Gujarati entitled satya na proyogo. Mahatma Gandhi (1869–1948) was a charismatic leader who brought the case for India's independence to world attention. His philosophy of nonviolence, for which he coined the term satyagraha, has influenced nonviolent resistance movements to this day.

The Swaraj and Home Rule Movement : Subsequent to the Sepoy Mutiny (1857), some Englishmen in India felt that a harmony between the ruling English and the Indian people has to be built and Sir Allen Octavian Hume founded the Indian National Union which gave way to the Indian National Congress (INC). The birth of INC marked the entry of new educated middle-class into politics and transformed the Indian political horizon. Intelligentsia from Bengal (among them, W.C. Banerjee) constituted the core of the activism and Viceroy Curzon, an arrogant and ambitious bureaucrat, divided Bengal into two reducing the size, population and restricting flow. Contrary to his plans, it only brought the Bengalis and rest of Indians together.

Minto who succeeded Curzon was a complex man and although he encouraged political reforms in India, he unleashed a series of violent attacks on Indians and Congressmen. In 1906 in Barisol the police canned INC delegates and in 1919 a British General opened fire on a peaceful protest rally in Jallianwala Bagh in an act of savagery that is unparalleled in Indian History. The freedom movement now took a violent turn and the white man's blood was to atone for the cruelty and repression of the Empire. New extremist and revolutionary leaders emerged (like Bal Gangadhar Tilak, Subhas Chandra Bose and Lala Lajpat Rai).

The Tantra : The Tantra ("Looms" or "Weavings"), refer to numerous and varied scriptures pertaining to any of several esoteric traditions rooted in Hindu and Buddhist philosophy. Most tantra were written between the 10th and 14th centuries CE. Tantra include a variety of mystical, occult, medical and scientific works.

While Hinduism is typically viewed as being Vedic, the Tantra are not considered part of the orthodox Hindu/ Vedic scriptures.Legend ascribes the origin of Tantra to Dattatreya, a semi-mythological yogi and the assumed author of the Jivanmukta Gita ("Song of the liberated soul"). Others traditionally confer authorship on the Indian god Shiva. Matsyendranath is credited with authorship of the Kaulajnana-nirnaya, a voluminous ninth-century tantra dealing with a host of mystical and magical subjects, and occupies an important position in the Hindu tantric lineage, as well as in Tibetan Vajrayana Buddhism.

Buddhist and Hindu Tantra, though having many similarities from the outside, do have some clear distinctions. Scholars are unable to determine whether the Hindu or the Buddhist version of Tantra appeared first in history. Buddhist Tantra is always part of the Mahayana school of Buddhism. Buddhist Tantra spread out from (North) India, chiefly to Tibet, where it became known as the Vajrayana school of Buddhism. It also had some influence on Chinese and Japanese Buddhism (notably Shingon).

The Telegraph : The Telegraph is a Kolkata based broadsheet newspaper in English. It is owned by the Ananda Bazar Group of publications. It has published continuously since 7th July 1982 and created history by being the only broadsheet newspaper in post independent India to increase its market share by taking away readership from the established market leader (The Statesman). In its short life span of 23 years, it has become the largest circulated English daily in the eastern region published from Calcutta. It is considered by the Audit Bureau

The Third Battle of Panipat : The Third Battle of Panipat took place on January 14, 1761 at Panipat (Haryana State, India) about 80 miles (130 km) north of Delhi, between the Maratha forces of north-western India aiding their allies, the Mughal Empire, and Afghan forces under Ahmad Shah Abdali. It is believed that nearly 100,000 people either died or were injured on both sides in the one-day battle, though some historians estimate the total to be nearer to 60,000.

The battle pitted the French-supplied and trained artillery of the Marathas against the famous light cavalry of the Afghans. The matchup would have been rather one sided in favour of the Marathas had not their own cavalry decided to charge prematurely leading to their defeat. Both forces were so heavily attritted that the Mughal Empire fell, the expansion of the Maratha's power ended, and Ahmad Shah's Durrani Empire suffered continual attacks by the growing Sikh power and eventually retired to the north of Kandahar. The Marathas had also pursued his fleeing army right up to Attock at the foothills of Afghanistan in 1756 under Raghobadada.

The Times of India (ToI) : The Times of India, one of India's leading daily newspapers, has the highest circulation amongst English language daily broadsheets in the world. It is published from eight cities across India. ToI was founded on November 3, 1838 as The Bombay Times and Journal of Commerce, and served the British residents of western India. It adopted its present name in 1861. Published on every Saturdays and Wednesdays "Bombay Times and Journal of Commerce" was launched as a bi weekly editions. It contained news of Europe, America and the sub-continent and was conveyed between India and Europe via regular steam ships.

The daily editions of the paper were started from 1850 and by 1861 Bombay Times was renamed as "The Times of India". By 19th century this news paper company employed more than 800 people and had good circulation in India and Europe. It is published by India's largest media group, Bennett, Coleman & Co. Ltd. This company, along with its other group companies are more popularly known as The Times Group, which also publishes The Economic Times (a leading financial broadsheet), Mumbai Mirror, the Navbharat Times (a Hindi daily broadsheet), and the Maharashtra Times (a Marathi daily broadsheet).

The Tribune : The Tribune is a daily newspaper published in Chandigarh, India. It was founded in 1881 by Sardar Dyal Singh Majithia, and was originally based in Lahore.

The University of Calcutta : Calcutta's College Street is not a tourist attraction but it may be an interesting place for some folks. The center of activity is the College Square. The University of Calcutta, established in 1857, is on the western side of the square. Next to it is the prestigious Presidency College originally the Hindu College. The Eden Hindu Hostel is behind the University. A little further off is the IISWBM, India's oldest management institution. South of the university is the Asia's oldest medical school—the Calcutta Medical College.

Other institutions around the College Square include the Hare School, the Hindu School and the Sanskrit College. The section of College Street in front of the Presidency College and the surrounding areas form a veritable book bazar which attracts readers of every kind. The Indian Coffee House is a favorite hangout for many Calcuttans. College Square is also the site of one of Calcutta's prestigious Durga Pujas.

The Upanishads : The Upanishads are part of the Hindu Shruti scriptures which primarily discuss meditation and philosophy and are seen as religious instructions by most schools of Hinduism. The Upanishads are mystic or spiritual interpretations on the Vedas, their putative end and essence, and thus known as Vedanta ("the end of the Vedas"). The teachers and students appear in a variety of settings (husband answering questions about immortality, a teenage boy being taught by Yama, etc.). Sometimes the sages are women and at times the instructions (or rather inspiration) are sought by kings.

The Vikram Sarabhai Space Centre (VSSC) : The Vikram Sarabhai Space Centre (VSSC) is located at Thumba near Trivandrum, a city of the Kerala state in India. It is a major space research centre of the Indian Space Research Organisation (ISRO),where space vehicles are developed for the Indian satellite programme.

The Vikram Sarabhai Space Center is ISRO's one of the main Research & Development establishment. Its facilities were built near the Thumba Equatorial Rocket Launching Station (TERLS), on the west coast of India, about 10 miles (16km) north of Thiruvananthapuram in Kerala State. Named after the late Professor Vikram Sarabhai (1919-1971), founder of the Indian Space Program. VSSC is an entirely national facility working on the development of sounding rockets; Rohini and Menaka, launchers; ASLV, PSLV and GSLV, along with the solid motor program.

Thekkady : Thekkady (Idukki district) is the location of the Periyar Wildlife Sanctuary, which is an important tourist attraction in Kerala state, India, close to the Kerala -Tamil Nadu border town Kumily, located about 160 miles from Trivandrum. The sanctuary is famous for its dense evergreen, semievergreen, moist deciduous forests and savannah grass lands. It is home to herds of elephants, sambar, tigers, gaur, lion-tailed macaques and Nilgiri langurs.

The Periyar Widlife sanctuary is spread across 777 sq km, of which 360 sq km is thick evergreen forest. The Periyar Wild Life Sanctuary was declared a Tiger Reserve in 1978. The splendid artificial lake formed by the Mullaperiyar Dam across the Periyar River adds to the charm of the park. The greatest attraction of Periyar are the herds of wild elephants that come down to play in the lake.

Thekkady has immense possibilities for Adventure Tourism. The Forest Department offers many programs including Periyar Tiger Trail, Nature walk, Bamboo Rafting etc. There are private organizations like AdventureKerala.com who promote adventure tourism in Thekkady.

Theni District : Theni District has been formed after bifurcation from erstwhile Madurai District as per G.O.Ms.No.679 Revenue Department Dated:25.07.96. Consequent on the bifurcation, one new Revenue Division with headquarters at Uthamapalayam and two new Taluks at Theni and Bodinaickanur were also created with effect from 01.01.97. Theni Municipal town was only a firka headquarters till 31.12.96. Consequent on the formation of the new District, Theni Municipal Town has been upgraded as the Taluk and District head quarters from 01.01.97. It is mainly a commercial town. It is also known for its big weekly shandy on every Sunday. Vaigai dam and

Kumbakarai falls in Periyakulam Taluk, Suruli falls in Uthamapalayam Taluk are the main places of attraction for tourists.

Theyyam : Theyyam or Kaliyattom is a ritual dance typical of the northern Malabar. It is not merely a dance but a cult, which is inseparable from the Hindu practices of the region. Elaborate description of such rituals are found in the Tamil literature of the Sangam period (500 BC-500 AD).

As a performing art, Teyyam offers an unusual experience. The painting of the face, the gorgeous attire and the imposing headdresses all speak of a developed artistic sensibility. Every Teyyam presentation has two parts, the Tottam or Vellattam, which involves preliminary ceremonies, and the spirited calling upon the deity for inspiration, and the dance. The accompanied instruments include drums, pipes and cymbals.

Thidampu Nritham : It is the 700 years old ritualistic art form of North Kerala. In this, the dancer moves to the rhythmic beats of the chenda carrying the thidampu (the idol of the deity) on his head.

Thirunavaya : Thirunavaya is a small village in Malappuram district of Kerala, south India. This village is famed as the theatre of the Mamankam festival. Thirunavaya was once the captial of Perumpadappu Rajas. They were forced to move their capital from Thirunavaya to Thiruvanchikkulam, when the Samoothiri captured Thirunavaya. Between 1353-1361 AD, the Samoothiri Raja fought a series of small battles with smaller states called the Thirunavaya War. After Thirunavaya was captured, the Samoothiri proclaimed himself as the Rakshapurusha (in Malayalam for chief protector) and announced that from then on, he had the sole right of conducting the Mamankam festival—a major Hindu festival of the Bhagvati deity held at Thirunavaya. Famous poet Melputhoor Narayana Bhattapathar was born at Melputhoor Illam, located 3.5 km from Thirunavaya, on the northern banks of Nila River, (Bharathapuzha).

Thiruvananthapuram : Thiruvananthapuram formerly known as Trivandrum, is the capital of the Indian state of Kerala and the headquarter of Thiruvananthapuram District. It is located on the west coast of India near the extreme south of the mainland. It is characterized by its undulating terrain of low coastal hills with narrow winding lanes and busy commercial alleys.

With a population of 889,191 it is the second biggest city in Kerala after Kochi. The city, being the State Capital houses many Central and State Government offices, organizations and companies. Apart from being the political nerve center of Kerala, it is also a major academic hub and houses several premier educational institutions including the Kerala University. Thiruvananthapuram is also home to many science and technology institutions, the most prominent being the Vikram Sarabhai Space Centre(VSSC). The city also has the first Technopark of its kind in India. Situated near Kazhakutoom, this Technopark houses many of the leading software giants in the world.

Thiruvananthapuram District : Thiruvananthapuram District is the southernmost district of Kerala. The headquarter is in the town of Thiruvananthapuram. The district has an area of 2192 km^2, and a population of 3234707 (2001), the second largest in Kerala. It is divided into four talukas: Thiruvananthapuram, Chirayinkil, Nedumangad, and Neyyattinkara. The urban bodies in the district are the Thiruvananthapuram corporation, Attingal, Neyyattinkara, Varkala and Nedumangad municipalities.

Thiruvathira : Thiruvatira is the women's festival of Kerala. It is celebrated in the Malayalam month of Dhanu.

The popular conception of this festival is that it is the commemoration of the death of Kamadevan; the cupid of our national mythology. Thiruvathirakali also known as Kaikottikkali is a dance in which a group of women dance in a circle around a lighted brass lamp. They are dancing to the rhythms of the songs they sing. They wear the traditional dress, consisting of two pieces, dhoti and an upper garment across the breast and look elegant and sprightly for the game. The leader of the group sings the first line which is repeated by the group to the simple rhythm of clapping hands. There are many songs which are exclusively sung as Tiruvathira songs, popular Kathakali songs are also included. The kinetic phrases are so simple that any new comer easily gets initiated to the game. This dance form had been keeping its basic posture for centuries. The bent of the body, hand movements and dance gestures are common to the region.

Thiruvathirakali : is a dance form which is a pointer to the old customs followed in Nair tharawads (joint families) where the women of the house dance elegantly around the ceremonial lamp or floral decoration on festive occasions to the accompaniment of the Thiruvathira pattu (song).

Thoothukudi : Thoothukudi, also known as Tuticorin, is a city in the state of Tamil Nadu, India. The city is also known as "Pearl City". It is a sea port city which serves southern Tamil Nadu, including the inland cities of Coimbatore, Madurai and Tirunelveli. It is one of the oldest cities in India with the history dating back to the 6th century BCE.

Thrissur : Thrissur is a city situated in the Thrissur District of Kerala state, India. It is an important cultural centre, and is known as the "cultural capital" of Kerala. It is famous for the Thrissur Pooram festival, the most colourful and spectacular temple festival of Kerala. The festival is held near the Vadakkumnathan temple, in April or May. It has a large number of well known temples around, including the temple town of Guruvayoor. The name Thrissur is derived from 'Tri-Shiva-Perur', which means the place with three famous Shiva temples which are said to be—the Vadakkunathan temple, Kottapuram Shiva temple and the Punkunnam Shiva temple. (Alternately, the name can be parsed as 'Thiru-Siva-Perur', the place with the holy name of Siva). Thrissur was also known as Vrishabhadripuram and Then Kailasam(Kailasam of the south) in ancient days.

Thrissur Pooram : Thrissur Pooram is the most colourful temple festival of Kerala, Thrissur Pooram attracts large masses of devotees and spectators from all parts of the State and even outside.

Celebrated in Medom (April-May) it consists of processions of richly caparisoned elephants from various neighbouring temples to the Vadakumnathan temple, Thrissur. The most impressive processions are those from the Krishna Temple at Thiruvambadi and the Devi Temple at Paramekkavu which is quite a significant event for its devotees.

This festival was introduced by Sakthan Thampuran, the Maharaja of the erstwhile Cochin State. Perhaps, there is no other festival in Kerala that draws such an unbelievable number of people to a single event. However Vadakkunnathan is a mere spectator at this festival, lending its premises and grounds for the great event. The pooram festival is also well known for the magnificent display of fireworks. Fire works start in the early hours and the dazzling display last three to four hours.

The Pooram Festival is celebrated by two rival groups representing the two divisions of Thrissur Paramekkavu and Thiruvambadi vying with each other in making the display of fireworks grander and more colourful. Each group is allowed to display a maximum of fifteen elephants and all efforts are made by each party to secure the best elephants in South India and the most artistic parasols, several kinds of which are raised on the elephants during the display. Commencing in the early hours of the morning, the celebrations last till the break of dawn, the next day.

The procession of the Thiruvambadi Pooram to the grounds of Vadakkumnatha Temple and back is not only important, but also quite enlivening. The marvellous as well as magical effect of the Panchavadyam, a combination of five percussion and wind instruments is to be felt and enjoyed. Among the varieties of festivals celebrated in Kerala, Thrissur Pooram is the most thunderous, spectacular and dazzling. There are three temples participating in the event. It is an expression of popular fascination for sound and colour, and because of the pageantry, it appeals to all people. The images of the deities from all temples of the village are taken on elephants to the main temple. The climax of the festival is the exhibition of thirty elephants and the famous fireworks at 2.30 am local time.

Thullal : It is characterised by simplicity of presentation, wit and humour. Kunjan Nambiar, one of the leading poets of Malayalam, originated this dance form. The dancer himself sings the lead to the accompaniment of the maddalam and elathalam. It is of three types — Ottanthullal, Seethankam thullal and Parayanthullal.

Thumba : Thumba is a small fishing village near Thiruvananthapuram, capital of Kerala, India. On November 21, 1963 it entered India into space-travel history when a group of scientists worked for six months to launch the country's first rocket from the newly created

Thumba Equatorial Rocket Launching Station (TERLS). A local Catholic church and its associated buildings served as the office, workshop and laboratory where the scientists built and fine tuned the rocket. The main person behind the project was Dr.Vikram Sarabhai and scientists under him included the current President of India Dr.A P J Abdul Kalam.

Dr Sarabhai chose Thumba as the ideal site because it is near the magnetic equator, at 8°32'N 76°52'E Now Thumba is home to Vikram Sarabhai Space Centre (VSSC) of Indian Space Research Organisation (ISRO). With three launch pads TERLS still continues to do weekly rocket launches for weather and atmospheric research. It is an international launch site for sounding rockets, a research funded by the United Nations. The old village community and the church still exist in the middle of the various VSSC office compounds.

Thumri : Thumri is a common genre of semiclassical Indian music from the North. The text is romantic and devotional in nature, and usually revolves around a girl's love for Krishna. The language is a dialect of Hindi called Braj bhasha. This style is characterized by a greater flexibility with the rag. Most commonly used rags are Pilu, Kafi, Khamaj, Tilak Kamod, Bhairavi etc. The compositions are usually set to kaherava of 8 beats, addha tal of 16 beats, dipchandi of 14 beats or jat of 16 beats. It arose in popularity during the 19th century in the Lucknow court of navab Wajid Ali Shah. At that time it used to be a song sung by courtesans accompaigned by dance. That was the bandish ki thumri or bol bant ki thumri. When this style of thumri went out of vogue, a new style became more popular, which is known as bol banao, sung in Varanasi.

Thunjath Ezhuthachan : Thunchaththu Ramanujan Ezhuthachan is known as the "Father of the Malayalam language". He was born around 450 years ago in

Malappuram district of Kerala, south India. He traveled extensively in search of knowledge and returned to Thrikandiyur, after mastering the religious sciences. Ezhuthachan tried to propagate the universal nature of the language. He wanted to bring language to level of a layman's understanding. The great teacher taught the people to respect and worship the language and the alphabet, a level of culture which is difficult to find even in the modern era. He refined the Malayalam language style and wrote his works for ordinary people, incorporating whatever is good with a strong sense of righteousness and worship. It was in Thunjan Parambu that Ezhuthachan modified the Malayalam alphabets and wrote the Harinamakeerthanam to popularize them. Even after centuries people from various parts of the state come to take sand from Thunjan Parambu to initiate their children to the alphabet. Every year, hundreds of people bring their children to write their first alphabets during the Vijayadasami festival, to Thunjan Parambu.

Tibet : Tibet is a region in Central Asia and the home of the Tibetan people. With an average elevation of 4,900 m (16,000 ft), it is often called the 'Roof of the World'. All or most of historic Tibet (depending on definition) is currently a part of the People's Republic of China (PRC).

Tibetan Buddhism : Tibetan Buddhism — formerly also called Lamaism, after their religious gurus known as lamas — is the body of religious Buddhist doctrine and institutions characteristic of Tibet and the Himalayan region. It is a multifaceted and integrated teaching, naturally implementing methods for all human-condition levels: Hinayana, Mahayana, Vajrayana (Tantric Path) and Ati Yoga (Dzogchen).

Tibetan Plateau : The Tibetan Plateau or Qinghai-Tibetan (Qingzang) Plateau is a large, elevated region in Central Asia, covering much of Tibet. It occupies an area of around 1000 by 2500 kilometers, and has an average elevation of over 5000 meters. Called "the roof of the world," it contains the world's tallest mountain range, the Himalayas, as well as Mount Everest, the world's tallest mountain. The plateau was formed by the collision of the Indo-Australian and Eurasian tectonic plates in the Cenozoic period (approximately 55 million years ago), although the process is still ongoing. The uplift of the plateau is thought to have had a significant effect on climate change, and it is believed to affect the Asian monsoon.

Tihar : Tihar is an interesting festival observed in Bhadarwah and Kishtwar in the months of Chaitra (March-April) in Kashmir. Springs and baulis receive a spring-cleaning and this is followed on the next day by worship of nagas (serpents), to whom rice and floral offerings are made.

Tihar Festival : Tihar is the "Festival of Lights" and symbolises the return of Lord Ram to his hometown from exile after victory over Ravana and covers a period of five days. The festival honours certain animals on successive days. The first day known as "Kak Tihar" is dedicated to crows and they are offered rice and some if caught are even garlanded. On the second day, which is known as "Kukkur Tihar", dogs are garlanded. On the third day the cows are honoured with garlands and their horns are painted in bright colours. It is the turn of the bullocks on the fourth day.

Tihar Jail : Tihar Jail, also called Tihar Prisons, is the largest complex of prisons of South East Asia, and is located in the western part of Delhi, India. It is approximately 8km from Chanakya Puri. The prisons is supposed to be a correctional institution. Its main objective is to convert it's inmates into normal members of the society by providing them with useful skills, education and rules. It is meant to improve the inmates' self-esteem and strengthen their desire to improve.

Tikka Khan : Tikka Khan (1915–2002) was Pakistan's Chief of Army Staff from March 1972–March 1976). He was born in the village of Jochha Mamdot (Tehsil Kahuta) near Rawalpindi in 1915 (in what was then British India). He fought in World War II as part of the British Indian Army, and was injured on multiple occasions during the fighting After his return from World War II, he was an instructor at the Indian Military Academy at Dehradun for some time. During the Partition of India, Major Tikka Khan remained in what is now Pakistan, and became an officer in the Pakistan Army.

He was promoted to the rank of Major General in 1962. One of General Tikka's greatest successes on the battlefield came in the spring of 1965, during the series of clashes between India and Pakistan in the Rann of Kutch. By most accounts, the Pakistani forces performed very well on the battlefield, routing the Indian forces; this led to a very high level of confidence among Pakistani Army commanders.

General Tikka Khan was at the Sialkot front during the 1965 India-Pakistan war, and successfully defended the city from an Indian attack. Due to his performance there, and his victory during the Rann of Kutch clashes, General Tikka became something of a hero to the Pakistani people, having the image of being an extremely tough commander and a loyal soldier who strictly followed the army chain of command.

Zulfikar Ali Bhutto appointed General Tikka Khan as the Chief of the Army Staff in March 1972. One of Tikka Khan's earliest responsibilities was to oversee Pakistan's nascent nuclear program, which Bhutto had initiated in early 1972. The goal of the nuclear program was to enhance Pakistan's security, and the program's pace was accelerated after India's 1974 nuclear test. Tikka Khan did not intrude into politics, and for the first time in many years, the policy making was left to the civilian Prime Minister Bhutto. Another major task undertaken by Tikka Khan was the repatriation and re-settlement of 90,000 Prisoners of War from India, which included thousands of civilians as well.

Tikka Khan's tenure ended in March 1976, and he was later appointed Defence Minister by Bhutto. Muhammad Zia-ul-Haq's July 1977 coup led to the arrest of both Bhutto and General Tikka Khan. Bhutto was executed in 1979, after which General Tikka Khan emerged as one of the leaders of the Pakistan People's Party (PPP), becoming its Secretary General, during a time when many party stalwarts abandoned it. General Tikka was imprisoned numerous times for his political activities during the late 1970s and 1980s, until Zia-ul-Haq died in August 1988 in an airplane explosion over Bahawalpur. General Tikka Khan was appointed the Governor of Pakistan's largest province, the Punjab, in December 1988. His tenure as the Governor was cut short by the dismissal of the Benazir government in August 1990, after which he retired from active politics.

As a politician, Tikka Khan will be remembered for his intense loyalty to the Bhutto political clan, whatever the political climate in the country, first to Zulfikar Ali Bhutto and then later to Benazir Bhutto. As a soldier, he will be remembered as a loyal man who would strictly observe the army chain of command and never disobey a senior officer. General Tikka Khan died on 28 March 2002 after several years of illness.

Tikuli Art : Tikuli art in Bihar originated from the gold foiled Tikuli, bindis with a glass base, adoring the forehead of the Queens and Aristocrats ladies of yore.

Today hard board, enamel paints and Madhubani motils are used to create produce for interior decorations and utility items like tablemats and coaster. Making of the hard board plates follows a Japanese technique. The erobate follows 15 stages. In 1982, the then Indian Prime Minister Mrs. Indira Gandhi, chose Tikuli as official gift for the International athletes participating in the Delhi Asiad. These art pieces are heat proof and water proof.

Tilkut : A sweet savoury made in the Indian state of Bihar. Tilkut is made of pounded 'tila' or sesame seeds (Sesamum indicum) and jaggery or sugar. The best tilkut is said to be from Gaya. References to this dry sweet is found in the in Buddhist literature as 'Palala'.

Tipi Orchidarium & Bhilukpong : Arunachal has the largest range of orchids in India. There is an Orchidarium at Tipi near the banks of the Bharali River in the West Kameng District, west of Tawang district. It houses 500 or more varieties of orchids which grow abundantly in different parts of Arunachal Pradesh. Some of the rarest species of Orchids are on display. In the Orchid research centre, scientists create new hybrid varieties of orchids using the latest techniques of biotechnology. The place is also ideal for rafting and angling in river Kameng.

The river is a perfect rafting spot and a fishing haven, perfect for Mahseer fish which can be found on the Jia Bhorali river that branches off from the Kameng river. Buses are available from Bomdila the headquarters of West Kameng district and Bhalukpong, the entry point only 3km from Tipi. Bhalukpong on the Assam- Arunachal border straddles the edge of the Kameng river and is surrounded by the evergreen forests of the Pakhui Game Sanctuary. Pakhoi sanctuary can be reached by crossing the Kameng river in a dug out canoe and is a lush rain forest of tangled moss, lichen and ferns. Nearest airport is Tezpur (52km) and the nearest railway station is Rangapara.

Tippani : It this dance, women from some parts of Saurashtra beat the floor with wooden mallets, and sing to the pace, while others dance in swirling skirts.

Tipu Sultan : Tipu Sultan, also known as The Tiger of Mysore (December 10, 1750, Devanahalli—May 4, 1799, Srirangapatnam) was the second son of Haider Ali by his second wife, Fatima or Fakr-un-nissa.

Tippu ruled the Kingdom of Mysore from the time of his father's death in 1782 until his own demise in 1799. Tipu was a learned man and an able soldier. He was reputed to be a good poet. He was also a strongly religious man, and practised the Sunni branch of Islam. He built a church, the first in Mysore, at the request of the French, he also built many temples and mosques. He was a noted linguist and cultural patriot.

He helped his father Haider Ali defeat the British in the Second Mysore War, and negotiated the Treaty of Mangalore with them. However, he was defeated in the Third Anglo-Mysore War and in the Fourth Anglo-Mysore War by the combined forces of Britain and of Mysore's neighbours. Tipu Sultan died defending his capital Srirangapatnam, on May 4, 1799.

Tipu's Summer Palace : This palace is at Albert Victor Road in Karnataka. The Haidar Ali started the construction of this palace and this wooden summer palace completed by Tipu Sultan in 1789. Its construction was alike of the Daria Daulat palace of Srirangapatnam. The 2- storeyed ornate palace is made of wood. The walls and ceilings are painted in brilliant colours with carvings. The building is now used to exhibit the modern photo of Tipu and his era.

Tira : This is also a ritual dance similar to Teyyam but existing only in the northern part of Kerala.

Tirah : Tirah is a mountainous tract of country in the west-central North-West Frontier Province, Pakistan. It lies between the Khyber Pass and the Khanki Valley, and is inhabited by the Afridi and Orakzai tribes. It is chiefly notable as the scene of the Tirah Campaign of 1897. It is a cul-de-sac in the mountains and the difficulty of its passes and the fierceness of its inhabitants had hitherto preserved it inviolable from all invaders.

Tirap : The Tirap district is located in the southeastern part of Arunachal Pradesh. It shares a state border with Nagaland and Assam, an international border with Myanmar and a district border with Changlang. Much of the land lies not very far removed from those of the sea level, although a large portion of the district comprises of the Patkoi Hills, which consists of the Namdhapa National Park. The park hosts a wide variety of wildlife species, from mithun to the Himalayan black bear, locally known as takin, to the wild goat.

Much of the tribal population consists of the Naga related Nocte, Konyak and Wancho, who traditionally followed Hinduism and Animism, although a sizeable minorty of Christians can be found among the Nocte and Konyak as well. Smaller communities of Tutsa, Tangsa and Singpho can be found in the district as well.

Tirich Mir : Tirich Mir (alternatively Terich Mir and Terichmir) is the highest mountain in the Hindu Kush region of northern Pakistan. The mountain was first climbed in 1950 by a Norwegian expedition comprised of Arne Næss, P. Kvernberg, H. Berg, and Tony Streather. Tirich Mir overlooks Chitral town. It can easily be seen from the main bazaar. It can also be seen from Afghanistan. The Chitralis believe that it is impossible to climb it, because of all the Jinns, demons, witches and fairies who live up there.

Tiruchirapalli : Tiruchirapalli (also spelt Tiruchchirapalli, commonly known as Tiruchi or Trichy, formerly known as Trichinopoly under British rule) is a city situated on the banks of the Kaveri River, centrally located in the Indian state of Tamil Nadu. The city is the administrative headquarters of Tiruchirappalli District. The name of the town, "Tiruchirapalli", originated as a tribute (thiru in Tamil means respected) to a Jain monk called "Chira": "Tiruchirapalli" means "the town of respected Chira". Tiruchirapalli has many historic temples, monuments, churches and mosques. It was an important town in the days of the later Cholas as well as during the early days of the British East India Company.

Tirukural : Tirukural is an important work of Tamil literature by Tiruvalluvar written in the form of couplets expounding various aspects of life. While most scholars place him during 100-300 AD, there are a few who consider him to have lived during 600 A.D. Tirukural contains 1330 couplets divided into 133 chapters of 10 couplets each. Each couplet consists of seven words, with four words on the first line and three on the second. It is sometimes claimed that Tiruvalluvar wrote more than 1330 couplets, and that the rest of the work has gone missing. However, this is unlikely since several different writers of later years in different areas of India all alluded to the standard 1330 verses, merely choosing to group them in different ways. Moreover, unlike some works in Tamil like Tirumandiram or works of Sarvajna in Kannada and Vemana in Telugu, not a single couplet outside this compact work of 1330 verses has been attributed to Tiruvalluvar!

Tirumala : Tirumala, the abode of the Hindu God Lord Venkateswara, is situated on a very ancient ridge of mountains in a southern district of Andhra Pradesh. It houses the richest Hindu temple, monitored by the Tirumala Tirupati Devasthanams. One has to go through

7 mountains to reach the temple. The temple is open for more than 22 hours in day, and it usually takes anywhere from 2 to 20 hours, depending on the season, to get to the Sanctom sanctorum from the time one registers into the queue system.

Tirupati is also the most visited temple in the world. It is estimated that more that 50,000 people visit the temple everyday; this makes it almost 19 million people in a year, almost double the estimated number of people visiting Vatican City. The lord in here is said to be Swayambhu, meaning that the statue was naturally formed and not sculpted by anyone. The Temple was built by King Thondaman.

In the holy shrine of Tirumala, lot of devotees offer their hair as sacrifice against their fulfilled wish. They also drop their offerings in the form of money, gold, silver or anything they wish in the holy hundi(a box to collect the offerings). According to Hindu mythology, all the offerings to Lord Venkateswara count to repay the loan taken by him from Kubera for his marriage expenses which will be repaid completely by the end of Kaliyuga.

Tirumala also has a naturally formed rock arch which at about 1500 million years old, the second oldest natural arch in the world. The oldest arch is at Arches National Park, Utah, USA. The length of this arch is 25 feet and the height 10 feet. The drive to Tirumala is an enchanting half an hour from Tirupati, the town at the base of the mountain. One gets to see abundant greenery and unique geological formations on the way to the hill shrine. There is also a walkway from the base of the mountain to the shrine. It is a strenuous walk and undertaken by ardent devotees as a penance. An average person takes about 3 hours to reach the temple from the starting point at the base of mountain.

Tirumala Nayak Mahal : Tirumala Nayak Mahal is 1.5km north of Meenakshi temple in Tamil Nadu. This Palace was built in 1636 by King Thirumalai Nayak with the help of an Italian Architect. The original Palace Complex was four times bigger than the present structure. This palace consisted mainly of two parts, namely Swargavilasa and Rangavilasa. The Sound and Light show, shown here is excellent. Show starts at 1845. This show dramatizes Madurai's past.

Tirumala Tirupati Devasthanams : Tirumala Tirupati Devasthanams is an independent trust which manages the Sri Venkateshwara temple at Tirumala, Tirupati. The chairman of the board is nominated by the state government of Andhra Pradesh. Hindus believe that this richest Hindu temple is the second most visited religious center after Vatican City. About 60,000 to 150,000 devotees visit the temple complex every day for the auspicious darshan (visit) of the deity donating nearly $2 million every month.

Complex queueing theories and emerging technologies have been evaluated and implemented to manage the large and unmanageable crowds by the TTD. The deity has also over 1000 kg of gold and diamond jewellery, making it one of the richest temple treasures. TTD has procured machines from MICO BOSCH to automate the making of Laddus, a sweet which is offered as Lord's prasadam. The TTD's stated goals include the restoration of Sanathana Dharma, reviving various failing temples of South India and running Vedic schools and Veda parishats.

Tirumalai Krishnamacharya : Sri Tirumalai Krishnamacharya (1888-1989) is credited with being instrumental in the resurgence of interest in hatha yoga. His students included Indra Devi, B.K.S. Iyengar, Sri K. Pattabhi Jois, and T.K.V. Desikachar—major yoga teachers in their own right. Born in 1888 in Mysore, India, Krishnamacharya received his first instruction in Sanskrit and yoga from his father. He went on to attend the Royal College of Mysore and later spent seven years studying in Tibet. He returned to Mysore in 1924 and later opened a yoga school. In 1976, Krishnamacharya's son and closest disciple, T.K.V. Desikachar, founded the Krishnamacharya Yoga Mandiram, a yoga center in Madras

Tirunellai Narayanaiyer Seshan : Tirunellai Narayanaiyer Seshan was the 10th Chief Election Commissioner of India, serving from December 12, 1990 to December 11, 1996. His firebrand leadership qualities earned him very creative sobriquets like 'Alsatian' by the Indian Press. An officer of the Indian Administrative Service, he also held the posts of director, Ministry of Atomic Energy; joint secretary, Ministry of Space; secretary, Department of Agriculture; Government of Tamil Nadu; Member (Personnel), Oil & Natural Gas Commission, Additional Secretary, Ministry of Space, Secretary to the Government of India, Ministry of Defence, and secretary, Internal Security. He went on to occupy the post of Cabinet Secretary—the seniormost position in the Indian Civil Service hierarchy, and member, Planning Commission of India, before being appointed the Chief Election Commissioner.

As the Chief Election Commissioner of India he made history by introducing innovative electoral reforms and making the Election Commission a powerful body. He may be rightfully termed as the most visible and controversial public figure who redefined the status and visibility of a CEC in India. His name became synonymous with transparency, effeciency and forward vision during his tenure as the CEC. He used this to hone his political ambitions by contesting for the post of President of India in 1997 (though he lost it to K.R. Narayanan). He came up with the vision of an election-card for every rightful voter in India, something that is being regarded as the US equivalent of the Social-Security card. He is often known for his crisp one-liners, be it during his service to his superiors and ministers OR while handling the media. He won the prestigious Magsaysay Award for Government Service in 1996.

Tirunelveli : Tirunelveli is a city in Tamil Nadu state of southern India. It is the headquarters of Tirunelveli District. It is located on the banks of the perennial Thamirabarani River, 75 km from Kanyakumari, the southernmost tip of India. The Thamirabarani contains traces of copper, hence its name (Thamiram means copper in Tamil). Tirunelveli can be easily reached from Madurai (3 hours) or Nagercoil (1 1/2 hours). It is one of the Ayyavazhi populated districts of Tamil Nadu.

Tirupati : Tirupati is located in the southeastern part of Andhra Pradesh, in Chittoor district. Known as the abode of the Hindu god 'Venkateshwara' (Lord Vishnu), Tirupati is famous for the 10th century Venkateswara temple (11kms) located on the seventh peak Venkatachala, in the sacred Tirumala hills at an elevation of 860m. The Puranic conception of the hill is that it represents the body of Adisesha (a seven hooded serpent) the seven hills being his seven heads, on top of which Lord Vishnu the protector of the world rests. One of the most important pilgrimage centers in India, the temple draws millions of pilgrims and is believed to be the busiest pilgrimage centre in the world.

There are several legends associated with the manifestation of the Lord at Tirumala in the Puranas. The temple has its origins in Vaishnavism. Once sage Bhrigu visited the aboard of the gods to settle a dispute among the scholars regarding the supreme power among the trinity. He first visited Siva and Brahma's aboard both of whom ignored him. An enraged Bhrigu then visited Vishnu who was fast asleep. In his anger he kicked Vishu on his chest. But Vishnu put up with the insult considering him as a great sage but Lakshmi, the consort of Vishnu did not. Lakshmi quarreled with Vishnu and left him. Feeling lonely in Vaikunta, Vishnu is believed to have come down to earth and settled here in hill Seshachalam, to rest and meditate. In course of time he was buried under an ant hill and later turned to stone. Years after, the cows of a local king which used to come here, milked of their own accord and returned home dry. The king came to know of it, discovered the underground form of Lord Srinivasa and placed the Lord in the now famous shrine at Tirupati.

The 2m high standing idol of Venkateswara or the Lord of the Seven Hills, on a lotus flanked by his consorts Bhudevi and Sridevi, is believed to grant any wish made in front of it. The most striking feature of the awe-inspiring black idol is its fabulous diamond crown, which is said to be the most precious single ornament in the world. The richest temple in India, it is a master piece of South Indian Dravidian Architecture. The Sanctorum 'Ananda Nilayam' has a glittering gold covered 'Vimana' and gold covered gates guard the sanctum sanctorum. The rulers of all the great dynasties of the southern peninsula have been ardent devotees and paid homage to Lord Sri Venkateswara in this ancient shrine.

The approach to the temple is through mango groves and sandal wood forest and devotees chanting 'Govinda' or 'Om Namo Venkatesaya' reach the top where the temple is situated. The daily program starts with 'Suprabhatam' (awakening the Lord) at three in the morning and end with the 'Ekanta Seva' (putting the Lord to sleep) at one in the night. Daily, Weekly and Periodical sevas and utsavams are performed to the Lord. Pilgrims can choose from the list and pay to get the 'Sevas' or 'Utsavams' done on their name. Anointing the idol with camphor, saffron and musk and the offering of their hair by pilgrims are important customs performed. A bath in the 'Swami Pushkarini' tank, adjacent to the temple is believed to cleanse devotees of their sins. A consecrated sweet is distributed as 'prasadam' to about 50,000 pilgrims on festival days. The pilgrims visit and pay homage to Adivaraha idol in the Sri Varaha Swami Temple, situated on the banks of the tank before visiting Sri Venkateswara Temple.

The devotees stand in line for hours together to obtain a glimpse of the presiding deity for a few fleeting seconds. Different darshans are arranged for the convenience of the pilgrims, the 'Sarvadarshan' -'darshan for all', free of cost, timings differ on different week days, Special darshan (paid darshan), 'Sudarshanam' -free or paid darshan's using a token system minimizing the waiting time and special darshan for the physically disabled and the aged. Brahmotsavam, the most important of the various festivals of the temple, is conducted usually in Bhadrapada i.e., in September for about 9 days. On account of Adika Masam, which comes in every third year, the Brahmotsavam celebrated then is especially grand and held under the name 'Navarathri Brahmotsavam'. The 'Garudotsavam' and the temple car festival 'Rathotsavam' is particularly popular. These Brahmotsavams attract thousands of pilgrims from various parts of the country.

Tirupati Thimmappa : Tirupati Thimmappa is very much alive in janapada (Dalit and Backward Castes) culture of south India. When people take piligrimage to Tirupati, they chant 'Tirupati Thimmappana Padakke Govinda Govindaa'. Gathering folklore knowledge of Indian Villages may give more in depth history and heritage of Tirupati Temple.

Tiruvallur : Tiruvallur is a town in Tamil Nadu state of southern India. It is the administrative headquarters of

Thiruvallur district. It is well known because of the Veera Raghava Swami temple which is one of the 108 sacred shrines of Vaishnavites. There is a pond nearby this temple, where the tank festival is held. There is a Siva temple near this shrine which is also quite popular among the locals. There is also a 40 feet tall Viswaroopa Panchamukha Anjaneya Swami (a.k.a. Hanuman) murti.

In the far past, this region was under a chain of regimes commencing from the Pallavas during the 7th century ending with the Nawab of Arcot during the early part of 19th century when it came under the British rule. In 1687, the Golkonda rulers were defeated and the region came under the Moghul emperors of Delhi. The towns and villages of this region were the scene of Carnatic wars. Battles are said to have been fought in this region during the struggle for supremacy between the English and French. The town of Pulicat was the earliest Dutch possession in India founded in 1609 which was ceded to the British in 1825. With this, the region came under the British rule which ended on the 15th August, 1947 with India becoming independent.

Tiruvalluvar : Tiruvalluvar was one of the greatest Tamil poets. Thirukkural, one of the greatest ethical works in Tamil language was written by him. Very little is known conclusively about the life of Tiruvalluvar. As per Tamil tradition, he is believed to have lived some time during the 1st millennium AD. While most scholars place him during 100-300 AD, there are a few who consider him to have lived during 600 A.D. He is said to have been a textile weaver by profession, who led an austere life. His devoted wife was named Vasuki. The term Tiru is the Tamil term of respect, equivalent to the North Indian/ Sanskrit Shri/Shree. This phrase of respect coupled with his supposed name Valluvan (pluralized by changing 'n' to 'r' as part of the Tamil honorific system), led to the name by which he is referred to today. The name Valluvan is ambiguous as well : it may have referred to his caste/ occupation and may not have been his real name. There is a distinct caste to this day with this name, among the Tamils whose traditional occupation used to be textile weaving who trace their ancestry to Tiruvalluvar. However, the question of whether the author was named after his community or vice versa, has never been satisfactorily answered.

Legends abound about the birthplace of Thiruvalluvar. According to one legend he is supposed to have been born and lived in Mylapore, an ancient part of present day Chennai city. Another legend associates him to Madurai, the ancient capital of the Pandya rulers. This second legend probably has its origins due to the fact that Pandya rulers promoted Tamil by patronising a lot of Tamil poets and Thiruvalluvar is supposed to be one of them. In fact, some folklore cite that Tirukkural was introduced to the world by Tiruvalluvar in Madurai's Tamil Sangam, a historical equivalent to a modern day's conference of eminent scholars and researchers, which was conducted by the Pandyas on a regular basis for a long number of years. There are also recent claims by Kanyakumari Historical and Cultural Research Centre (KHCRC) that Valluvar was a king who ruled Valluvanadu in the hilly tracts of Kanyakumari district of Tamil Nadu. Though this recent claim comes through research, a lot of questions remain unanswered. For instance there existed during the 9th century A.D. a Valluvanadu in Kerala itself.

Tiruvannamalai : Tiruvannamalai is a town in the state of Tamil Nadu in India situated 185 km from Chennai/Madras and 210 km from Bangalore (Karnataka). It is the headquarters of the Tiruvannamalai district. The town is a pilgrimage site, known for its Arunachaleswara Temple, located at the foot of the hill Arunachala. The annual ten-day Karthigai Deepam festival is celebrated in Karthigai Tamil month (November - December). The tenth day is the major festival day, where at the top of the hill, many lamps made of a wick in ghee are lit.

Every month in the night of the full moon-day many devotees (200.000 up to 1.000.000) worship Shiva by walking around the hill barefoot, a distance of about fifteen kilometres (3-5 hours walk). There are eight lingams and many mandapas, or holy tanks, around the Arunachala hill. The great Advaita Vedanta guru Bhagwan Sri Ramana Maharishi lived in Tiruvannamalai from about 1900 until his mahasamadhi, or death, in 1950. The very tranquil ashram by the name of Ramanashramam is near a hill called Arunachala on the west side of town. The ashram has cows, monkeys, dogs and peacocks (including an albino), reflecting Ramana Maharshi's love for animals. There is also a large silent meditation hall, a cafeteria, a bookstore, and rooms for devotees to stay in. Food is provided daily by the ashram to the long line of villagers who come asking for it.

Tiruvarur : Tiruvarur is town in Tamil Nadu state of southern India. The town is the administrative headquarters of Tiruvarur district. Tiruvarur is famous for Sri Tyagaraja temple and the annual chariot festival perfomed at the month of Chitrai (April/May). Tiruvarur was the birth place of three great Carnatic musicians Tyagaraja, Muthuswami Dikshitar and Syama Shastri.

Tiruvarur District : Tiruvarur district is one of the 30 districts in the Tamil Nadu state of India. The district occupies an area of 2161 km² and has a population of 1,165,213 (as of 2001). It is lies between Nagapattinam district on the east and Thanjavur district on the west, and is bounded by the Palk Strait on the south. The district headquarters is at Tiruvarur town. The Tiruvarur district, along with the Nagapattinam district was part of the Thanjavur district before 1981. After that, the present taluks of Tiruvarur district and Nagapattinam district were separated from the Thanjavur district, and formed the Nagapattinam district. The present Tiruvarur district was formed in 1997 by bifurcating the then Nagapattinam district.

Tista River : Tista river is an important river of the northern region of Bangladesh. According to Hindu mythology, it originated from the breast of Devi Parvati (Goddess Parvati). Actually it originates in Chitamu Lake in the Sikkim Himalayas at an altitude of about 7,200 m and comes down first to the Darjeeling plain and then to the Duar plain of West Bengal (India). It flows through a magnificent gorge known as Sivok Gola in Darjeeling. It is a wild river in the Darjeeling Hills where its valley is clothed with dense forest, but its drainage area in the mountains is only 12,500 sq km. It enters Bangladesh at the Kharibari border of Nilphamari district.

Titas River : Titas River is a river in south-eastern Bangladesh. It originates from the state of Tripura in India, and enters Bangladesh near Agartala (India) and Akhaura (Brahmanbaria District, Bangladesh). The length of the river is about 98 km. It falls into the Meghna River near Ashuganj.

Titumir : Titumir was a rebel against the zamindars and British colonial system in 19th century Bengal, part of British India. He rebelled against rich landlords and colonial British rulers and put up an impressive resistance. Along with his followers, he built a Bamboo fort (Bansher-Kella in Bangla). After a battle with British soldiers, Titumir succumbed to death on November 19, 1831. Titu Mir, real name Sayyid Mir Nisar Ali, was born on 27 January 1782 (14 Magh 1182 according to Bangla calendar), in a small village named Chandpur, Bashirhat Thana, Chabbish Parguna district (currently in West Bengal, India). Titu Mir's initial education was begun in his village school, and after his primary education, he moved to a local Madrassa. By time he was 18 years of age, Titu Mir had become a Hafiz of Qur'an, and a scholar of Hadith. He also became well accomplished in Bengali, Arabic, and Persian.

In 1822, Titu Mir went on a pilgrimage to Mecca to perform Haj, and on his return he commenced organizing peasants against Zamindars and the British colonialists. Titumir opposed a number of discriminatory measures in force at that time which included taxes on beard and mosque. The rift between Titu Mir and his followers on one side, and the local Zamindars supported by the-then British rulers of India on the other side, continued to widen, and armed conflicts surfaced at several places.

The followers of Titumir, believed to have reached 5000 number by that time, readied themselves for prolonged armed conflicts, and they even built a castle, made of bamboos at Narikelbaria. Titu Mir declared freedom from the British, and regions currently comprising districts of Chabbish Parguna, Nadia and Faridpur came under his control. The troops of Zamindars and the forces under the British met with a series of defeats.

Finally, the British forces, armed with superior weapons, mounted a concerted attacks on 14 November 1831, on Titu Mir and his followers. With their simple swords and spears, Titu Mir and his forces could not withstand the might of modern weapons, and were overwhelmed. The bamboo castle was destroyed, and Titu Mir was martyred along with several of his followers.

T Jayakanthan : He (born April 24, 1934) is a Tamil writer, essayist, journalist, pamphleteer, film-maker and critic. He was an iconoclast who ridiculed social anomalies and was known for his bold and revolutionary ideas.

T K V Desikachar : T.K.V. Desikachar is the son and primary student of Sri Tirumalai Krishnamacharya, a prominent yogi credited with being a driving force behind the resurgence of Hatha yoga in recent decades.

T K V Desikachar, started his career as a civil Engineer. Having been inspired by his father's teachings on Yoga in Madras (now Chennai), he left his engineering career and became a student of his in the sixties. In 1976 as a gurudakshina (offering) to his father and teacher, Sri Tirumalai Krishnamacharya, he established Krishnamacharya Yoga Mandiram (KYM), which is now a leading institute of Yoga and Yoga Studies based in Chennai, India. Today, TKV Desikachar is known and respected the world over as an authority on Yoga. He studied with his father for over 30 years.

Teaching regularly in India and overseas, TKV Desikachar, has participated in many international conventions and conferences. His books include the "Health, Healing and Beyond" and "The Heart of Yoga: Developing a Personal Practice". He has recently authored the first ever translation of the classical yoga text "Yogayajnavalkya Samhita". He has also co-authored with his son Kausthub, a book titled "Vedic Chant Companion". His latest work "The Viniyoga of Yoga", co-authored with Kausthub and Frans Moors, deals with the application of asana and pranayama to various needs,

Tlawmngaihna : In Mizoram, there was an excellent custom called tlawngaihna by which one was duty bound to help others. Under this custom everyone was required to be courteous and considerate and to help others always and every time, irrespective of one's inconvenience. Every one would try to surpass others in unselfishness and cooperation. This was an excellent custom in the daily life of a Lushai. For example : while traveling together, if one of the party would fall sick, all would wait for him to recover and would then resume the journey together.

With the advent of Christianity the institution of Zawlbuk and the custom of tlawmngaihna gradually died. The Christian in a village would not join a Zawlbuk and hence when the majority in 'a village become Christians, the zawlbuk in the village languished and ultimately become extinct. Similar was the fate of tlawmngaihna. When the people were turning away from their old beliefs, the customary network of duties and obligations was also snapped. New structures and institutions like village churches, schools, medical centres and administrative centres etc, were coming up. The people started depending, individually and collectively, more on the church and the Government for guidance and help.

TMSS : Also called TMSS or simply Thengamara. Thengamara is an operative Non-governmental organisation in Bangladesh that works with a number of poverty alleviation programs, with an emphasis on microcredit lending.

T P Kailasam : T. P. Kailasam (1884 - 1946) born July 29, 1884, was one of the foremost playwrights and writers of Kannada literature. His sense of humour, contribution to Kannada theater won many hearts and earned him the title Prahasana Prapitamaha (grand old man of humorous plays). Born in a Tamil family settled in Southern Karnataka, and educated in Great Britain, Kailasam on his return to India worked for the upliftment of Kannada. His life was dedicated to theater and his contributions revolutionised it. His sense of humour and its application in his plays left an everlasting impression on Kannadigas.

He opposed the company theatre's obsession with mythology and stories of royality and shied away from overloading his plays with music. Instead, he introduced simple sets which were realistic. Kailsam chaired the Kannada Sahitya Sammelana held at Madras (now Chennai) in 1945. His speech, one of the shortest was also one of the most effective ones made by any, who have chaired the prestigious gathering.

Toba Tek Singh : Toba Tek Singh is a district in the Punjab province of Pakistan. It was created in 1982 when it was carved out and separated from the district of Faisalabad. It took its name from the city of Toba Tek Singh, which in turn was named after a Sikh religious figure. Toba Tek Singh occupies 3252 square kilometers and is made up of large areas of lowlands that flood regularly during the rainy season; the floods originate frequently from the Ravi River that runs along the southern and southeastern borders.

Tochi river : Tochi river is located in North Waziristan, Federally Administered Tribal Areas, Pakistan. Tochi river flows eastward, in North Waziristan, to join the Kurram River and the Indus. It surrounds Waziristan in the North while the Gomal River river surrounds South Waziristan.

Toda people : The Toda people are a small pastoral tribe of Southern India who reside in the Nilgiri hills. The Toda number less than 1,000 and are an isolated people who speak Toda, a Dravidian language.

The Toda dress consists of a single piece of cloth, which is worn like the plaid of a Scottish highlander. The women cover their whole body with this mantle. Their sole occupation is cattle-herding and dairy-work. They practice polyandry, a practice in which a woman marries all the brothers of a family. The ratio of females to males is about three to five. The Toda are most closely related to the Kota both ethnically and linguistically. The Todas worship their dairy-buffaloes, but they have a whole pantheon of other gods. The only purely religious ceremony they have is Kona Shastra, the annual sacrifice of a male buffalo calf. Toda villages, called munds, usually consist of five buildings or huts, three of which are used as dwellings, one as a dairy and the other as a shelter for the calves at night. These huts, of an oval, pent-shaped construction, are usually 10 feet high, 18 feet long and 9 feet wide. They are built of bamboo fastened with rattan and thatched. Each hut is enclosed within a wall of loose stones. The inhabitants of a mund are generally related and consider themselves one family. The Todas numbered 807 in 1901 and their current population stands at around 1,100.

Toddy : Palm wine, also called palm toddy or simply toddy, is an alcoholic beverage created from the sap of various species of palm tree. The drink is particularly common in parts of Africa, South India and in the Philippines, where it is known as tuba.

Tolkappiyam : The Tolkappiyam is a work on the grammar of the Tamil language. Written in the form of poems (or short hymns) around the 3rd century BC by Tolkappiyar, is said to be the world's oldest surviving grammar for any language, except Sanskrit. The name Tolkappiyam can be split as Tolkappiyam = Tonmai + kappiyam. Tonmai means archeologically old and Kappiam is a literature master piece or epic. All the words, poems and literature that came in Tamil language after that followed the grammar as explained by Tolkappiyam. It also includes classification of habitats, animals, plants and human beings. The discussion on human emotions and interactions is particularly significant.

Tomara : The Tomara (also known by other variations of that name, such as Tomar, Tanwar and Toor) are a clan of Rajputs. They ruled certain minor states in northern India during the 8th-12th and the 15th-16th centuries. In the 8th century, the Tomaras established a state in what is now Haryana, and founded the city of Dhiliki (later Delhi) in 736. That state was defeated by the Chàuhans in 1162, who in turn were defeated by Muhammad Ghori in 1194 AD. This latter event led to the founding of the Delhi sultanate.

As the sultanate weakened in the early 15th century, the Tomaras established themselves at the strategic fortress of Gwalior in northern Madhya Pradesh; the ruler Man Singh Tomara built the fortress-citadel that still stands there. The Mughal emperor Akbar captured Gwalior in 1559. After the defeat of the Tomara state by the Chauhans in 1168 AD, some Tomars moved to Rajasthan and established a minor state centered around the town of Patan near Jaipur. Other Tomars who left Delhi settled around Panipat in Haryana. Significant numbers of Tomaras, known as Tonwar Thakurs, live in Morena District northwest of Gwalior; The district was formerly known as Tonwarghar.

Tomb of Bibi Pari : The tomb of Bibi Pari, is located in the center of Lalbagh Fort, is the most impressive of the surviving buildings of the fort. Eight rooms surround a central square room that contains the mortal remains of Bibi Pari. The central room is covered by a false octagonal-shaped dome, wrapped by a bronze plate. The entire inner wall of the central room is covered with white marble, while the four rooms at the sides had stone skirting up to a height of one metre. The walls in the rooms at the four corners are skirted with beautifully-glazed floral tiles. The tiles have recently been restored; two of the original tiles have been retained. The room at the south eastern corner contains a small grave, popularly known to be of that of Shamsad Begum, possibly a relative of Bibi Pari.

The archaeological excavations have also revealed strata of the Sultanate, as well as of the pre-Muslim periods, from where terracotta heads and plaques have been found. Thus, it is now justified to say that though the Mughals founded Dhaka, it was definitely inhabited long before the Muslims came to Bengal.

Tomb of Sheikh Salim Chishti : One of the most significant of Sufi shrine, the tomb of Sheikh Salim Chishti is one of the finest and famous examples of marble work masterpieces in India. It is situated in the north half of the great courtyard of the 'Jami Masjid' (Royal Mosque) in the city of 'Fathehpur Sikri' in Agra. The tomb was built where the renowned Sufi mystic Sheikh Salim Chisti had his hermitage and had sat in meditation during his lifetime. The shrine was built in 1570.

Fathehpur city was founded in Sikri village, 40km from Agra by the Mughal Emperor Akbar in honour of the Saint Sheikh Salim Chishti. Emperor Akbar came to Sikri in search of the saint to ask his blessing for a son when all else had failed. The Sufi saint who was Emperor Akbar's advisor and teacher predicted that the king would have three sons. The prediction came true, and Akbar's son Jahangir was named as Salim after the saint, and raised by the Sufi holy man. The saint passed away in 1571. To perpetuate the memory of the saint, Akbar constructed a charming mosque in the midst of Sikri complex with its palaces, courts, baths and gardens. The white marble mausoleum of Sheikh Salim Chishti with its unusual carvings, has an ethereal quality about it.

The entrance has four thin pillars with unusual Gujarati style serpentine struts that curve upwards to the roof which are highly decorative. These brackets are filled with marble inlay work (jali), containing minute geometrical and floral designs, with a moulded-pendant at lower end and a half chakra at upper end. Around the arched entrance are inscribed the names of God, the Prophet and the four Caliphs of Islam. Shahjahan added exquisite pietra dura work later as a mark of respect for the saint.

Tongi : Tongi is a city in Dhaka Division, Bangladesh. It is located at around 23°53'24?N, 90°24'21?E and has a population of 350,000. Tongi is a place where Biswa Ijtema is held every year. Tongi is located near Turag River

Tonk : Tonk is a town in Rajasthan state, India. The town of Tonk is situated 1462 ft. above sea-level, 100 km (60 miles) by road south from Jaipur, near the right bank of the Banas River. It is the administrative headquarters of Tonk District. Tonk was also the capital of the eponymous princely state of British India from 1817 to 1947. The founder of the princely state of Tonk was Amir Khan, a Muslim freebooter of Afghan descent, and a notorious Pindari leader of the early 19th century. In 1817, upon submitting to the British during the Pindari War, he received the territory of Tonk and the title Nawab. The state was part of the Rajputana agency and consisted of six isolated tracts, some of which were under the Central India Agency. Upon India gaining its independence in 1947, the Nawab of Tonk acceded unto the Union of India; most of the area of the state of Tonk later became part of Rajasthan state, while some of its eastern enclaves became part of Madhya Pradesh.

Topi : Topi is a small town in NWFP, Pakistan. It is located near the world's largest earth-filled dam, Tarbela Dam, which is also the largest hydroelectric generation project in Pakistan. The town of Topi became known after the Ghuulam Ishaq Khan Institue of Technology (GIKI), named after an ex-president, was establihed here. GIKI provides state-of-the-art education in various technologies.

Tosra River : Tosra river is one of the trans-boundary rivers lying over Tibet, Bhutan, India and Bangladesh. The river originates from eastern Tibet and crosses the Chumbi valley. In this part, the river is known as the Chumbi. Then it receives the name Am-Chu and flows south over Tibet and Bhutan. The river enters Bangladesh after crossing Kuchbihar and meets the Brahmaputra 22.5 km southwest of Dhubri. West of Kuchbihar the Tosra creates an offshoot, the Dharla to join with the Jaldhaka river. The Tosra also receives a tributary from the Raidak river at 29 km southeast of Kuchbihar. The upperstream of the Tosra from the confluence is known as the Raidak or the Dudhkumar.

Tour de Pakistan : The Tour de Pakistan is an annual cycling race held in Pakistan. It is modeled after the Tour de France. The race begins in Quetta and ends in Peshawar. The event is 22 stages long and 2200 kilometre in length.

Trango Tower : The Great Trango Tower (6286 m / 20608 ft) is part of the Trango massif, which is located across the Baltoro Glacier in the Karakoram mountain range in Pakistan's Northern areas. The Trango Towers consist of four summits with sharp ridges. Great Trango Tower was first climbed in 1977 by Galen Rowell, John Roskelly, Kim Schmitz and don freakazoid by the easiest route up the western side. The east face of Great Trango is the world's tallest vertical rock face, and was first climbed in 1984 by the Norwegians Hans Christian Doseth and Finn Dæhli, who were killed on the descent.

Trango Towers : Great Trango Tower (6286 m / 20608 ft) is part of the Trango massif, which is located across the Baltoro Glacier in the Karakoram mountain range in Pakistan's Northern areas. The Trango Towers consist of four summits with sharp ridges. Great Trango Tower was first climbed in 1977 by Galen Rowell, John Roskelly, Kim

Schmitz and Dennis Hennek by the easiest route up the western side. The east face of Great Trango is the world's tallest vertical rock face, and was first climbed in 1984 by the Norwegians Hans Christian Doseth and Finn Dæhli, who were killed on the descent.

Tranquebar : Tranquebar was a Danish colony in India from 1620-1845. It is spelled Trankebar or Trangebar in Danish, which came from the native Tamil Tarangambadi, meaning "place of the singing waves". It is located in Nagapattinam district about 100 km south of Pondicherry, near the mouth of a distributary of Kaveri river

It was founded by the Danish East India Company in 1620 when the main fort in Trankebar city, known as Fort Dansborg, was built by a Danish captain named Ove Gedde as the residence of the governor and other officials for about 150 years. It is now a museum hosting a collection of artefacts from the time of Danish presence in the region. Churches, the fort and the city gates are now being restored for tourism. It was sold to Britain in 1845, whereafter much of it fell into disrepair.

Transcendental Meditation : Transcendental Meditation or TM is a form of meditation developed in 1955 by Maharishi Mahesh Yogi, a disciple of Guru Dev. There have been some studies on Transcendental Meditation but critics have raised questions about the integrity of the scientists who conducted the studies, and the possible negative effects of Transcendental Meditation.

In 1957, at the end of a great "festival of spiritual luminaries" in remembrance of the previous Shankaracharya of the North, Swami Brahmananda Saraswati, his disciple Maharishi Mahesh Yogi (or simply "Maharishi") announced the formal beginning of TM. In the movement's initial stages, Maharishi operated under the auspices of an organization he called the "Spiritual Regeneration Movement".

In the early 1970s, Maharishi launched his "World Plan" to establish a TM teaching center for each million of the world's population, which at that time would have meant 3,600 TM centers throughout the world. Since 1990, Maharishi has co-ordinated his global activities from his headquarters in the town of Vlodrop in the municipality of Roerdalen in the Netherlands.

The TM Movement founded a nationally accredited university in Iowa, USA, the Maharishi University of Management in 1971; a number of schools around the world; a city in south-east Iowa, Vedic City (founded 21 July 2001); political parties in many countries around the world known as the Natural Law Party, the US branch having closed on April 30, 2004 in favour of the Global Country of World Peace, founded in 2002.

Trans-Karakoram Tract : The Trans-Karakoram Tract is a small area that was transferred by a border agreement from the Pakistani-administered Northern Areas to China in 1963 with the proviso that the settlement was subject to the final solution of the Kashmir dispute. The transfer is disputed by India which claims the Tract as part of Jammu and Kashmir state. A similar but larger area of Kashmir held by China is the Aksai Chin region northeast of Ladakh. The Tract is one of the most inhospitable areas of the world with some of the highest mountains including Broad Peak, Gasherbrum and Masherbrum and adjacent to the highest battlefield in the world at Siachen Glacier.

Travancore : Travancore or Thiruvithaamkoor was a princely state in India with its capital at Trivandrum (Thiruvananthapuram). The state comprised most of south Kerala and the modern Kanyakumari district of Tamil Nadu and it had a 19-gun salute in the British Empire. Its flag was red with a silver dextrally coiled sacred chank

(Turbinella pyrum Linnaeus). Travancore was merged with the other Malayalam-speaking state of Cochin on 1 July 1949 to form Travancore-Cochin, and later with the Malabar district of Madras State on 1 November 1956 to form the south Indian state of Kerala.

The region was ruled by the Ay Dynasty during the first Sangham age (circa 300 BC – 600 AD) and was the scene of many battles between the Kulashekaras and the Cholas during the second Sangham age (circa 850–1400 AD), when Vizhinjam, the capital, was sacked by the Cholas. Later the area was termed Venad, and the rulers were very weak, being vassals of Nayaks of Madurai or facing rebellions from the powerful feudal land lords (Ettuveetil pillamar and the Yogakaar).

Treaty of Amritsar : The Treaty of Amritsar of 1846 settled a dispute over territory in Kashmir, with the United Kingdom ceding some land to Maharaja Ranbir Singh.

Treaty of Rawalpindi : The Treaty of Rawalpindi was (signed on August 8, 1919 and amended November 22, 1921) a treaty made between the United Kingdom and Afghanistan during the Third Anglo-Afghan War. In it, the United Kingdom recognised Afghanistan's independence, agreed that British-Indian empire would never extend past Khyber Pass, and stopped British subsidies to Afghanistan. The Treaty of Rawalpindi is celebrated on Afghan Independence Day, August 9.

Treaty of Sugauli : The Treaty of Sugauli was a treaty signed after the Anglo-Nepalese War in 1816 between Nepal and the British East India Company. The Anglo-Nepalese War (1814-16) was a total disaster for Nepal. According to the Treaty of Sagauli, signed in 1816, Nepal lost Sikkim, the territories west of the Kali River (Kumaon and Garhwal), and most of its lands in the Tarai. The

British East India Company was to pay 200,000 rupees annually to Nepal to make up for the loss of revenues from the Tarai.

Treaty of Titalia : The Treaty of Titalia (1817) was signed between the chogyal (monarch) of Sikkim and the British East India Company. The treaty, which was negotiated by Captain Latter in February 1817, guaranteed security of Sikkim by British and returned Sikkimese land annexed by the Nepalese over the centuries. it followed the Anglo-Nepalese War of 1816 in which the Nepalese were routed by the British forces. In return, the British were given trading rights and rights of passage up to the Tibetan frontier. The treaty was named after Titalia, a place on the current-day West Bengal-Bihar border. In the Gazette of Sikkim, 1894, by H. H. Risley, it was written that "the Treaty of Titalia British India has assumed the position of Lord's paramount of Sikkim and a title to exercise a predominant influence in that State has remained undisputed."

Trichambaram Temple : Trichambaram Temple is situated 20 km from Kannur district of Kerala state, south India. It is near Taliparamba town, famous for its spices trade. The temple is believed to have got the name from Thiru Shambara or the holy shambara in reverence to Maharishi Shambara. The deity of the temple is Sree Krishna. The sculptures on the walls of the sanctum sanctorum are a class by themselves. The temple also contains one of the most exquisite collection of mural paintings in south India. Trichambaram Temple has three ponds attached to it, with the temple for Durga being surrounded by water on all sides. The annual temple festival (Utsavam) is a colourful event. The fortnight-long festival begins on Kumbham 22 of Malayalam calendar (which generally falls on March 6) every year with the kodiyettam (hoisting of a religious flag) and comes to an end on Meenam 6 (which generallay falls on March 20) with Koodipiriyal (Ending of this festival). In between these dates, for 11 days, thitambu nriththam (a sort of dance with idols of Sri Krishna and Balarama) is held at Pookoth Nada (1 km from Trichambaram temple).

Trimbakeshwar : Trimbak or Trimbakeshwar is an ancient Hindu temple dedicated to Lord Shiva, one of the twelve Jyotirlingas. It is located in the town of Trimbak, in the Nasik district of Maharashtra, India. The source of the Godavari river, the longest river in peninsular India lies in the hills surrounding the temple.

Trimbakeshwar, which is 28 km (18 mi) from Nashik City, Maharashtra, India, is a religious center having one of the twelve Jyotirlingas of the world. The extraordinary feature of the Jyotirlinga located here is that it has three faces embodying Lord Brahma, Lord Vishnu and Lord Mahesh(Shiva). All other Jyotirlinga have Shiva as the main deity. The entire black stone temple is known for its appealing architecture and sculpture and is at the foothills of a mountain called Brahmagiri. Godavari River originates on Bramhagiri mountain and meets to the sea near Raj Mahendri, AP. This place is famous for lots of religious rituals(vidhis). Narayan-Nagbali, Kalsarpa Shanti, Tripindi vidhi are done here.

The Trimabakeshwar town has good number of Brahmin houses and is also a centre for Vedic Gurukuls (kind of boarding school). It also has Ashrams & Muths devoted to Ashtanga Yoga—the Hindu art of Living. The place is known for its scenic beauty in rainy season and is surrounded by lush green hills untouched by pollution.

Trimbakeshwar Temple : This temple situated in Trimbak, 30 km West of Nasik, contains one of the twelve Jyotirlingas (naturally occuring Lingas) in India. The temple has beautiful carvings. There is a belief that anybody who visits Trimbakeshwar attains salvation. It is considered to be the holiest place to perform Shraddha ceremony as mentioned in 'Nirnaya Sindhu'—a religious book of Hindus. Non Hindus are not allowed inside the temple but one can get a clear view from outside. The river Godavari rises here from a hill called Brahmagiri. Nearby there is the 'Gangasagar bathing tank' into which the Godavari river dribbles in, from its source. A bath in these waters is supposed to wash away sins.

Trinamool Congress : The All India Trinamool Congress, earlier West Bengal Trinamool Congress, (WBTC), was a political party in West Bengal, India, led by Mamta Banerjee. Founded in 1998, it consisted largely of defectors from the (then) electorally unsuccessful Indian National Congress in Bengal. In the Lok Sabha elections in 1999 AITC got 2.6% of votes and eight seats, the Communist Party of India (Marxist) retaining control of most of the remaining seats in the State Assembly. However the Trinamool Congress managed to win control of Calcutta (Kolkata) in municipal elections in 2000, only to lose it again to the CPI (M) in June 2005. Ahead of the 2004 Lok Sabha elections AITC merged with P.A. Sangma's break-away fraction of the Nationalist Congress Party. The new party is called Nationalist Trinamool Congress.

Trinket Island : Trinket Island (29 sq km) is part of the Nicobar Islands chain, located in the northeast Indian Ocean between the Bay of Bengal and the Andaman Sea. It is located east of Kamorta island and, like the Nicobar Islands generally, is under the sovereignty of the nation of India. As of 2001, the Indian census catalogued 436 persons living on Trinket in four villages, Trinket (population 244), Safebalu, Tapiang and Hockcook.

Like the other Nicobar and Andaman Islands, Trinket was devastated by tsunamis generated by the 2004 Indian

Ocean Earthquake. The island, which had a low and flat topography, was severely eroded by the powerful waves, suffering the loss of 19.4% of its surface area, from 36 sq. km. down to 29 sq. km. Initial reports that the island had been split apart were later confirmed by satellite imagery. On Trinket, the tsunami caused 91 deaths and the total devastation of the island's communities and economy. Shortly after the disaster, the entire remaining population of the island was evacuated to neighboring islands, principally Nancowry Island.

Tripura : Tripura is a state in North-east India. The capital is Agartala and the main languages spoken are Bengali and Kokborok. Tripura (Twipra) used to be a royal state before independence.The Tribal Kings (Habugra) had the title of Manikya and ruled Tripura for hundreds of years until its incorporation into India in 1949. The capital of the Kingdom was based in Udaipur which was known as Rangamati on the banks of the river Gomati (Kormoti) in South Tripura. The capital was shifted first to Old Agartala and then the present Agartala in the 19th Century. As a revolt against the monarchic rule, the Ganamukti Parishad movement was launched. The movement was victorious and Tripura was integrated with India. It was heavily affected by partition and its population now consists of Bengalis (most of whom came as refugees from Bangladesh after independence in 1971) living side by side with the native tribal population.

Trishuli : Trishuli is the name of Himalayan mountain peak,which is 7,074 m high in the Pithoragarh district of Uttaranchal,India. The peak was scaled for the first time in 1966 by a team led by C. K. Mitra.Trishuli West is another peak with an elevation of 7,035 m.Both peaks are situated ahed of Milan valley.Trishuli West is climbed for the first time in 2001 through south west ridge.A total of three ascent to Trishuli West had been recorded in

2001.These peaks are the part of Trishuli massif formed by the peaks of Trishuli-Trishuli West—Hardeol (7,151 m)-Changabang or Kalanka.

Tropical Cyclone 05B : Tropical Cyclone 05B was the deadliest Indian Ocean tropical cyclone since the 1991 Bangladesh cyclone, and deadliest Indian storm since 1971. The storm made landfall just weeks after another Category 4 hit the same general area. A tropical disturbance developed in the South China Sea in mid-to-late October. It tracked westward with limited development until it reached the Andaman Sea on October 24. The convective area slowly consolidated, and it became Tropical Depression 5B on October 25 over the Malay Peninsula.

The depression tracked northwestward under the influence of the Subtropical Ridge to its north. Warm water temperatures and favorable upper level winds allowed further strengthening, and it became Tropical Storm 5B on October 26, 210 miles (345 km) south-southwest of Yangon, Myanmar. The storm continued to strengthen, and intensified to a cyclone on the 27th in the open Bay of Bengal.

On October 28, the cyclone rapidly intensified to a peak of 160 mph winds, the equivalent of a Category 5 hurricane. Just prior to its Indian landfall, the cyclone weakened slightly to a 155 mph cyclone. On October 29, the cyclone hit the Indian state of Orissa near the city of Bhubaneswar. The ridge to the north blocked further inland movement, and the cyclone stalled about 30 miles (50 km) inland of the ocean. It slowly weakened, maintaining tropical storm strength as it drifted southward. The cyclone re-emerged into the Bay of Bengal on October 31, and dissipated on November 3 over the open waters.

Tsongmo Lake : Tsongmo Lake (also called Changu Lake) is a large lake in the East Sikkim district of the

Indian state of Sikkim. Etymologically "Tso" means lake and "Mgo" means head, thus literally meaning "source of the lake" in the Bhutia language. The cerulean lake is about forty kilometres away from the capital Gangtok at an altitude of 3,780 m (12,400 feet). It is oval-shaped, with a length of about one kilometre and has an average depth of fifteen metres. The tarn, with its refulgent waters is situated on the Gangtok-Nathula route.

Tsongmo lake is declared a sacred lake by the local Buddhist and Hindu population. During the winter months, the lake freezes over. It is fed by the melting snow during the summer months from May to August. Flora around the lake include the rhododendron, the state tree, primulas, iris and poppies. The Brahmini ducks, red panda and migratory birds frequent the lake. Due to the heavy promotion of tourism in the state, many locals have set up shop here offering yak rides, yak cheese, trinkets, and local curios.

Tsukhenye Festival : In Nagaland, Tsukhenye festival is also an important festival for the Chakhesang. Earlier it was usually celebrated at the end of the 3rd lunar month of March. But now it is being observed on 16th May. Tsukhenye is a festival which celebrates the culmination of all leisure activities and a festival for welcoming a new fruitful life and year.

The Chang usually observe six major festivals in year, out of which three festival namely Poang Lem, Jeinyu Lem, Kundang Lem were monitored by Haongang Clan. The remaining three festivals Muong Lem, Naknyu Lem, Monyu Lem were monitored by Ung Clan. In this way the tradition was maintained for generations and is followed till date.

Tuensang : Tuensang is the district headquarter of Tuensang district,the easternmost and the largest (area) district of Nagaland.The town was founded in 1947 for the purpose of administrating the erstwhile North Eastern Frontier Agency (NEFA) that comprised the present day Tuensang, Mon, Longleng and Kiphire districts.It is located at an altitude of 1371 metres above sea level.The town's population is around 30,000(2001 census) and is the fifth largest urban centre in Nagaland after Dimapur-Chumukedima, Greater Kohima, Alichen-Mokokchung-DEF and Wokha. Changs, Sangtams, Yimchungers, Aos, Khiamungans, Semas and Phoms are the main Naga tribes that constitute the town's population.

Tughlaq Dynasty : The Tughlaq Dynasty of north India started in 1321 CE in Delhi when Ghazi Tughlaq assumed the throne under the title of Ghiyath al-Din Tughluq. The Tughluqs were a Muslim family of Turkish origin. Their rule relied on their alliances with Turkish, Afghan, and other Muslim warriors from outside South Asia.

The empire grew under his son and successor Muhammad bin Tughlaq, but the latter became notorious for ill-advised policy experiments such as shifting the capital from Delhi to Daulatabad and introducing copper coins without effective regulation against forgery.

After Muhammad bin Tughlaq his cousin Feroz Shah Tughlaq assumed the throne. He was a very benevolent ruler but was somewhat weak militarily. After Feroz died in 1388, the Tughlaq dynasty started to fade out and there were no able leaders; the dynasty was almost over within 10 years.

Tughlaqabad Fort : Tughlaqabad Fort is a ruined fort and city in Delhi built by Ghiyas-ud-din Tughlaq of the Delhi Sultanate which was abandonded in 1327. It seems that even when he was far from being a king Ghiyas-ud-din Tughlaq had dreamed of raising his city, Tughlaqabad.

Earlier, Ghiyas-ud-din had been a general (he rose to being the governor of an important province like Punjab, but that's another story) in Ala-ud-din Khalji's army. Once, while on the road with Ala-ud-din, Ghiyas-ud-din, on spotting this area, mentioned to the sultan what an ideal setting it seemed to provide for a new city. Upon this the king indulgently (and, knowing Ala-ud-din, also perhaps patronizingly) replied, 'When you become king, build it.' Knowing full well, as every boss, that while he was around there was not a shadow of a chance of anyone else taking his place. After the death of Ala-ud-din various events conspired to put the general on the throne at last. Then he fulfilled his long-cherished dream.

The fort is half-hexagonal in shape and Ghiyas-ud-din seems to have built defenses around and in it till he was blue in the face. The outer walls are built around the silhouette of the surrounding land and, what with their height and width, add formidably to the natural barriers. They were also well defended. On the north, east and west sides it is protected by trenches that go far down, and in the south a lake acts sentinel.

Tukaram : Sant Tukaram, respectfully referred to as Shri Tukaram, and colloquially referred to as "Tuka" was a seventeenth century Marathi poet saint of India, with a very great stature in the Bhakti movement of Maharashtra, so much so that in the popular mind he is the very peak of that centuries long outbreak of love for god. The days of his life are contentious with scholars assigning various dates to his birth. The four most popular options are 1568, 1577 1608 and 1598 AD, so we do have a wide choice. There is lesser dispute that he died in 1650 AD, a public event wherein he was supposed to have bodily been lifted up to salvation by his favourite deity, Vithobha of Pandharpur, who was an avatar of Krishna. As to the rest his poetry did the talking and it still does.

He is considered one of the favourite saints of Maharashtra especially the Varkari sampradaya (community). Tukaram was a great devotee of Krishna, considered an incarnation of Vishnu, the supreme God in Vaishnavism He was born in Dehu, very close to modern Pune city in Maharashtra. His father was a small trader or peddler and he was barely literate all his life. His family were successful grain sellers but the priestly class considered him lowborn.

Tulsi lake : Tulsi lake is the second largest lake in the Indian city of Mumbai. It is situated in the Borivali National Park in northern Mumbai. It is the northern-most lake in Mumbai. The Powai-Kanheri hill ranges serve as the catchment area for rain water which feeds the lake. It meets part of the city's water requirement, especially to the South Mumbai region. Its overflow level is measured at 139.17 metres. Vihar Lake and Powai Lake are the other two lakes in the vicinity.

Tulsidas : Goswami Tulsidas was a Awadhi poet and philosopher. He was born in Rajpur, India in the district of Banda in Uttar Pradesh, during the reign of Humayun. Tulsidas wrote twelve books and is considered the greatest and most famous of Hindi poets. He is regarded as an incarnation of Valmiki, the author of Ramayana written in Sanskrit. He wrote Ramacharitamanasa (The Lake that is the Story of Lord Rama), an epic devoted to Lord Rama. This Awadhi version of Ramayana, like many translations of the original Sanskrit Ramayana, is read and worshipped with great reverence in many Hindu homes in northern India. It is an inspiring book that contains sweet couplets in beautiful rhyme called 'chaupai'. Vinaya Patrika is another important book written by Tulsidas. He is considered one of the northern Indian Sants.

Tulu : Tulu is a Dravidian language of India with fewer than two million speakers. Most of its speakers are in the district of South Kanara in the west of the state of Karnataka. The original written script of the language, similar to Malayalam script, is rarely used today. It is normally written in the Kannada script.

There is a controversy whether Tulu script originated from Malayalam script or vice versa. However inscriptions available both of Tulu and Malayalam says Tulu is much older language than Malayalam. In fact, Tulu is much older than Kannada itself. However, 19th century German missionaries used the Kannada script to transcribe Tulu works, and it soon fell out of use due to the fact that Tulu was a lingual minority in the princely state of Mysore. Tulu is generally spoken as the local language by the Mangaloreans. Daily use of the language has propelled its popularity to higher than that of Kannada, the state language. The local population relates closely to any tulu speaker and this fact has its own far reaching consequences and it is now a recognized language in the southern districts of Karnataka.

Tulu Nadu : Tulu Nadu is a region of the southwestern coast of Karnataka, India, consisting of the districts of Dakshina Kannada and Udupi. These districts were formerly the single district of Dakshina Kannada or South Kanara, but Udupi district was separated in August 1997. This is the region in which Tulu is spoken. The population of these districts in 2001 was 3,005,897. Mangalore and Udupi are the chief cities.

Besides Tulu, Kannada (the state language) and Konkani are spoken in the area. Also, a sizeable population of Muslims, Bearys, speak a dialect of Malayalam. The Tulu speakers are known as Tuluvas. Tulu Nadu lies along the Malabar Coast, and shares a number of geographic, culinary, and social traits with the neighbouring Konkan and Kerala regions. Like them, Tulu Nadu is bounded on the west by the Arabian Sea and on the east by the

Western Ghats. Tulu cuisine is popular across South India in the form of 'Udupi restaurants', which are primarily vegetarian. The Tulu language was also once spoken in Uttara Kannada or North Kanara, which for this reason is sometimes considered part of Tulu Nadu as well.

Tulu Nadu was governed by feudatories of the Vijayanagara Empire until the 17th century. In the 18th, it was conquered by Haidar Ali, the ruler of Mysore, and Mangalore became Mysore's chief naval entrepôt. After the British defeated Haidar's successor Tipu Sultan in 1799, the region was attached to the Madras Presidency before reverting to the linguistic state of Mysore in the aftermath of independence. Mysore has since been renamed Karnataka.

Tunga : The Tunga is a river in the Indian state of Karnataka. The Tunga river is born in the Western Ghats, on a hill known as Varaha Parvata, at a place called Ganga Mula. From here, the river flows through four districts in Karnataka - Dakshina Kannada, Udupi, Chikmagalur and Shimoga. 147 km long, the Tunga merges with the Bhadra river at Koodli, a small town near Shimoga, Karnataka. The river is given the compund name Tungabhadra from this point onwards. The Tungabhadra flows eastwards and merges with the Krishna river in Andhra Pradesh. The river is famous for the sweetness of its water. It has a dam built across it at Gajanur, and a larger dam has been built across the compound Tungabhadra river at Hospet. A famous religious center on the banks of the Tunga is Shringeri.

Tungabhadra : The Tungabhadra is a river of southern India. It is the chief tributary of the Krishna River. It formed by the confluence of two rivers, the Tunga and the Bhadra, which rise in the eastern slope of the Western Ghats, in the state of Karnataka. The Tungabhadra flows east across the Deccan Plateau, joining the Krishna in

Andhra Pradesh state, from where the Krishna continues east to empty into the Bay of Bengal. The wedge of land that lies north of the Tungabhadra, between the Tungabhadra and the Krishna, is known as the Raichur Doab.

Tura Peak : A majestic hill stands on the eastern flank of Tura, the largest town in the Garo Hills region of the Meghalaya State. It peaks eight hundred and seventy two metres above sea level over looking Tura. A tourist-bungalow, an observatory and a Cinchona-plantation are located at Tura Peak and its environs. A magnificent view of the lower Brahmaputra Valley as well as the golden yellow plains of Bangladesh is available all year round to viewers on Tura Peak.

Turi : Turi are a Pathan tribe on the Kohat border of the North-West Frontier Province of Pakistan. The Turis inhabit the Kurram Valley, which adjoins the western end of the Miranzai Valley. They speak Pashto and ranking as Pathans, they are by origin a Tttrki tribe, of the Shiah sect, who subjected the Bangash Afghans some time early in the eighteenth century. They are strong, hardy, and courageous, and are rated horsemen. Their early dealings with the British government were inclined to turbulence, and they were concerned in the Miranzai expeditions of 1851 and 1855. But the only expedition specially sent against them was the Kurram expedition of 1856. Since then they have settled down and engaged in trade. During the Second Afghan War they supplied Sir Frederick Roberts with guides and provisions. In 1892 they voluntarily accepted British administration. They now furnish a large part of the tribal militia in the Kurram Valley.

Tusu Makar : Here the most common festival is Tusu or harvest festival comes during the winter in the last day of Poush month in Jharghand. It is also for the unmarried girls. For them Tusu is super excellent with grace and elegance who may fulfil their desire. Though there is no history behind this festival, there are some ritual custom and what it has its tremendous store of scintillating songs full of life and taste.

Two-Nation Theory : Two-Nation theory was the basis of creation of Pakistan. It stated that Muslims and Hindus were two separate nations by every definition; therefore Muslims should have a separate homeland in the Muslim majority areas of British India (1858-1947), where they can spend their lives according to the teachings of Islam.

The ideology of Pakistan took shape through an evolutionary process. Historical experience provided the base; with Sir Syed Ahmad Khan began (1817-1898) the period of Muslim self-awakening; Allama Iqbal (1877-1938), also remember as poet of East, provided the philosophical explanation; Mr. Jinnah (1876-1948) translated it into a political reality; and the Constituent Assembly of Pakistan, by passing Objectives Resolution in March 1949, gave it legal sanction. It was due to the realization of Muslims of South Asia that they are different from the Hindus that they demanded separate electorates. When they realized that their future in a 'Democratic India' dominated by Hindu majority was not safe; they put forward their demand for a separate state.

The Muslims of South Asia believe that they are a nation in the modern sense of the word. The basis of their nationhood is neither territorial, racial, linguistic nor ethnic; rather they are a nation because they belong to the same faith, Islam. On this basis they consider it their fundamental right to be entitled to self-determination. They demanded that areas where they were in majority should be constituted into a sovereign state.

As early as in the beginning of the 11th century, Al-Biruni (973-1048) observed that Hindus differed from the Muslims in all matters and habits. The speech made by Jinnah at Minto Park, Lahore on March 22, 1940 was very similar to Al-Biruni's thesis in theme and tone. In this speech, he stated that Hindus and Muslims belong to two different religious philosophies, with different social customs and literature. They neither intermarry, nor eat together, and indeed belong to two different civilizations whose very foundations are based on conflicting ideas and concepts. Their outlook on life and of life is different. He emphasized that in spite of the passage of about 1,000 years the relations between the Hindus and Muslims could not attain the level of cordiality. The only difference between the writing of Al-Biruni and the speech of Jinnah was that Al-Biruni made calculated predictions, while Jinnah had history behind him to support his argument.

Tyagaraja : Tyagaraja was one of the most important composers of Carnatic music. He is regarded as one of the "trinity" of Carnatic music composers, along with Muthuswami Dikshitar and Syama Sastri. He was a devotee of Rama.

Tyagaraja was named after Lord Tyagaraja, the presiding deity of Thiruvarur. His family was a pious Telugu-speaking smartha brahmin family of the vaidiki Mulukanadu sub-caste. Tyagaraja started his musical training under Sri Sonti Venkataramanayya at an early age. Tyagaraja regarded music as a way to experience the love of God. His objective while performing music was to repeat the name of God and contemplate on His Divine Pastimes, thereby reducing the vices of the mind, not to display his mastery over Raga and Tala. He had to struggle quite a bit to compose music in which Bhava, that is, emotion, was crowned

As an 8-year-old, he composed Namo Namo Raghavaya Anisham in Desikathodi. Much later in life, his guru, Sonti Venkataramanayya, wanted to listen to Tyagaraja's new talent and invited him to perform at his house in Thanjavur. On that occasion, Tyagaraja presented Endaro Mahaanubhavulu, the fifth of the Pancharatna Krithis.

Intensely pleased with Tyagaraja's song, Sonti Venkataramanayya told the king about the genius of Tyagaraja. The king sent an invitation, accompanied as was traditional with many rich gifts, to Thyagaraja, inviting him to grace the royal court. To the unworldly Tyagaraja, the prospect of wealth or fame was no incentive; he clearly had no inclination for a career life at court, which doubtless in that age, as in every other, entailed petty rivalries and jealousies. He rejected the kings invitation outright, composing another gem of a kriti, Nidhi Chala Sukhama on this occasion.

Angered at his rejection of the royal offer, Tyagaraja's brother took revenge by throwing his idols of Rama Pattabhisheka in the nearby River Cauvery. Tyagaraja, unable to bear the separation with his Lord, made a pilgrimage to all the major temples in South India and composed many more songs in praise of the deities of those temple. He is said to have finally found the idols with the help of Rama himself. Tyagaraja attained Moksha on a Vaikunta Ekadasi.

Tyagaraja Music Festival : Thiruvaiyaru is the pace where the great saint and musician Tyagaraja lived and attained samadhi. Here an eight day music festival, Tyagaraja Aradhana is held every year in January. This Carnatic Music festival attracts music lovers from all corners of the country. Thiruvaiyaru is situated 13kms from Thanjavur.

U

Uch : Uch, also known as "Alexandria at the Head of the Punjab", is a historical city in Pakistan. Once it was an important city of ancient India. It is believed that in 325 BC Alexander the Great founded a city called Alexandria at the site of the last confluence of Punjab rivers with the Indus river. The website of the Embassy of Pakistan, Washington, D.C, however, describes Uch as follws: " Uch Sharif, 75 km from Bahawalpur, is a very old town. It is believed that it was founded in 500 BC. Some historians believe that Uch was there even before the advent of Bikramjit when Jains and Buddhists ruled over the sub-continent. At the time of invasion by Alexander the Great, Uch was under Hindu rule." Some historians believe that Mithankot or Chacharan Sharif was the settlement of Alexandria founded by Alexander the Great. Muhammad bib Qasim conquered the city; during the muslim period Uch was a center of Islamic studies for the subcontinent of India. There are several tombs of famous mystics (Sufis) in Uch, notably the tombs of Syed Jalaluddin Bukhari and his family.

Udaipur : Udaipur is a city in Rajasthan, India. It is the historic capital of the former kingdom of Mewar, and the administrative headquarters of Udaipur District. Udaipur is famous around the world as the City Of Lakes or Venice of East. The Pichola Lake, Udai Sagar, Fateh

Sagar and Badi Sagar in this city are considered some of the most beautiful lakes in the state.Fateh Sagar contains a small island, which contains USO, or Udaipur solar observatory. It is known for its Rajput-era palaces. Particularly famous is the Lake Palace, which entirely covers a small island in the Pichola Lake. Many of the palaces, like Lake Palace and Fateh Prakash Palace, have been converted into luxury hotels. Udaipur is also home to the Udaipur Solar Observatory, one of the six stations participating in the international Global Oscillations Network Group (GONG) which is aimed at the determination of the physical properties of the solar interior.

Udanti Sanctuary : The Udanti Sanctuary occupies the South-Eastern portion of Gariaband Tehsil of Raipur District and adjoins Orissa State in Eastern side. It covers an area of 247.59 Sq. Kms. The Sanctuary is principally created to protect the wild buffaloes. The other species are also abundant in the area.

Uday Shankar : Uday Shankar (1900-1977) is one of the most renowned dancers and choreographers of India, who brought the Indian dance to international attention. Born in Udaipur, Shankar formed his own company in 1929 and toured until 1938. While in London at the Royal College of Art, he choreographed two Indian ballets, Krishna and Radha and A Hindu Wedding. He formed a troupe of 'Hindu dancers' from among his family and friends and in March 1931 at the Theatre Champs-Elysées in Paris, he presented *Tandava Nritya.* In 1939 he set up the Uday Shankar India Culture Center at Almore, with a galaxy of great Gurus like Shankaran Namburi in Kathakali, Kandappal Pillai in Bharatnatyam, Amobi Sing in Manipuri dance and Allauddin Khan in classical music. He was a man of superb showmanship and perfectionism. By the sheer impact of his physical presence on stage he transformed the traditional forms into the most memorable works. He is widely accepted as the Father of Modern Dance in India. Some of Uday Shankar's famous works include the innovative ballet, 'Labour and Machinery' and a path breaking film, *'Kalpana,'* on the theme of dance.

Udham Singh : Udham Singh (December 26, 1899 – July 31, 1940), born Sher Singh and also known as Ram Mohammed Singh Azaad, was a Punjabi militant, nationalist, and freedom fighter. Singh is considered to be one of the front-ranking revolutionaries and martyrs of the Indian freedom struggle; for this reason, he is also sometimes referred to as Shaheed-i-Azam Sardar Udham Singh (the expression "Shaheed-i-Azam" means "king of martyrs"). Along with Bhagat Singh, Udham Singh is also believed to be one of the earliest Marxists/Bolsheviks in India.

At various stages in his life, Singh went by the following names: Sher Singh, Udham Singh, Udhan Singh, Ude Singh, Uday Singh, Frank Brazil, and Ram Mohammed Singh Azaad. Whilst living in England in 1940, Singh Shot dead Sir Michael O'Dwyer, former Governor General of the Punjab. This was in revenge for the Amritsar Massacre, when General Reginald Edward Harry Dyer's ordered British troops to fire on unarmed Indian protesters. This occurred during Michael O'Dwyer's rule and is believed by many to have occurred with latter's full connivance "to teach the Indians a lesson, to make a wide impression and to strike terror through-out Punjab". Although the Indian press generally condemned the incident, numerous Indians regarded Singh's action as justified and an important step in India's struggle to end British colonial rule in India.

Udupi : Udupi District in Karnataka was created in August 1997. The three northern taluks, Udupi, Kundapur and Karkal, were separated from Dakshina Kannada district to form Udupi district. The administrative headquarters of

Udupi district is Udupi. Population (2001) 1,109,494, a 6.88% increase from 1991.

The primary languages of Udupi district are Tulu, Kannada, and Konkani. Udupi and Dakshina Kannada districts are sometimes referred to as Tulu Nadu, as they constitute the Tulu-majority region. Udupi restaurants that are popular all over India and have found its way into other countries also. Udupi restaurants are typically south Indian vegetarian restaurants.

The famous sriKrishna temple is located in Udupi.Udupi is the place where Sri Madhwacharya,one of the greatest proponents of the Vaishnava faith began his philosophical journey

Ugadi : It is the Telugu New Year day celebrated on Chaitra Suddha Padyami, the first day of the bright fortnight in the month of Chaitra. This festival is known as Gudi Padwa in Maharashtra and Ugadi in Karnataka and Andhra Pradesh. It is a day of great joy and happiness. There is a strong belief that this day's happenings fore shadow the course of events in the entire year head. Everybody in the house gets up early in the morning takes an oil bath and puts on new clothes. Torana, (festoons of mango leaves), are tied to all the doors of the house The front yards are washed with cow dung water and decorated with different designs. Bhakshya otherwise known as Purampoli, is the special sweet cooked on this day. A special preparation called Ugadi Pachadi (chutney) is a must in very house.

Fresh tamarind with fresh water, jaggery, fresh mangoes and fresh margosa flowers form the ingredients of Ugadi Pachadi. They are mixed in a new decorated earthen pot and then kept before the presiding deity of the house hold. After puja, everybody partakes of the Ugadi Pachadi and only then goes for meals in the company of all. The significance of this Pachadi is, the mixture of bitter margosa flowers and sweet jaggery is that life also is a mixture of sorrow and joy. Men and women take part in sports and games, cock-fights and competitions, girls and boys find delight in having informal singing competitions.

In the evening people gather in temples or in common places. The village purohit worships the new Panchangam or Almanac. Then he announces the influence of various planets during the new year over the wind, rains and crops, cattle, wealth and human beings. Every body is eager to know his own future for the year according to his Rashi. In towns and cities poet's gatherings and musical concerts are held.

Ujjain : Ujjain (also known as Ujain, Ujjayini, Avanti) is an ancient city of central India, in the Malwa region of Madhya Pradesh, on the eastern bank of the Kshipra River. In ancient times the city was called Ujjayini, and is referred to as Ozene by Ptolemy. It is the administrative center of Ujjain District and Ujjain Division. It is one of the seven sacred cities of the Hindus, and the Kumbh Mela religious festival is held there every twelve years. It has been the first meridian of longitude for Hindu geographers since 4th century BCE. It is also home to Mahakal, one of the twelve Jyotirlinga shrines to the god Shiva.

The earliest references to the city, as Ujjaini, are from the time of the Buddha, when it was the capital of the kingdom of Avanti. Ujjain was the traditional capital of King Chandragupta II, also known as Vikramaditya, at whose court the nine poets known as the navaratna (nine jewels) of Sanskrit literature are said to have flourished. It marks the first meridian of longitude in Hindu geography. It is also reputed to have been the residence of Asoka (who subsequently became the emperor), when he was the viceroy of the western provinces of the Maurya empire. It was invaded by the Delhi Sultanate lead by Iltutmish in 1235 causing widespread destruction and systematic desecration of temples.

Under Mughal emperor Akbar it became the capital of Malwa, and during the last half of the 18th century it was the headquarters of the Maratha leader Sindhia. The Sindhias later established themselves at Gwalior, and Ujjain remained part of Gwalior state until Indian Independence in 1947. Gwalior state bacame a princely state of the British Raj after the Maratha defeat in the Third Anglo-Maratha War, and Gwalior, Ujjain, and the neighboring princely states were made a part of the Central India Agency. After Indian independence, the Sindhia ruler of Gwalior acceded to India, and Ujjain became part of the Madhya Bharat state. In 1956, Madhya Bharat was merged into Madhya Pradesh state.

Ujjayanta Palace : Ujjayanta Palace, standing right in the heart of the city of Agartala, is a famous royal House, covering an area of one sq. km.. Styled in Greek Sculpture, Ujjayanta Palace was built by Maharaja Radhakishore Manikya in 1901 at the cost of 10 lakh of rupees. The palace is set with the huge lughole style gardens, adorned by pools and fountains, the superbly tiled floors, curved wooden ceilings and exquisitely crafted doors. The three storied mansion has a mixed architecture with three domes (the centre one being 86' high).

Its well laid out gardens have two large tanks on either side and the fountains are laid out in the patterns of Mughal gardens.

Ulema : Ulema is a common romanisation for the plural of Arabic Alim "Scholar", namely 'Ulama'. The same word appears in Turkish as Ulema and in Persian as Olæma. The ulema are Muslim scholars engaged in the several fields of Islamic studies. They are best known as the arbiters of shari'a, that is, the Islamic law. While the 'ulama are understandably well versed in fiqh, some of them also go on to specialize in other sciences, such as philosophy (falsafah), dialectical theology (kalam) or Quranic hermeneutics (tafsir). The fields studied, and the importance given them, will vary from tradition to tradition, or even from seminary to seminary.

Ulsoor Lake : Ulsoor lake is a perfect gateway dotted with picturesque islands in Karnataka. This pretty picnic spot is on the north eastern fringe of the city centre. Here one can enjoy boat ride or swim in the near by pool. One of Kempegowda's watch towers stand near by.

Umananda Temple : The Shiva temple stands on Peacock island in the midst of river Brahmaputra. The temple built by an Ahom king in 1594, can be reached by crossing the river via country boats plying from Kachari Ghat in Guwahati. Ferries make regular crossings from 7am to 5pm. The site is especially busy during the annual Shivaratri festival, when devotees from all over the state come to worship the god.

Umar Saif : Dr. Umar Saif was the first Pakistani to receive a Ph.D. in Computer Science from University of Cambridge, where he was admitted to the doctorate program when he was only 19 years old. Subsequently, Dr. Saif joined the Laboratory for Computer Science and Artificial Intelligence (CSAIL) at the Massachusetts Institute of Technology (MIT), where he worked on the core technologies for project Oxygen — a US$40 million project sponsored by the US Department of Defense and an industrial Alliance of world-class companies.

While at MIT, Dr. Saif also managed the multi-million dollar collaboration on future computing technologies between University of Cambridge and MIT sponsored by the Cambridge-MIT Institute (CMI) and a consortium of hightech companies.

Umarkot : Umarkot is city in the province of Sindh, Pakistan. It was relatively more prominent during the time of the Mughals and during the British Raj. The great Mughal king Akbar was born in Umarkot when his father Humayun lost the battle against Sher Shah Suri and was on the run. Akbar later became the King of India and was a popular figure with both Hindus and Muslims. Umarkot has many sites of historical significance such as Akbar's birthplace and Umarkot Fort. The city is well connected with the other large cities like Karachi, the provincial capital and Hyderabad.

Una : Una is one of the Districts of Himachal Pradesh, India, and shares its border with Punjab. The terrain is plain with small hills. Una has been identified as a main industrial hub, as the city finds its place on a roadmap for future industrial sprees. Over the years, Una has turned into transit town for travelers going to the Buddhist town of Dharamsala or the Himalayas. Una is home to the "Killa", which is a historical fort, ancestral home of the descendants of the first guru of the Sikhs, Guru Nanak.

Undivided India : Undivided India has several socio-political, historical, and geographical meanings. Officially, it is a term which refers to the major part of the South Asia which comprised the British Raj, and included the current sovereign states of India, Bangladesh, and Pakistan. Undivided India did not include all geographical regions and nations of the South Asia like Nepal and Bhutan, but included most of the Princely states of India. References to undivided India are found in some legal enactments including India's Citizenship Act, 1955, which states that for the meaning of undivided India (in the context of this Act), the undivided India means India as defined in the Government of India Act 1935, as originally enacted. There are innumerable other references to undivided India, in a variety of contexts, but mostly indicating India with boundaries as it existed just before the partition of India into India and Pakistan.

Union Councils of Pakistan : A Union Council or Village Council in Pakistan is an elected local government body consisting of 21 councillors, and headed by a Nazim. "Union Council" is the more generic term, whereas "Village Council" is used for rural areas. The territory represented by a Village Council usually comprises a large village and surrounding areas, often including nearby small villages. The term "Union Council" may be used for localities that are part of cities. The territory of a Union Council or Village Council is usually part of a Tehsil (county). Less commonly, a Union Council may be part of a City District.

United Bengal Movement : United Bengal Movement a political proposal to solve the communal question on the eve of the termination of British rule in India. In April-May 1947 it became clear that the Partition of India was ineviatable. Huseyn Shaheed Suhrawardy, the Premier of the province of Bengal, formally launched his idea of a sovereign state for undivided Bengal. Almost simultaneously Sarat Chandra Bose came forward with his proposal for a Sovereign Socialist Republic of Bengal. There had been differences of opinion between Suhrawardy and Sarat Bose regarding the sovereign status of Bengal, but the primary motive of both of them was to resist the partition of the province. While the former wanted a completely independent state for united Bengal outside the union of India, the latter visualised Bengal to be a sovereign socialist republic within the Indian union

United Liberation Front of Asom (ULFA) : The United Liberation Front of Asom is a separatist organization from Assam. It was formed by the historic

Ahom structure Rang ghar on April 7, 1979. The ULFA is one of many separatist organizations operating in North-East India.

United News of India : United News of India is one of the two primary Indian news agencies. It began its operations on March 21, 1961, though it was registered as a company in 1959 itself.

University Grants Commission (UGC) : The University Grants Commission of India is a central government body that provides funds for government-recognised universities. It is the body that provides recognition for universities in India. Its central office is in New Delhi, and it also has a southern regional office in Hyderabad. University Grants Commission (Pakistan) : University Grants Commission of Pakistan, is the sole body in the country with the responsibility to ensure quality education. UGC supervises the overall functioning and the grant of funds to all the public sector universities in Pakistan. There are many regional offices of UGC all over the country. There are many inspection teams of the UGC, which inspect the institutes, and then give them the letter of recommendation or vice versa.

University of Azad Jammu and Kashmir : University of Azad Jammu and Kashmir was established in 1974 at Muzaffarabad, Azad Kashmir, Pakistan. The University of Azad Jammu & Kashmir is a multi-campus and multi-discipline university. It consists the Main Campus, based at Muzaffarabad, and four University Colleges. The Main Campus is a spectral combination of Basic Sciences and Humanities. The science group includes Department of Botany, Chemistry, Mathematics, Physics, Zoology, Computer Sciences and Information Technology and the Institute of Geology while Kashmir Institute of Economics, Department of English, Law and Art and Design make up the Humanities group. Also located at Muzaffarabad is Kashmir Information Resource Center.

University of Balochistan : University of Balochistan was established in 1974 at Quetta, Balochistan, Pakistan. It has more than 6,000 students and one campus, 35 different fields of studies and 5 faculties.

University of Calcutta : University of Calcutta (also known as Calcutta University) is the first modern university in the Indian subcontinent. It is a state-government administered urban-based affiliating and research university. It has its main campuses in College Street, Rajabazar, Alipore and a host of affiliated colleges in greater Calcutta.

University of Chittagong : University of Chittagong is a public university situated at Hathazari Upzila (Thana) of the district of Chittagong, Bangladesh. The university was established in 1966. Dr. Muhammad Yunus, founder of Grameen Bank and a pioneer in Microcredit theory in Economics, started his first experiments from this campus at the neighboring village of Zobra. Dr. Zamal Nazrul Islam, a noted mathematician and physicist, is another faculty member. The university is located in a remote place from the city (22 Km north of City of Chittagong. Therefore, it has free shuttle trains service from 7:00 A.M. to 8:00 P.M. for students. There are bus services for the faculties and other staffs.

University of Dhaka : The University of Dhaka (commonly referred to as Dhaka University or just DU) is the oldest university in Bangladesh. Established in 1921 under the Dacca University Act 1920 of the Indian Legislative Council, it is modelled after British universities. It is a multi-disciplinary university and is among the top universities in the region. With more than 30,000 students and upwards of 1,300 teachers, the University of Dhaka is the largest public university in Bangladesh. It is the only university in Bangladesh to have been listed in AsiaWeek's listing of top 100 Universities in Asia (64th).

Initially, the university worked hard to build up an outstanding record of academic achievement, earning for itself the reputation of being the 'Oxford of the East'. The university contributed to the emergence of a generation of leaders who distinguished themselves in different occupations in East Bengal. Until the Partition of Bengal in 1947, it maintained its unique character of being one of the few residential institutions of higher learning in Asia. In 1947, it assumed academic authority over all educational institutions above the secondary level falling within East Bengal. In the process, it became a teaching-cum-affiliating institution. This transformation, coupled with its unprecedented growth in the years that followed, put strains beyond reckoning on its human as well as material resources.

The university demonstrated an inherent strength in its activities during its eventful and often critical existence of over 80 years. Today, it provides about 70% of the trained human resources of Bangladesh engaged in education, science and technology, administration, diplomacy, mass communication, politics, trade and commerce, and industrial enterprises in all sectors. Students and teachers of this university have played a major part in shaping the history of Bangladesh.

University of the Punjab : University of the Punjab is located in Lahore, Punjab, Pakistan. University of the Punjab is the oldest and largest university of Pakistan. It was formed after the first meeting of Senate on 14 October 1882. It was the fourth university formed during the British colonial rule in South Asia.

Dr. G. W. Leitner, a well-educated Hungarian and a naturalized British citizen, became its first Registrar. Dr. Leitner contribution was instrumental in the establishment of University of Punjab.

Until the independence of Pakistan in 1947, the University of the Punjab was fulfilling the educational needs of a vast region of the South Asia. The independence of Pakistan reduced the geographical limits of the jurisdiction of the University.

On-campus teaching and research programs of the University are organized under more than 60 institutes, departments, and constituent colleges or centers. The university offers over one hundred degree, diploma or certificate programs. Addition to on-campus teaching and research activities, the University oversees and regulates the academic activities of over 410 affiliated colleges and institutes, imparting undergraduate, postgraduate and professional education.

Upanayanam : When the child attains eight years, the wearing of the thread, is ceremoniously done in Brhmins of Kerala. This is only in the case of the boys. It is taking the child to the preceptor for initiation. Along the sacred thread, the hide of the antelope called Krishnajinam is also worn by the boy.

Upma : Upma (Tamil), also known as "Uppindi" in Telugu and Uppittu in Kannada, is a wholesome Indian dish made of Wheat Rava. It is remarkable that in all the south Indian languages, the name of the dish has a similar etymology. The word "Uppu" means "Salt" in all these languages; the word for the dish derives from "Salt-and-flour".

There are many ways Upma is prepared; indeed, every south Indian lady will impart a small difference in flavour when making her Upma. This variation is obtained by varying or emphasising some particular spice, thereby making for variation

Apart from Rava, Upma is widely made with Rice Rava, Vermicelli and Cous-cous also. The Rice Upma, which is mainly popular in the southeren parts of Karnataka is referred to as Akki Tari Uppittu (Rice coarse flour uppittu). Since rice is easier to digest than Wheat is, akki tari uppittu has also become a recommended edible for patients along with Idli and Ganji

Upper Dir : Upper Dir is an area in the North-West Frontier Province of Pakistan. Dir is administratively subdivided into Upper Dir and Lower Dir districts. Dir district is 5,280 square kilometres in area and part of the Malakand division, lying along the Afghanistan border between Chitral and Peshawar. Almost all of it lies in the valley of the Panjkora which rises high in the Hindu Kush at Lat. 35.45 and joins the Swat River near Chakdara, where the district is usually entered, at Lat. 34.40. Apart from the tehsils of Adenzai round Chakdara and Munda in the south-west, Dir is rugged and mountainous with peaks rising to 16,000 feet in the north-east and to 10,000 ft. along the watersheds with Swat to the east and Afghanistan to the west. The

Upper Gangetic Plains Moist Deciduous Forests : The Upper Gangetic Plains moist deciduous forests is a tropical moist broadleaf forest ecoregion of northern India. It lies on the alluvial plain of the Ganges and Yamuna rivers, with an area of 263,100 square kilometers (101,600 square miles), covering most of the state of Uttar Pradesh and adjacent portions of Uttaranchal, Haryana, Madhya Pradesh and Bihar. The ecoregion is bounded on the north by the Himalayan subtropical pine forests, Terai-Duar savannas and grasslands and Himalayan subtropical broadleaf forests of the Himalaya foothills, to the west by the drier Northwestern thorn scrub forests and Kathiarbar-Gir dry deciduous forests, on the south by the Narmada Valley dry deciduous forests of the Malwa and Bundelkhand uplands, and on the east by the more humid Lower Gangetic plains moist deciduous forests.

The ecoregion has a tropical climate. Rainfall is highly seasonal, falling mainly during the June-to-September southwest monsoon. In ancient times the region was mostly forested, with sal (Shorea robusta) the predominant tree. Many trees lose their leaves during the winter dry season. The ecoregion is currently densely populated, and the fertile plains have largely been converted to intensive agriculture, with only a few enclaves of forest remaining.

Upper Sind Frontier : Upper Sind Frontier, with Jacobabad as the administrative headquarters, was one of the districts of Undivided India during the period of the British Raj. The district was part of the Sind province, which was then under the jurisdiction of Bombay Presidency. Currently, the regions is a part of Pakistan.

U R Ananthamurthy : U. R. Ananthamurthy is a leading thinker and writer in the Kannada language. Born in Melige village in Thirthahalli taluk on December 21, 1932 had his early education in Durvasamatha Sanskrit school. His main works include Samskara, Bhava, Bharathi Pura, and Avasthe. He has written numerous short stories as well.

Several of his novels and short fiction have been made into movies. Educated at Oxford in English literature, he came back to his homeland to write in Kannada, his mother tongue. He is a recipient of the Padma Bhushan.

U R Rao : U. R. Rao is a space scientist and former director of the Indian Space Research Organisation. He is presently the President of the Council of Management of the Physical Research Laboratory in Ahmedabad.

Urdu : Urdu is an Indo-European language of the Indo-Aryan family which developed under Persian, Turkish, and Arabic influence in South Asia during the time of the Delhi Sultanate and Mughal Empire (1200-1800).

Taken by itself, Urdu is approximately the twentieth most populous natively spoken language in the world, and is the national language of Pakistan as well as one of the 24 national languages of India. However, Urdu is often considered to be part of a wider Hindustani language, in which case it is the fourth most populous language in the world.

In Pakistan, Urdu is spoken and understood by a majority of urban dwellers in such cities as Karachi, Islamabad, Lahore, Rawalpindi, Peshawar, Quetta, Hyderabad, Sialkot, Gujranwala, Faisalabad, Multan and Sukkur. Urdu is used as the official language in all provinces of Pakistan. It is also taught as a compulsory language up to high school in both the English and Urdu medium school systems. This has produced millions of Urdu speakers whose mother tongue is one of the regional languages of Pakistan such as Punjabi, Sindhi, Pashto, Kashmiri, Balochi, Seraiki, Brahui, etc. Urdu is the lingua franca of Pakistan and is absorbing many words from regional languages of Pakistan. The regional languages are also being influenced by Urdu vocabulary. Most of the nearly five million Afghan refugees of different ethnic origins who stayed in Pakistan for over twenty five years have also became fluent in Urdu. It is fair to conclude that the center of Urdu language has shifted from Delhi and Lucknow in India to Karachi and Lahore in Pakistan.

In India, Urdu is spoken in Uttar Pradesh, Kashmir, Delhi, Bhopal, Bangalore, Hyderabad, Mumbai and other central parts of India. Some Indian schools teach Urdu as a first language, have their own syllabus and exams, Indian madrasas also teach Arabic as well as Urdu.

Newspapers like Daily Salar, Paasban are published and distributed in cities like Bangalore.

Urdu is also spoken in urban Afghanistan. Outside the South Asia, it is spoken by large numbers of workers in the major urban centres of the Persian Gulf countries and Saudi Arabia. Urdu is also spoken by large numbers of immigrants and their children in the major urban centres of the United Kingdom, the United States, Canada, Norway and Australia.

Urdu is the national language of Pakistan. It shares official language status with English. Although English is used in most elite circles, and Punjabi has a plurality of native speakers, Urdu is the lingua franca, and it is expected to prevail. Urdu is also one of the official languages of India, and in Indian controlled Jammu and Kashmir and the state of Andhra Pradesh, Urdu has official language status. While the government school system in most other states emphasizes Standard Hindi, universities in cities such as Lucknow and Hyderabad, Urdu is spoken and learned and is regarded as a language of prestige.

Urs (or Ziarats) : The *Urs (or Ziarats)* is a typical Kashmiri festival. It is held annually at the shrines of Muslim saints on their death anniversaries. There is a saying " It snows when the Urs of Meesha Sahib is held, it is windy when the Urs of Batamol Sahib takes place, it rains on the occasion of the Urs of Bahauddin". These Urs are popular despite the rigours of weather. This is celebrated in different parts of Srinagar, not only by Muslims but Hindus and Sikhs also. An interesting feature of the Urs celebrations at Batamaloo (the locality in Srinagar named after the saint Batamol Sahib) and in Anantag (Rishi Mol's anniversary) is that both Muslims and Hindus abstain from taking meat during the course of the festival.

The inter-communal participation is the main feature of the Urs celebrations. The anniversary of Rishi Pir, a Hindu saint, held on the fifth day of the full moon of Baisakh, at his home in Srinagar is attended by Muslims also.

Urumulu or Thunder Dance : Urumulu or thunder dance is found only in Anantapuram district in Andhra Pradesh. The instrument employed in this dance is called urumu. It is a percussion instrument which sounds like thunder. The instrument is made out of brass or bell metal—a hollow round pipe. Both sides are covered with goat skin fixed on to iron rings and tightened with ropes at the top of the drum. It hangs from the left shoulder on the belly of the artiste and it is tied to the right side of the waist. The left side of the instrument is rubbed with a thin stick and the right side is beaten with a thick stick.

The urumu dancers belong to the scheduled caste. They are a pious and virtuous group of people who observe religious austerity and worship goddess Akkamma. They abstain from drinking and eating meat. They present urumu dance to please their deity. It is a ceremonial dance. They move in circles adopting different styles and foot steps and play on urumu. They put on big turbans and strings of beads or coins like metal pieces around their necks. They smear their faces with turmeric and also put on Namam on their foreheads. They wear long shirts covering from neck to feet and an upper garment hanging from both shoulders. While dancing they sing devotional songs on Lord Kadiri Narasimhaswami, Dasavataras and goddess Akkamma.

Ushakothi Sanctuary : Established in 1962 over a forest area of about 285 square kilometres, the Ushakothi Sanctuary is situated at a distance of about 22 kilometres from Sambalpur in Orissa. To the west of the Sanctuary lies Hirakud dam. Principally comprising of dry deciduous forest type, floral species like sal, sandalwood, arjun, neem, acacia, casuarinas are of frequent occurrence. The fauna includes, amongst others, tigers, elephants, sambar leopards and bison. Presently there are about 15 tigers and 35 elephants in the sanctuary. It is rich in avifaunal wealth and the main attraction of this sanctuary are racket tail drangos and flying squirrel. For night halts there is one two roomed forest rest house inside the sanctuary.

Ustad Amir Khan : Ustad Amir Khan (1912-1974), born in a family of musicians in Indore, India, was a well-known Hindustani classical vocalist. He developed his own singing style and helped popularise taranas.

Besides singing in concerts, he also sang film songs based on ragas, most notably for the films Baiju Bawra and Kshudhita Pashan. He died a premature death in a car accident in Calcutta on February 13, 1974.

Ustad Amjad Ali Khan : Ustad Amjad Ali Khan is an Indian sarod player and composer. Khan was born in Gwalior (Madhya Pradesh) in 1945, is the sixth-generation sarod player in his family and his ancestors have developed and shaped the instrument over several hundred years. "You could say it's my family instrument", says Khan, "Whoever is playing the sarod today learned directly or indirectly from my forefathers."

Khan was taught by his father Haafiz Ali Khan, a musician to the royal family of Gwalior; he was born to the Bangash lineage rooted in the Senia Bangash School of music and is the sixth generation inheritor of this lineage. He was awarded India's second highest civilian award, the Padma Vibhushan in 2001.

Ustad Bade Gulam Ali Khan : Ustad Ali Khan the great classical vocalist was born in Lahore, Punjab into a family of Musicians. His father Ali Baksh Khan was a well known vocalist and Sarangi player, while his uncle Kale Khan was also an extremely renowned musician. Ustad's fine musical voice, intelligence and innate discipline contributed to his great success as a vocalist. Bade Gulam Ali Khan trained rigorously under Kale Khan his uncle for 10 years, practicing from dawn to midnight. He was unsurpassed as the master of 'Thumri' Tradition. The Ustad's melodious voice had an effortless range and style which gripped the listeners. He has recorded several Khayals and Thumris. Some of them are 'Yad piya ki aaye', 'Katena birahaki raat', Tirachhi Nazariya ke baan', 'Premke fandeme aakar sajani', 'Aaye na baalam', 'Kya karun sajani', 'Naina more taras rahe hatn' and 'Prem ki maar katarand' these albums recorded many years ago, are still popular with listeners not only in India but also abroad.

Bade Gulam Ali's study of music was extensive. He had knowledge and definite ideas about any aspect of music. During partition he went to Pakistan but came back and settled in India where he had innumerable admirers. His brother Ustad Barakat Ali Khan, and Bade Gulam Ali's younger son, Munawar Ali who always accompanied him on the tanpura and imbibed his father's musical knowledge, are talented in their own rights. Ustad Bade Gulam Ali Khan passed away in 1968, leaving behind a priceless and glorious heritage of music.

Ustad Bismillah Khan Sahib : The legendary Indian shehnai maestro Ustad Bismillah Khan Sahib is the third classical musician to be awarded the Bharat Ratna (in 2001), the highest civilian honour in India. Bismillah Khan is perhaps single handedly responsible for making the shehnai a famous classical instrument.

Khan was born on 21 March 1916. His ancestors were court musicians in the princely state of Dumraon in Bihar and he trained under his uncle, the late Ali Bux 'Vilayatu', a shehnai player attached to Benares's Vishwanath Temple. He brought the shehnai to the center stage of Indian music with his concert in the Calcutta All India Music Conference in 1937. It was Khan Sahib who poured his heart out into Raga Kafi from the Red Fort on the eve of India's first Republic Day ceremony.

Khan has honorary doctorates from the Banaras Hindu University and Visva Bharati University, Santiniketan. He has been awarded the Sangeet Natak Academi Award, the Tansen Award of the Madhya Pradesh government and also the prestigious Padma Vibhushan. Despite his fame, Khan's lifestyle retains its old world Benares charm. His chief mode of transport is still the cycle rickshaw. A man of tenderness, he believes in remaining private, and that musicians are supposed to be heard and not seen. He is a pious Shia Muslim and also, like many Indian musicians regardless of creed, a devotee of Mother Saraswati.

Utpal Dutt : Utpal Dutt (March 29, 1929, Barisal in the then Undivided Bengal (now in Bangladesh)- August 19, 1993, Calcutta, India) was an Indian actor, director and writer. He studied English literature at the St. Xavier's College, affiliated to the University of Calcutta. He was active primarily in Bengali theatre, but did tour several times with the Shakespearean International Theatre Company. Dutt staged what he called "Epic Theatre" (a term he borrowed from Bertolt Brecht) to bring about discussion and change in Bangladesh. Utpal Dutt was also a very good comedian and his style of comedy is unparalled. He acted in the comedy movies Guddi Golmaal and Shaukeen. He was also a lifelong Marxist and an active supporter of the Communist Party. He staged many street theatres in favour of the Communist Party. He was also jailed for his views.

Uttamar Kovil : Uttamar Kovil is a temple town near Tiruchirapalli in Tamil Nadu, India. It is known for the

Uttamar Kovil (Uttamar means The good one and Kovil means Temple). It has the shrines of Brahma, Vishnu and Shiva in the same complex, making this a unique temple with shrines for all three gods and their consorts in the same place. There are very few temples where Brahma, the first of the trinity, is worshipped in statue form, which makes this temple an imortant place of worship.

Uttapam : Uttapam is a Dosa-like dish that is made by cooking ingredients in a batter. The batter is made of a 1:3 ratio of urad dal and rice (1:1 ratio of boiled to non-boiled rice). Uttapam is usually made with tomatoes or an onion-chilli mix.

Uttar Pradesh (UP): Uttar Pradesh is the most populous and fifth largest state in the Union of India. It is the most populous subnational entity (aka state) in the world. Uttar Pradesh covers a large part of the densely populated Gangetic plain. It shares an international border with Nepal and is bounded by the Indian states of Uttaranchal, Himachal Pradesh, Haryana, Delhi, Rajasthan, Madhya Pradesh, Chhattisgarh, Jharkhand and Bihar. The administrative and legislative capital of Uttar Pradesh is Lucknow; its high court is based at Allahabad. Other notable cities in Uttar Pradesh include NOIDA, Agra, Aligarh, Varanasi (Benares), Gorakhpur, Kanpur and Meerut.

Uttara Kannada : Uttara Kannada is a district in the southern Indian state of Karnataka. It is sometimes called North Canara, or North Kanara. It is bounded on the northwest by the state of Goa, on the north by Belgaum district, on the northeast by Dharwad district, on the east by Haveri district, on the southeast by Shimoga district, on the south by Udupi district, and on the west by the Arabian Sea. The district has an area of 10291 km^2, and a population of 1,353,299 (2001 census), a 10.90% increase since the 1991 census. The town of Karwar is the administrative headquarters of the district.

Uttara Mimamsa: The Uttara ("later") Mimamsa school, more commonly known as the Vedanta, concentrates on the philosophical teachings of the Upanishads rather than on the ritualistic injunctions of the Brahmanas.

While the traditional Vedic 'karma kanda' (ritualistic components of religion) continued to be practiced as meditative and propitiatory rites gearing society (through the Brahmins) to Self-knowledge, more jnaan (knowledge) centered understandings began to emerge, mystical streams of Vedic religion that focused on meditation, self-discipline and spiritual connectivity rather than more practical aspects of religion like rituals and rites. The more abstruse Vedanta (meaning literally the end or the goal of the Vedas) is the essence of the Vedas, encapsulated in the Upanishads which are commentaries on the four original books (Rig, Yajur, Sama and Atharva). Vedantic thought drew on Vedic cosmology, hymns and philosophy. The first Upanishad, the Brihadaranyaka, appeared as far back as three and a half thousand years ago. While thirteen or so Upanishads are accepted as principal, over a hundred exist. The most influential Vedantic thought, advaita vedanta, based on the Upanishads, considers the consciousness of the Self—Jivatma—to be continuous with and indistinguishable from the consciousness of the Supreme Spirit or Brahman—Paramatma.

The Upanishads are acknowledged by scholars and philosophers from both East and West, from Rabindranath Tagore, Mahatma Gandhi and Aurobindo Ghosh to Erwin Schrödinger, Henry David Thoreau and Ralph Waldo Emerson, to be beautiful in poetry and superlatively rich in philosophy. But they do not form a unified system or set of writings.

The upanishads are traditionally classed into twelve or thirteen primary Upanishads, perhaps the oldest of which is the Brihadaranyaka Upanishad, believed by some to have been first written down as early as c.1500 BCE.

The cryptic way in which the aphorisms of the Vedanta sutras are presented leaves the door wide open for a multitude of interpretations. This led to a proliferation of Vedanta schools in six sub-schools. Each of these interprets the texts in its own way and has produced its own series of sub-commentaries—all claiming to be faithful to the original. Four of them are given here.

Uttarakhand : Uttarakhand presently called Uttaranchal is the ancient name for the stretch of Indian Himalayas that borders the Himachal ranges in the west, and Nepal in the east. Literally North Country or Territory in Sanskrit, its peaks and valleys were well known in ancient times as the abode of gods and site of Hinduism's most sacred pilgrimage spots. From 1948 to 2000, the region formed the hilly segment of northernmost Uttar Pradesh state, until its separation as part of the new Uttaranchal state in 2000. Until 1998, Uttarakhand was the name most commonly used to refer to the region, as various political groups including most significantly the Uttarakhand Kranti Dal (Uttarakhand Revolutionary Party est. 1979), began agitating for separate statehood under its banner. Bringing together the erstwhile rival hill kingdoms of Garhwal and Kumaon, the movement gained significant momentum in 1994 when it achieved almost unanimous acceptance among the people as well as the national political parties.

However, the term Uttaranchal came into vogue when the BJP-led central government initiated a new round of state reorganization and imposed its preferred name. Chosen for its allegedly less separatist connotations, the name change generated enormous controversy among the rank and file of the separate state activists, however they were not quite as successful as Jharkhand state that successfully thwarted a similar move to impose the name Vananchal. As such, Uttarakhand remains popular in the region to this day, even while Uttaranchal has been promulgated and popularized globally through its official usage.

Uttarakhand Kranti Dal : The Uttarakhand Kranti Dal is a political party in India. It was established in 1979 to fight for a separate state composed of the hill districts of Uttar Pradesh. This demand was partially achieved with the creation of Uttaranchal state in 2000. In the first ever state assembly elections in 2002, it won only 4 out of 70 seats, and were outmaneuvered by the Congress and BJP who were late comers to the separate state movement, but succeeded in capturing its momentum for electoral gain.

Uttaranchal : Uttaranchal became the 27th state of the Republic of India on November 9, 2000. Uttaranchal borders China in the north and Nepal to the east, while its neighbour states are Himachal Pradesh to the west and Uttar Pradesh (of which it formed a part before 2000) in the south. The region is traditionally refered to as Uttarakhand in old literature and scriptures which derives from the Sanskrit for North Country. The provisional capital of Uttaranchal is Dehra Dun which is also a rail-head and the largest city in the region. The small hamlet of Gairsen has been mooted as the future capital owing to its geographic centrality but controversies and lack of resources have led Dehra Dun to be the provisional capital. The High Court of Uttaranchal is situated in Nainital though most of the litigation is in Dehra Dun or Haridwar. The lawyers in Dehra Dun have been striking work on Saturdays ever since the state was formed demanding that a bench be set up at Dehra Dun

Uttarapatha : Ancient Buddhist and Brahmanical texts reveal that Uttarapatha was the name of northern division of Jambudvipa of ancient Indian traditions. Initially, the term Uttarapatha referred to the northern high road..the main trade route that followed along the river Ganges, crossed the Indo-Gangetic watershed, ran through the Punjab to Taxila (Gandhara) and further to Zariaspa or Balkh (Bactria) in Central Asia. The eastern terminus of the Uttarapatha was Tamraliptika or Tamluk located at the mouth of Ganges in west Bengal. It was the longest ancient land route which had become very popular due to increasing maritime contacts with the sea-ports on the eastern coast of India during the Mauryan rule. Later, Uttarapatha was the name lent to the vast expanse of region which the Uttarapatha or the northern high road traversed. The boundaries of Uttarapatha, as a region, are nowhere precisely defined in the Buddhist or any other ancient Indian source. According to some writers, the Uttarapatha included the whole of Northern India, from Anga in the east to Gandhara in the north-west, and from the Himalaya in the north to the Vindhya in the south.

V

Vaastu Shastra : Vaastu Shastra (Vaastu- physical environment and Shastra- knowledge/ text/ principles) is one of the traditional Hindu canons of town planning and architecture. These canons are codified in texts such as Manasara Silpa Shastra (by Manasara), Mayamatam (by Maya), Viswakarma Vaastushastra (by Viswakarma), Samarangana Sutradara (by Raja Bhoja), Aparajita Praccha (by Viswakarma's son Aparajita) and Silparatna. Other treatises such as Agni Purana and works by Kautilya and Sukracharya are not popular even though they preceded the previously mentioned documents. Distinction of style exists due to each documents place of origin. Mayamata and Mansara Silpa Shastra are considered Dravidian because they are from South india whereas Viswaskarama Vaastu Shastra is considered Aryan due to its North Indian origin. Vaastu Shastra deals with various aspects of designing and building living environments that are in harmony with the physical and metaphysical forces/ energies of the cosmos such as the gravitational, electromagnetic and supernatural. Building practices based on limited interpretations of these principles are still sustained in specific areas of India.

Vachanamrut : The Vachanamrut or the nectarine discourses of Bhagwan Swaminarayan is the most sacred and foundational scripture of the Swaminarayan

Sampraday. It contains the profound wisdom of the Vedas, Upanishads, Brahmasutras, Bhagvad Gita, Bhagvat Purana, Dharma shastras like Yagnavalkya Smruti, Vidurniti, and epics like the Ramayan and Mahabharat. It is the essence of ancient Indian wisdom given by Bhagwan Swaminarayan and compiled by His four contemporary scholarly-sadhus who were known for their asceticism and scholarship in Sanskrit, besides their devotion to Him. In fact every statement of the Master is packed with and based on His in-depth religious knowledge, spiritual insights and practical experience. It contains practical and philosophical answers to the sincere enquiries of all types of aspirants regarding life in this world and the life hereafter.

Vada : Vada (or Wada or Vade) is a popular Indian snack. It originates from South Indian states of Tamil nadu and Karnataka but now it is popular all over. The most popular one is the Vadai from Tamil nadu or the Uddina Vade from Karnataka: Similar to a doughnut, a circle with a hole in the center Traditionally Vadais are prepared during festivals along with other dishes. But it is now a common sight in most Indian Fast-Food restaurants nowadays...Popular variations of Vada are Masala vada, Maddur vada, Bonda, Dahi Vada etc etc..

Vada Pav : Vada Pav (also spelled Wada Pav) is an Indian vegetarian fast food commonly eaten in Maharashtra, India. It consists of a vada, served in a bun (pav). The vada is usually potato-based. Potatoes are mashed/diced and coated with an herb-seasoned batter, then deep fried. The finished vada is then wrapped in bread and served with condiments such as chutney and red chili powder.

Vada pavs form a breakfast for many of the local people of Maharashtra. It is a scrumptious snack sold nearly everywhere in Maharashtra. The snack is often served at breakfast and at tea time in many of the region's small eateries. On long distance trains, it is sometimes served as well. Like hot dogs and other roadside fast food, care must be taken in ensuring that the product is not undercooked.

The vada pav was first made when Ashok Vaidya, a snack seller outside Dadar railway station, decided to experiment. The combination of batata vada and split pav continues to be Mumbai's sledgehammer answer to the burger.

Vadakkunnathan Temple : Vadakkunnathan Temple at Thrissur also known as Rishabhari or Thenkailasam (the Kailash of the south) is one of the ancient and most prominent Shiva kshetram's (temples) of Kerala. Situated on top of a beautiful hillock, the temple is a classical example of the Kerala style of architecture depicting many decorative murals and works of art. Vadakkunnathan temple houses a museum of ancient wall paintings, wood carvings and art pieces of immense historical value. It is famous for its spectacular Pooram Festival celebrated annually in April -May every year. It is a stunning event, combining the majestic elephant pageantry with the frenzied playing of drums and cymbals, rounded off with a fireworks extravaganza.

Vadakkunnathan temple is believed to be built by Lord Parasurama, one of the incarnations of Lord Vishnu. The temple complex is a massive one covering an area of about nine acres. The vast maidan about 65 acres around the temple is called Tekkinkadu or forest of teak woods. Once, many years ago there used to be a beautiful teak forest here, now the ground is scattered by dozens of peepal trees. The four magnificent gateways called Gopurams facing the four directions and the massive masonry wall around the temple quadrangle gives the temple an imposing appearance. The multi-shrined internal temple complex (nalambalam or chuttamabalam) is situated in the center of this vast enclosure. There are five separate shrines inside the nalambalam for five separate deities. These central shrines are dedicated to Shiva, Parvati, Ganapati, Sankaranarayana and Sri Rama (Vishnu).

Lord Shiva, more popularly known as Vadakkunnathan, is the principal deity and the circular srikovil (shrine) of Shiva is on the northern side. The unique feature of the temple is that, the idol of Shiva i.e the Shivalingam facing west, is worshipped in the form of a mound of ghee or clarified butter. This is formed by the daily abhisheka with ghee over the years. The ghee never melts in spite of several lamps in the sanctum or even in hot weather nor has any bad smell or is infested by insects or pests. The centuries-old ghee is considered to possess medicinal qualities and cures many ailments. The eleven feet high mound of ghee is embellished with fifteen cascading crescents of gold and three serpent hoods at top. The main offering is ghee and Kadali bananas. The outside wall of the shrine has a big painting of Mohini holding a mirror.

Vadodara : Vadodara, also known as Baroda, is the third-most populated town in Gujarat after Ahmedabad and Surat, and is one of four towns in the state with a population of over 1 million, the other being Rajkot. It is located on the Vishwamitri river, southeast of Ahmedabad and is known as the Cultural Capital of Gujarat. It is the administrative headquarters of the Vadodara District.

Vadodara is home to almost 1.729 million people (as of 2005), the beautiful Lakshmi Vilas Palace and the Maharaja Sayajirao University of Baroda (M.S.U.) which is famous for various departments, including the fine arts, performing arts, technology and medicine streams. It has a high literacy rate by Indian standards of 82% (2001). About 15,000 people lived in slums in Vadodara according to the provisional results of census 2001. Major industries include petrochemicals, engineering, pharmaceuticals, and plastics.

Vagad : Vagad is a region in southeastern Rajasthan state of western India. It includes the districts of Banswara and Dungarpur, and is bounded on the north by Mewar region of Rajasthan, on the west and southwest by Malwa region of Madhya Pradesh, and on the southeast and east by Gujarat state. It mostly lies in the upper watershed of the Mahi River and its tributaries.

Vaghelas : The Vaghelas were an Indian dynasty of Gujarat. The Vaghelas were based in the town of Dholka, and were feudatories of the Solanki dynasty, who ruled Gujarat from the 10th to the 13th centuries. The Solanki went into decline in the thirteenth century, and by 1243 the Vaghelas were firmly in control of Gujarat. They restored stability to Gujarat for the latter half of the 13th century, and the Vaghela kings and officials were dedicated patrons of the arts and temple-building.

Virdhaval was the first Vaghela king, and two of his ministers, Vastupal and Tejpar, built the exquisite Dilwara Temples on Mount Abu in Rajasthan, and temples at the Girnar and Shetrunjay hills. His successor Vishaldev built temples at Dabhoi and founded Vishalnagar. Karandev was the last Vaghela king, who died in the 1297 conquest of Gujarat by Ala-ud-din Khilji, Sultan of Delhi.

Vaigai : The Vaigai is a river in Tamil Nadu state of southern India. It originates in the Periyar Plateau of the Western Ghats range, and flows northeast through the Kambam Valley, which lies between the Palni Hills to the north and the Varushanad Hills to the south. As it rounds the eastern corner of the Varushanad Hills, the river turns southeast, running through the region of Pandya Nadu. Madurai, the largest city in the Pandya Nadu region and its ancient capital, lies on the Vaigai. The river empties into the Palk Strait in Ramanathapuram District.

Vaikasi Vaisdakam : Vaikasi is the second month of Tamil Calendar. Temples dedicated to Subrahmanya or Muruga celebrate the Vaisdakam festival. The full moon day is a day of great festivity for Subrahmanya or Muruga, the son of Lord Shiva. At Tiruchendur and Thiruparankundran, devotees carry milk pots and this day is considered as a day of enlightenment. It is on this day that the Buddha Purnima is celebrated—the day on which Gautama Buddha is said to have been born, got enlightenment and attained Nirvana.

Vaikom Muhammad Basheer : Vaikom Muhammad Basheer (b. at Thalayolapparambu in Vaikom, 21 January 1908; d. at Beypore in Calicut, 5 July 1994) is a modern Malayalam fiction writer. He was a thinker, humanist, freedom fighter, novelist and short story writer. The Indian government recognized his contributions by awarding him the prestigious Padma Sri in 1982

Vaikom Satyagraham : Vaikom Satyagraham (1924 - 25) was a satyagraham (movement) in the southern Indian state of Kerala against untouchability in Hinduism. The movement was centered at the Shiva temple at Vaikom, near Kottayam. The movement resulted in abolishment of untouchability in his realm by the then King of Travancore.

Mahatma Gandhi also participated in this Satyagraham, and several other national leaders of India including C. Rajagopalachari, Acharya Vinoba Bhave and E.V. Ramswami Naykar had associated themselves with this struggle.

Vaikom Satyagraham : Vaikom Satyagraham is Satyagraham contact against untouchability in Hinduism in

Kerala at the famous Shiva temple at Vaikom, near Kottayam. This was a movement commeneced in the years 1924-25 for eradication of untouchability.

Mahatma Gandhi also participated in this Satyagraham, and several other national leaders of India including C. Rajagopalachari, Acharya Vinoba Bhave and E.V. Ramswami Naykar had associated themselves with this struggle.

Vaisakhi : Vaisakhi marks the beginning of the new Spring year and the end of the harvest in India. Vaisakhi falls in the Nanakshahi calendar (neither in the Amantha- nor in the Purnimantha-calendar) on the first day of Vaisakh and marks the sun entering Mesha Rasi (this fact is called Mesha Sankranti). Vaisakhi is therefore determined by the sun and not the moon. It usually falls on April 13, falling on April 14 once every thirty-six years. It coincides with 'Rongali Bihu' in Assam, 'Naba Barsha' in Bengal, Puthandu in Tamil Nadu and 'Pooram Vishu' in Kerala.

At the Vaisakhi festival of 1699, at Keshgarh Sahib near Anandpur, Guru Gobind Singh, the Tenth Guru of the Sikhs founded the Akal Khalsa (Community of the Pure). Guru Gobind Singh, had organised for followers from all over India to meet him at the Vasakhi Fair in Anandpur.

For Sikhs, this seasonal festival also has great importance as the founding of the (Soldiers of the Timeless One) at Anandpur Sahib, the famous Golden Temple of Amritsar, India. The Akal Khalsa played an important role in resistance against Mughal rule. This act of total surrender of one's life to the service of the AKAL(God), the Timeless One, and at the feet of Guru Gobind Singh created the Sikh religion. For many centuries after that, the first male child of many Hindu families in Punjab was ordained as a Sikh.

To mark the celebrations, devotees, irrespective of their religion, throng gurdwaras—the Sikh place of worship—and temples in different parts of the area. The celebrations start early as devotees, with flowers and offerings in their hands, proceed towards the gurdwaras and temples before dawn. Processions through towns are also common.

Vaishali : Vaishali is a district in Bihar state, India. The history of Vaishali district is very ancient, and finds mention in the Indian classic Mahabharata, as well as in Buddhist and Jain tradition.

Vaishali derives its name from King Vishal of the Mahabharata age. Even before the advent of Buddhism and Jainism, Vaishali was a vibrant republican state; in fact, it was the first republic in the world, similar to those later found in ancient Greece. In that period, Vaishali was an ancient metropolis and the capital city of the republic of the Vaishali state, which covered most of the Himalayan Gangetic region of present-day Bihar state, India. Very little is known about the early history of Vaishali. The Vishnu Purana records 34 kings of Vaishali, the first being Nabhaga, who is believed to have abdicated his throne over a matter of human rights and believed to have declared: "I am now a free tiller of the soil, king over my acre." The last among the 34 was Sumati, who is considered a contemporary of Dasaratha, father of the Hindu god, Lord Rama.

Vaishali finds repeated references in texts pertaining to both Jainism and Buddhism, which have preserved much information on Vaishali and the other Maha Janapadas. Based on the information found in these texts, Vaishali was established as a republic by the 6th century BC, prior to the birth of Gautama Buddha in 563, making it the world's first republic.

In the republic of Vaishali, Lord Mahavir was born. Buddha delivered his last sermon at Vaishali and announced his Nirvana there. Vaishali is also renowned as the land of Ambapali (also spelled as Amrapali), the great Indian courtesan, who appears in many folktales, as well as in Buddhist literature. Ambapali later adopted Buddhism. The district of Vaishali came in to existence on 12/10/1972. Earlier it was the part of old Muzzafarpur district.

Vaisheshika : The Vaisheshika system, which was founded by the sage Kanada, postulates an atomic pluralism. In terms of this school of thought, all objects in the physical universe are reducible to a certain number of atoms. God is regarded as the fundamental force who causes conscioussness in these atoms.

Although the Vaishesika system developed independently from the Nyaya, the two eventually merged because of their closely related metaphysical theories. In its classical form, however, the Vaishesika school differed from the Nyaya in one crucial respect: where Nyaya accepted four sources of valid knowledge, the Vaishesika accepted only perception and inference as being such.

According to the Bhagavad Gita, outwardly performing all actions but inwardly renouncing their fruits, the wise being, purified by the fire of transcendental knowledge, attains peace, detachment, forbearance, spiritual vision and bliss.

The Yoga system is considered by some to have arisen from the Samkhya philosophy. Its primary text is the Bhagavad Gita, which explores the four primary systems: Karma-Yoga; Buddhi-Yoga; Dhyana-Yoga; and Bhakti-Yoga. In the Bhagavad Gita itself the Yoga system is described as being many millions of years old. It is essentially described as a universal method of union with The

Supreme. There has been much debate on the personal/ impersonal nature of the Supreme by various Yoga practitioners over the years.

The sage Patanjali wrote an extremely influential text on Raja Yoga (or meditational) entitled the "Yoga Sutra". The most significant difference from Samkhya is that the Yoga school not only incorporates the concept of Ishvara (a personal God) into its metaphysical worldview, which the Samkhya does not, but also upholds Ishvara as the ideal upon which to meditate. This is because Ishvara is the only aspect of Purusha that has not become entangled with prakrti. It also utilizes the Brahman/Atman terminology and concepts that are found in the Upanishads, thus breaking from the Samkhya school by adopting concepts of Vedantic monism. The Yoga system lays down elaborate prescriptions for gradually gaining physical and mental control and mastery over the "personal self", both body and mind, until one's consciousness has intensified sufficiently to allow for the awareness of one's "real Self" (the soul, or Atman), as distinct from one's feelings, thoughts and actions. Realization of the goal of Yoga is known as moksha, nirvana and samadhi. They all speak to the realization of the Atman as being nothing other than the infinite Brahman.

Vaishnavism : Vaishnavism is one of the principal divisions of Hinduism. Its adherents worship Vishnu as the supreme God or one of his avatars and are principally monotheistic whilst also incorporating elements which could be described as panentheistic in nature. Bhaktas, or worshippers of Vishnu are called Vaishnavites, an English term that originated from Vaishnava in Sanskrit).

Vaishnavas believe that Vishnu-Narayana is the one supreme God and all other gods and creatures are subservient to Him. All of the sects mentioned above except the last fall under this group.

Advaita Vashnavas believe that no soul is actually separated from God, and that every soul is ultimately one and the same. Thus each soul could be considered as equally divine. Thus Vishnu in the saguna (with attributes) form is characterized by harmony and perfection. But in nirguna (without attributes) form, He is in a state unblemished by matter and is without attributes.

Normally the term "Vaishnava" is used to refer to people of the first category alone, who represent the vast majority of Vaishnavas. But there are a small number of people in the second group, e.g., Smartas who worship Vishnu as their favourite God, or Ishta Deva.

Vaishnavo Devi : The holy cave shrine of Vaishno-Devi is situated in the Trikuta Mountains of lower Himalayas in the state of Jammu and Kashmir. The shrine is approachable on foot along a 12 kms trek from Katra town at the foot of the hills. Vaishno Devi, is mother goddess worshiped here in the forms of Maha Kali, Maha Saraswathi and Maha Lakshmi. Thousands of Pilgrims from all over the world visit the holy shrine throughout the year except in winter.

Vaishno Devi, a devotee of Lord Vishnu, used to pray to Lord Rama and had taken vow of celibacy. One day, Bhairon Nath, a demon-God, saw her and gave chase. The Goddess felt thirsty at Banganga (1kms from Katra) and shot an arrow into the earth from where water gushed out. 'Charan Paduka', marked by the imprints of her feet, is the place where she rested. She then meditated in the cave at Ardhkanwari (6kms) now a temple. It took Bhairon Nath nine months to locate her.

Vaishno Devi assumed the form of Maha Kali and cut off Bhairon Nath's head, which fell at the place where the Bhairon Temple is now located. Vaishno Devi journeyed up to the mountains and took the present cave shrine as her home. The boulder at the mouth of the holy cave, according to the legend, is the petrified torso of Bhairon Nath who was granted divine forgiveness by the benevolent Mata in his dying moments.

All pilgrims are required to get passes at Katra for the yatra (pilgrimage) from Tourism Reception Centre, Katra Bus Stand. Facilities for food, water and public utility are available all along the trek. Overnight accommodation available enroute at Sanji Chhat and also at the shrine. Pony or Palanquin services are available for those who find it difficult to climb the trek. The cave shrine is narrow and pilgrims have to walk through a running stream of cold water Charan Ganga to get to the sanctum sanctorum.

Vaishya : In the Hindu caste system, a Vaishya is a member of the third of the four major castes of the varna system of traditional Indian society, comprising of merchants, farmers, landowners and artisans. Etymologically, the word derives from the root vish meaning "to work". Vaishya communities include Arora, Bohra, Aggarwal, Khatri, etc. In Buddhist literature, they are termed as Grihapati. Surnames of Vaishyas include Agrawal, Oswal, Porwad, Maheshwari, Barnwal etc. According to the Manu-smriti, the Vaishyas are sprung from the belly of Brahma.

Vajrayana : Vajrayana Buddhism is often viewed as the third major 'vehicle' (Yana) of Buddhism, alongside the Theravada and Mahayana. The Vajrayana is an extension of Mahayana Buddhism consisting not of philosophical differences, but rather the adoption of additional techniques (upaya, or 'skilful means').

Vakataka : The Vakataka was an Indian dynasty. They ruled in the today's parts of Maharashtra and Madya Pradesh from third century to fifth century and are the most important follow-up dynasty of the Satavahana and are contemoraries to the Gupta. The dynasty founder was called Vindhyashakti (250-270), which also the name of the goddess Vindhya mountains was. It was Brahman and probably came from there.

Vallabhacharya : Vallabhacharya (1479 - 1531) was the founder of the Vallabha sect in Indian philosophy. He called his system of thought Shuddhadvaita (pure monism). He was from a region that is currently in the Indian state of Andhra Pradesh, though the bulk of his fame lies in the region that is currently in the state of Gujarat. According to the version of Vaishnava Theology he espoused; the glorious Krishna in His sat-chid-ananda form is the Absolute Brahman. He is permanently playing out His sport (leela) from His seat in the goloka which is even beyond the divine Vaikuntha, the abode of Vishnu and Satya-loka, the abode of Brahma the Creator, and Kailas, the abode of Shiva. Creation is His sport.

Vallabhi : Vallabhi (modern Vala) is an ancient city located in Saurashtra peninsula in Gujarat, in western India, near Bhavnagar. Also known as Vallabhipura, it was the capital of the ancient Maitraka dynasty.

Legend has it that a Rajput named Vijayasen founded the city around the 3rd century. The Maitrakas, descending from general Bhatarka, a military governor of Saurashtra peninsula during Gupta ruler Skanda Gupta (455 AD-467 AD), had ruled the peninsula and parts of southern Rajasthan from Vallabhi from the fifth to the eighth centuries.

Vallabhi has been a famous Jain center, and there is a possibility that the Maitrakas (Sun-worshippers) may have embraced Jainism later on. But when Chinese traveller Hieun-Tsang visited Vallabhi during second quarter of 7th century CE, he found its ruler to be a Buddhist follower.

When Itsing, another Chinese traveller visited Vallabhi in the last quarter of 7th century, he found the city as a great center of learning including Buddhism. Gunamati and Sthiramati are stated to be two famous Buddhist scholars of Vallabhi at the middle of seventh century CE. Vallabhi was famous for its catholicity and the students from all over the country, including the Brahmana boys, visited it to have higher education in secular and religious subjects. We are told that the graduates of Vallabhi were given higher executive posts.

Vallathol Narayana Menon : Vallathol Narayana Menon (popularly known as Vallathol) was a famous poet in Malayalam. He was born in Palakkad District of Kerala state, south India. He died in March 1958. He set up the Kerala Kalamandalam at Cheruthuruthy, near the banks of river Bharathapuzha. Later this place was renamed Vallathol Nagar.

Valley of Flowers : Valley of flowers is the name of the Himalayan area in Uttaranchal, India. In 1931 the English mountaineer Frank Smythe stumbled across the Bhyundar Valley, an 8 km long glacier corridor in Chamoli Garhwal. This area, surrounded by snow-capped mountains and carpeted with over 500 species of flowers, soon became a protected site. It was declared a national park in 1982. The Valley of Flowers stretches over an expanse of 87.50 km^2. This part of Uttaranchal, in the upper reaches of Garhwal, is inaccessible through much of the year. The area lies on the Zanskar range of the Himalayas with the highest point in the national park being Gauri Parbat at 6,719 m above sea level.

Flowers mostly orchids, poppies, primulas, calendulas, daisies and anemones carpet the ground. Alpine forests of birch and rhododendron cover a part of the area, and are home to tahr, snow leopard, musk deer, red fox, common langur, bharal, serow, Himalayan black bear and a huge variety of butterflies. There is no settlement in the national park and grazing in the area has been banned. The park is open only in summers between June and October, being covered by heavy snow during the rest of the year.

Valley of Flowers National Park : Valley of flowers National Park was a set up in 1981 in Chamoli district covering an area of 87sq.km. The nearest town from the park is Karna parayag at a distance of 33km. The rail head is 290 km at Rishikesh. The nearest airport is at Dehradun which is 330 km from the park.

Valluvar Kottam : Valluvar Kottam, located at the intersection of the Kodambakkam High road and the Village road, is one of the modern landmarks of modern Chennai, Tamilnadu state, South India. The monument was constructed in 1976 in the memory of Thiruvalluvar, the classical Tamil poet and saint who wrote his famous Thirukkurals about 2000 years before. All the 133 chapters of the Thirukkural which include 1330 verses are inscribed on bas-relief in the front hall corridors. The construction of Valluvar Kottam is like a temple chariot, and it is a replica of the temple chariot in Thiruvarur. A magnificent life-size statue of the immortal saint Thiruvalluvar stands majestically atop the 39 meter high chariot. The auditorium of Valluvar Kottam can accommodate around 4000 people.

Valmiki : Maharishi Valmiki is the author of the Hindu epic Ramayana. The story of Valmiki is steeped in legend. One version has it that Valmiki was originally a dacoit called Ratna who haunted the forests and preyed upon the unwary travellers. One day a sage called Narada passed through the forest. Ratna saw him and immediately attacked him. Narada asked him why he did his foul deeds to which Ratna replied that it was to take care of his family, which consisted of his aged parents, wife and children. The sage then wanted to know if they would be willing to share in the punishment for his misdeeds. Ratna was sure they would but the sage advised him to go and ask them. Ratna tied the sage to a tree and ran home to ask his family if they would share in his punishments. His family replied in the negative, saying that it was Ratna's duty to take care of them and they were not responsible for the path he chose to do so. Disappointed, Ratna returned to the forest and confessed to the sage. The sage told him to repent for his sins and to stop his evil ways and to chant the name of Lord Rama. Legend has it that Valmiki meditated in one place till an ant-hill formed on top of him without him realising it. Hence the name Valmiki (which means ant-hill in Sanskrit). Valmiki became a maharishi (great sage).

There is another legend behind his writing the Ramayana. One day, Valmiki was in the forest when a hunter shot a bird. Valmiki was so touched by the pain of the bird that he composed and sang a sad song. Brahma was greatly moved by the touching song. He appeared before Valmiki and asked him to compose the life of Sri Rama in a similar verse. Brahma gave the gift of insight of Sri Rama's life to Valmiki. Valmiki began to compose the great eternal song and poem of the life of Sri Rama—The Rāmayana. Valmiki's Ramayana is the very first poem in Sanskrit. Therefore, it is called the Adikavya or the "The first poem" and Valmiki is also known as the Adikavi, which means "The first poet". Legend has it that it was Valmiki who offered refuge to Sita the wife of Lord Rama, and the queen of Ayodhya when she was banished from the kingdom. It was in his hermitage in the forest that Rama and Sita's twin sons Lava and Kusha were born and brought up.

Valmiki National Park : Valmiki National Park occupies the core area of 335.64 sq.km, of more than

800sq. km of the Valmiki Sanctuary located in the West Champaran district of Bihar bordering Nepal. Valmiki was established as the 18th tiger reserve in 1990 and ranks fourth in the density of tiger population. The park is bounded by the Royal Chitwan National Park of Nepal in the north and the river Gandak on the western side with the Himalayan Mountains as a backdrop. Adjacent to the sanctuary, in the forests in Chitwan National Park of Nepal, is the historic Valmiki Ashram.

The park consists of moist Sal bearing forests, dry Sal bearing forests, moist mixed deciduous forests without Sal, cane and tropical seasonal swamp forests containing reed beds and wet grasslands. The species found in the park include tiger, sloth bear, wolf, various species of deer, serow, leopard, python, peafowl, chitals, sambars, nilgais, leopards, hyenas, Indian civets, Jungle cats, Hog deer, wild dogs etc. One horned rhinoceros and Indian bison often migrate from Chitwan to Valmikinagar. There are 8 villages in the buffer area but no habitation in the core area.

The Kodarma Wildlife Sanctuary on the Patna-Ranchi road provides opportunity for watching tigers, bears and different varieties of deer. The Madampur Sanctuary situated in the north-west corner of Champaran district is approachable by a metalled road from Bettiah and from Bagha station on the N.E railway. The animals to be seen here are tigers, sambars, leopards, spotted and barking deer, pigs and fairly large variety of ground and water birds.

Van Vihar National Park : Van Vihar National Park is a national park in India located 6 km from Bhopal, the capital city of Madhya Pradesh. Declared an national park in 1983, the park covers an area of about 445 ha. Among the animals found here are: the tiger, jackal, hyena peacock, drongo and python.

Vanara Sena : The Vanara Sena (Army of Monkeys) was an organization of young Indian boys and girls created by the young Indira Gandhi in the late 1920s and early 1930s, as the children's wing of the Indian National Congress, the lead organization of the Indian Independence Movement.

The Sena played a small but interesting role in the Indian Independence Movement. Indira and her young comrades organized rallies and flag marches of young students, gave speeches and sang patriotic songs, and more importantly helped circulate prohibited and sensitive literature and other publications of the Congress Party to supporters. In an often-told story, Indira smuggles out from the police-watched house of her father Jawaharlal Nehru an important document in her schoolbag that outlines plans for a major revolutionary initiatve in the early 1930s to a local Congress office.

Vandalur Zoo : The Vandalur Zoo, also known as the Arignar Anna Zoological Park, in Vandalur, is located about 30 kilometers from the city of Madras. Founded in 1979, this zoo was preceded by the old Madras Zoo (founded 1855), which was one of the first in India, and the first to hold an All-India Zoo Superintendents Conference (1955, as part of the Centenary celebrations).

By 1975, the city had grown so much, and conditions at the old Madras Zoo were so bad, that a decision was taken to shift the zoo. The Government of Tamil Nadu and its Tamilnadu Forest Department came to the rescue. Thirty Kilometers from the city, 1300 acres (5.2 km^2) were set aside for development of the zoo. There is also a Rescue and Rehabilitation centre.

Vandana Shiva : Vandana Shiva (born November 5, 1952) is a physicist, philosopher, ecofeminist, environmental activist and writer. Vandana was born in Dehra Dun,

Uttaranchal State, which was formerly a part of the Indian state of Uttar Pradesh. She participated in the Chipko movement during the 1970s.

The movement, whose main participants were women, adopted the tactic of hugging trees to prevent their felling. In 1982, she founded the Research Foundation for Science, Technology and Ecology. Initiatives of this foundation are the organic farming programme Navdanya, the Bija Vidyapeeth (or Seed University, International College for Sustainable Living), and Diverse Women for Diversity. Another of Vandana Shiva's initiatives is the Living Democracy Movement.

She received the Right Livelihood Award (also known as the Alternative Nobel Prize) in 1993 "...For placing women and ecology at the heart of modern development discourse." Other awards she has received include the Global 500 Award of the United Nations Environment Programme (UNEP) in 1993, and the Earth Day International Award of the United Nations (UN). Vandana Shiva is one of the leaders of the International Forum on Globalization, (along with Jerry Mander, Edward Goldsmith, Ralph Nader, Jeremy Rifkin, etc.), and a figure of the global solidarity movement known as anti-globalization movement.

Vande Mataram : Vande Mataram is the national song of India. The song was composed by Bankim Chandra Chatterjee in a highly Sanskritized form of the Bengali language. The song first appeared in his book Anandamatha, published in 1882 amid fears of a ban by British Raj, though the song itself was actually written six years prior in 1876. "Vande Mataram" was the national cry for freedom from British oppression during the freedom movement.

Large rallies, fermenting initially in West Bengal, in the major metropolis of Calcutta (Kolkata), would work themselves up into a patriotic fever by shouting the slogan "Vande Mataram," or "Hail to the Mother(land)!" The British, fearful of the potential danger of an incited Indian populace, at one point banned the utterance of the motto in public forums and jailed many freedom fighters for disobeying the proscription. To this day, "Vande Mataram" is seen as a national mantra describing the love of patriots for the country of India. Rabindranath Tagore sang 'Vande Mataram' in 1896 at the Calcutta (Kolkata) Congress Session. Poet Sarala Devi Chaudurani sang 'Vande Mataram' in the Benares Congress Session in 1905. Lala Lajpatrai started a journal called Vande Mataram from Lahore.

Vangiya, Sahitya Parishad : Vangiya Sahitya Parishad a literary society. L Leotard and Kshetrapal Chakraborty founded 'The Bengal Academy of Literature' at the Shobhabazar residence of Binay Krishna Dev on 23 July 1893. Though development of bangla literature was its aim, yet almost every function of the society was performed in English. Even the monthly journal of the organisation The Bengal Academy of Literature was in English. To avoid this inconsistency Umesh Chandra Batabyal proposed to publish the journal also in Bangla on 18 February 1894 under the title Vangiya Sahitya Parishad. On 29 April the same year, the name of the society itself was changed to 'Vangiya Shahitya Parishad' (Vangiya Sahitya Parisad) and since then the journal of the society is being published under the title Sahitya Parishad Patrika.

Vansda National Park : Vansda National Park, a protected area representing the thick woodlands of the Dangs and southern Gujarat is situated in the Navsari District of Gujarat state, India.

Vansda, the town from which the name of the park is derived, is an important trading place for the surrounding area where the majority of the population is represented by adivasis. Vansda-Waghai state highway runs through the park, so does the narrow gauge rail link connecting Ahwa to Billimora. Established in 1979 as a National Park, the deciduous forest area having groves of "Katas" bamboo owes its beauty to no felling of trees since 1952. Nestled in the Western Ghats of Sahyadri range, it has a unique flavour of flora and fauna population. Apart from the Botanical garden, some of the other attractions include local tribes, "Gira Falls", and the "Conversation center".

Vapi : Vapi is a town on the banks of Damanganga River in the Valsad District of the southern Gujarat, India. Vapi falls under the taluka administration of Pardi. Around 28 km south of the district headquarter city of Valsad, it is surrounded by Union Territories of Daman on the west and by Dadra and Nagar Haveli on the east. Economic and industrial growth of the recent decades has, however, blurred the physical boundaries, and the small stretch of roughly 21 km of Daman-Vapi-Silvassa has almost become a monolith.

Varahagiri Venkata Giri : Varahagiri Venkata Giri was born on 10 August, 1894 at Berhampore in Ganjam district at that time in the Madras Presidency and now in Orissa. He came of a rather well-off Brahmin family. His father Shri V.V. Jogaiah Pantulu was a prosperous lawyer at Berhampore and the leader of the local Bar. He also took a prominent part in the nationalist movement. In the twenties he joined the Swarajya Party founded by Pandit Motilal Nehru and Chittaranjan Das and was a member of the Central Legislative Assembly from 1927 to 1930. He was also elected to the Madras Legislative Council after the introduction of the Act of 1935. Jogaiah was also interested in the Bengal Nagpur Railway Workers' Union.

In 1923 he became one of the founders of the All India Railwaymen's Federation. He was twice elected President of the Trade Union Congress, in 1926 and 1942.

As a leading trade unionist he attended many international gatherings. In 1927 he attended the International Labour Conference at Geneva. He also attended the Trade Union Congress at Geneva. In 1931-1932 he attended the Second Round Table Conference in London as the Workers' Representative.

During the Civil Disobedience Movement in the early thirties Giri, as a prominent labour leader, did much to organize trade unions in support of the nationalist movement. He was a member of the Indian Legislative Assembly from 1934 to 1937. In a house dominated by stalwarts like Satyamurty, Bhulabhai Desai, Jinnah, Govind Ballabh Pant, Madan Mohan Malaviya, Asaf Ali and others, Giri soon made his mark as a forceful speaker, specially on labour questions.

In the 1936 General Election in Madras, after the introduction of the Act of 1935, Giri was put up as the Congress candidate in Bobbili against the Raja of Bobbili, the most powerful political personality in the Madras Presidency. The Raja of Bobbili was the leader of the Justice Party and the Chief Minister of the Province; and the constituency was the traditional family strong-hold. The contest was like David tackling Goliath. In this contest between a feudal leader and a popular leader, the victory of the people's man heralded a decisive turning of the political tide. After the election when C. Rajagopalachari formed the Congress Ministry in Madras in 1937, V.V. Giri was naturally taken into the Cabinet and given the portfolio of Labour. Again after the General Election of 1946 in Madras Giri was taken into the Cabinet formed by T. Prakasam and given the portfolio of Labour. Later Giri was appointed India's High Commissioner in Ceylon.

Before long he returned to his favourite forum, the lelgislature. He was a member of the Lok Sabha from 1952 to 1957. From 1952 to 1954 he was a member of the Union

Cabinet and was given the portfolio of Labour. When an issue arose that involved the interest of labour, Giri resigned to uphold his cherished principles. Eventually, the Government had to come round to his viewpoint.

After 1957 began a long spell of gubernatorial assignments for Giri. Successively he served as Governor of Uttar Pradesh, Kerala and Mysore. He won friends everywhere, initiated new activities and became a mentor for the younger generation. It was during these years that he imparted new depth and dimension to social work as the President of the Indian Conference of Social Work, to which office he was elected in 1958.

In 1967, during the period of turmoil, he was invited to be the Vice-President. Fate willed that Dr. Zakir Hussain should not complete his term as the President. On his death on 3 May, 1969, V.V. Giri had to officiate as the President. Giri was so clear about his manifest destiny that without bothering about party support he offered himself as a candidate for the Presidential election, confident of popular approval. He was elected (1969) the fourth President of the Republic with the acclaim of the people. With him the arena of the election shifted from the close preserve of politicians to the broad wishes of the people.

Giri has written two important books, one on "Industrial Relations" and the other on "Labour Problems in Indian Industry". He has been a socialist of long standing, but never a doctrinaire socialist, always a pragmatist. His approach is at once practical and human. In his opinion of the tree of socialism the root is man. Even today he gives expression to his economic and social thoughts in terms of "jobs for the millions".

Varahamihira : Varahamihira (505 – 587) was an Indian astronomer, mathematician, and astrologer born in Ujjain. Varahamihira worked as one of the Navaratnas for

Chandragupta Vikramaditya. His book Pancasiddhantika (or Pancha-Siddhantika, The Five Astronomical Canons) dated 575 AD gives us information about older Indian texts which are now lost. The work is a treatise on mathematical astronomy and it summarises five earlier astronomical treatises, namely the Surya, Romaka, Paulisa, Vasistha and Paitamaha Siddhantas. Varahamihira is said to have origins from Eastern Iran from a sect known as Maga Brahmins. Varahamihira made important contributions to Mathematics. He was also an astrologer,& is considered among the greatest Acharyas of modern astrology. He is the only author who has written treatises on all the three main branches of HIndu / Vedic astrology.

Varanasi : Varanasi is a Hindu holy city on the banks of the river Ganga (Ganges) in the modern north Indian state of Uttar Pradesh. Varanasi is to Hindus, what Mecca is to Muslims and Vatican to Catholic Christians. Varanasi has a unique culture, quite different from other places in the region. This culture has developed through thousands of years during which it has been one of the major cultural centres of northern India. The whole Varanasi culture revolves around the river Ganga, which is the heart and soul of the city. Varanasi has its own 'Gharanas' (style of music) in classical Indian music. Varanasi has produced some of the most well-known musicians, philosophers, poets, writers in Indian history. To name a few, Kabir, Munshi Premchand,Jaishankar Prasad, Pandit Ravi Shankar, Ustad Bismillah Khan were/are from Varanasi. It even has its own dialect, which is quite different from other dialects of the region. It has been a seat of knowledge from about 700 BC onwards. Its universities attracted students from all over the then-known world. Varanasi is also known as the Cultural Capital of India.

Varkari Sampraday : The Varkari sampraday(sect) is so called because the followers consider it essential to visit

Pandharpur at least twice a year, on the two Ekadashi (11th day by lunar calendar) in the Hindu calendar months of Ashadh (which falls sometime in August) and Kartik (which falls sometime in November). This pilgrimage is called vari in the Marathi language and thus one who performs it in the path of devotion (Bhakti Marga) is a varkari.

Varkaris worship Vithal or Vithoba, the presiding deity of Pandharpur who is considered same as Shri Krishna. Varkaris can be categorized as vaishnavites Saints from Maharashtra like Dnyaneshwar, Namdeo, Tukaram, Eknath and many others spearheaded the and strengthened the sect with their teachings. The varkaris perform the pilgrimage to Pandharpur even today wherein they walk with the palkis of the saints from their places of origin all the way to Pandharpur.

Varman Dynasty : Varman Dynasty ruled in south-eastern Bengal towards the end of the 11th and first half of the 12th century AD. The history of the Varmans is known from three copperplates and the Bhuvanesvara inscription of Bhatta Bhavadeva. The Varman kings claim their descent from the Yadava dynasty ruling over Simhapura, which has been identified with modern Singapuram in Kalinga (northern Orissa) between Chicacole and Narasannapeta. Four Varman kings of southeastern Bengal are known to have ruled for about 60/70 years. The Senas ousted them during or shortly after the reign of Bhojavarman.

Vasant Panchami : Vasant Panchami is a Hindu festival celebrating Saraswati, the goddess of knowledge, music, and art. It is celebrated every year on the fifth day of the Indian month Magh (January-February), the first day of spring. During this festival children are taught their first words; brahmins are fed; ancestor worship (Pitri-Tarpan) is performed; the god of love, Kamadeva, is worshipped; and most educational institutions organise special prayer for Saraswati. The color yellow also plays an important role in this festival, in that people usually wear yellow garments, Saraswati is worshipped dressed in yellow, and yellow sweetmeats are consumed within the families.

Vasco da Gama : He was a Portuguese explorer, one of the most successful in the European Age of Discovery, and the first person to sail directly from Europe to India. Commissioned by King Manuel I of Portugal to find Christian lands in the East (the King, like many Europeans, was under the impression that India was the legendary Christian Kingdom of Prester John), and to gain Portuguese access to the commercial markets of the Orient, da Gama extended the sea route exploration of his predecessor Bartholomew Dias, who had first rounded Africa's Cape of Good Hope in 1487, culminating a generation of Portuguese sea exploration fostered by the nautical school of Henry the Navigator.

Da Gama's voyage was successful in establishing a sea route from Europe to India that would permit trade with the Far East, without the use of the costly and unsafe Silk Road caravan routes, dominated by Muslims, in the Middle East and Asia. However, the voyage was also hampered by its failure to bring any trade goods of interest to the nations of Asia Minor and India. The route was fraught with peril: only 54 of his 170 voyagers, and two of four ships, returned to Portugal in 1499. Nevertheless, da Gama's initial journey led directly to a several-hundred year era of European domination through sea power and commerce, and 450 years of Portuguese colonialism in India that brought wealth and power to the Portuguese throne.

Vasco da Gama (often shortened to Vasco) is a city in Goa state on the west coast of India. It is named for the Portuguese explorer Vasco da Gama. Vasco is Goa's largest town with an estimated 2005 population of over 100,000, and is the chief port town of Goa as well as the headquarters of the Mormugão taluka. The city lies on the western tip of the Mormugão peninsula, at the mouth of the Zuari River, about 30 km from Panaji, Goa's capital.

Vataman : Vataman or Vataman Chowkdi is a small village in the western state of Gujarat in India located at a crossroads about an hour and a half from Ahmedabad or Amdavad airport on the road to Palitana. There is a beautiful Jain derasar dedicated to Bhagwan Adinath or Lord Rishabha that was consecrated with great fanfare and devotion by Anilaben and Sureshbhai Bapalalbhai Shah of Palanpur and Mumbai in April 2003. The main temple also houses statues of Lord Mahavir Swami, Lord Parashvanath, Lord Vasupujyaswami and Lord Kunthunathswami.

Vatsyayana : Mallanaga Vatsyayana is the name of an Indian philosopher in the Carvaka or Lokyata tradition, who lived some time in the Gupta period (4th to 6th centuries [[Common Era|CE). He is known as the author of the Kama Sutra, and of the first commentary on Gotama's Nyaya Sutras.

Vautha Fair : For five days, you watch the elegantly embellished donkeys, put up proudly for sale at this annual fair in November, not far from Ahmedabad.

Vayalar Ramavarma : Vayalar Ramavarma (March 15, 1928 - October 27, 1975) was a modern Malayalam poet and lyricist. His works include Sargasangeetham, Mulankaadu, Padamudrakal, Aayisha, Oru Judas janikkunnu. Born in the village of Vayalar, in Aalappuzha district, Kerala, Vayalar belonged to an aristocratic family but became a poet of the proletariat inspired by revolutionary ideals. He was awarded Kerala Sahithya Academy Award (Kerala literary academy award) in 1961—

for Sargasangeetham, the President's gold medal for best movie song lyrics in 1974, and the Kerala state film award for best lyricist thrice. The Vayalar award for Malayalam literature, given on October 27 each year, was instituted in his memory. Vayalar wrote about 2000 songs for 223 Malayalam movies, many of which reflect the sorrows and happiness of common man.

Vazir Agha : Vazir Agha is a Pakistani writer, poet, critic and essayist, who lives in Sargodha. His rivalry with another writer Ahmed Nadeem Qasmi is very famous in the literary circles of the Urdu literary world. According to literary commentators, "this fight has served both gentle men in some way but has ruined Urdu literature and Urdu language writers of the country at large".

Vedanta : Vedanta means the anta or culmination or essence of the Vedas. It is a principal branch of Hindu philosophy. As per some, it is a form of Jnana Yoga (one of the four basic yoga practices in Hinduism; the others are: Raja Yoga, Bhakti Yoga, Karma Yoga), a form of yoga which involves an individual seeking "the path of intellectual analysis or the discrimination of truth and reality." As per others, Vedanta encompasses all the four yogas. The sage Badarayana is supposed to be the proponent of this philosophy and author of the Brahma Sutras based on the Upanishads. In late nineteenth and early twentieth centuries, Vedanta was propounded voraciously in the West by Vivekananda. He was followed by many other Indian sages in due course, including Yogananda, and others who came to North America to preach Vedanta and make it popular in the West.

The concept of Brahman—the Supreme Spirit or the eternal, self existent, immanent and transcedent Supreme and Ultimate Reality which is the divine ground of all Being—is central to Vedanta. The concept of God or

Ishvara is also there, and the Vedantic sub-schools differ mainly in how they identify God with Brahman.

Mimamsa is one of the three major divisions of Hindu theistic philosophy. It is further divided into Purva Mimamsa, also simply called Mimamsa, which deals with explainations of the fire-sacrifices of the Vedic mantras and Brahmanas, and Uttara Mimamsa, also called "Vedanta", which explicates the esoteric teachings of the Aranyakas and the Upanishads. The school of Vedanta is further divided into six main sub-schools.

Vedas : The Vedas, collectively refers to a corpus of ancient Indo-Aryan religious literature that are considered by adherents of Hinduism to be revealed knowledge. The word Veda means Knowledge and is cognate with the word "wit" in English (as well as "vision" through Latin). Many Hindus believe the Vedas existed since the beginning of creation. The texts of the Vedas have several references to specific patterns in the ancient flows of the Ganges River, which coincide with the sites of its ancient (but now dried) tributaries.

Many historians regard the Vedas as the oldest surviving text of humanity. The newest parts of the Vedas are estimated to date back to around 500 BCE. The oldest text (RigVeda) found is now dated to around 1,500 BCE, but most Indologists agree that a long oral tradition possibly existed before it was written down. They represent the oldest stratum of Indian Literature and according to modern scholars are written in forms of a language which evolved into Sanskrit. They consider the use of Vedic Sanskrit for the language of the texts an anachronism, although it is generally accepted.

Vedavathi River : The Vedavathi River is a river in India. It rises from the Western Ghats and flows through the states of Karnataka and Andhra Pradesh before joining river Tungabhadra. River Vedavathi is also called river Hagari in parts of Andhra Pradesh. Two rivers, Veda and Avathi arise in eastern part of Sahyadri Hill range, flow east word, concert near Pura and become river Vedavathi. On the bank of river Vedavathi, there is a famous temple of Shri Anjaneya at Kellodu, Hosadurga Taluk.

Vedic Civilization : The Vedic Civilization is the Indo-Aryan culture associated with the Vedas, the earliest known records of Indian history. Mainstream scholarship places the Vedic civilization into the 2nd and 1st millennia BCE, many Hindu scholars date its beginnings as early as the 7th millennium BCE starting from Mehrgarh Culture. The use of Vedic Sanskrit continued up to the 6th century BCE, when the culture started to be transformed into classical forms of Hinduism.

Vedic Religion : The religion of the Vedic civilization is the predecessor of classical Hinduism, usually included in the term. Its liturgy is reflected in the text of the Vedas. The religion centered on a clergy (the Brahmins) administering sacrificial rites. Texts considered to date to the Vedic period, composed in Vedic Sanskrit, are mainly the four Vedas, but the Brahmanas, and some of the older Upanishads are also considered Vedic. The Vedas record the liturgy connected with the rituals and sacrifices performed by the purohitas. To the rishis, the hymns of the Rigveda and other Vedic hymns divinely revealed and they were rather "hearers", of divine revelation. (shrauta means "what is heard"). The mode of worship was performance of sacrifices and chanting of hymns. The priests helped the common man in performing rituals. People prayed for abundance of children, cattle and wealth.

The main deities of the Vedic pantheon were Indra, Agni (fire), and Soma. Other deities were Varuna, Surya (the Sun), Mitra, Vayu (the wind). Goddesses included

Ushas (the dawn), Prithvi (the Earth) and Aditi. Rivers, especially Sarasvati, were also considered goddesses. Deities were not viewed as all-powerful. The relationship between the devotee and the deity was one of transaction, with Agni (the sacrificial fire) taking the role of messenger between the two. Strong traces of a common Indo-Iranian religion remain visible, especially in the Soma cult and the fire ritual also preserved in Zoroastrianism. The Ashvamedha (horse sacrifice) has parallels in the 2nd millennium BC Andronovo culture, in India allegedly continued until the 4th century AD.

Vedic Sanskrit : Vedic Sanskrit is the language of the Vedas, the earliest sacred texts of India. The earliest of the Vedas, the Rigveda, was composed in the 2nd millennium BC, and use of the Vedic dialect was continued for the composition of religious texts until roughly 500 BC, when the later Classical Sanskrit language began to emerge.

The Vedic form of Sanskrit is an early descendant of Proto-Indo-Iranian (spoken around 2000 BC), and still comparatively similar (being removed by maybe 1500 years) to the Proto-Indo-European language. Vedic Sanskrit is the oldest attested language of the Indo-Iranian branch of the Indo-European family. It is also still closely related to Avestan, the oldest preserved Iranian language.

Vedic University : Vedic University is where the Vedas are taught. Vedic knowledge is said to be eternal, it is timeless and ageless. Hinduism is based on the Vedic knowledge. One such Vedic University existed in Sitanagaram near Guntur in the South-Eastern part of India. It is run by the Jeer Educational Trust of Sri. Chinna Jeeyar Swamy. Also another vedic university is being built by Jeer Educational Trust at Shamshabad near Hyderabad of Southern India.

Veena : Veena is a stringed instrument. It consists of a large body hollowed out of a block of wood. The stem of the instrument is also made of wood. The bridge is placed on the flat top of the body of the veena and the neck attached to the stem is usually carved into weird figure like the head of the dragon. A gourd which is smaller than the rounded part of the body is fixed underneath the neck. Twenty one metallic frets are fixed on the stem by means of a resinous substance.

The veena has seven strings. Of them four are main strings that pass over the frets and are attached to the pegs of the neck. The other strings are used as side strings for rhythmic accompaniment. These strings pass over an arched bridge made of brass. They lie flat over the top of the body and are secured to the main bridge.

The veena is played by sitting cross-legged upon the floor and holding the veena in front. The small gourd on the left touch the left thigh, the left arm passing round the stem so that the fingers rest easily upon the frets. The main body of the instrument is placed on the ground, partially supported by the right thigh. There are different varieties of veena. Some of them are Mahanataka veena, Saraswati veena, Rudra veena, Vichitra veena etc. Saraswati veena is known as the queen of veena's.

Veer Natyam : Veer Natyam is performed to worship Veerbhadra, who was believed to have been created by Lord Shiva from his Jatajhuta or hair. It is commonly performed in Draksharama, which is supposed to be the birthplace of Veerbhadra. The dance is accompanied by musical instruments like Tambura, Soolen, Dholu, Thasha and Veeranam.

Veethi Bhagavatam : Veethi Bhagavatam is a solo performance that originated from Kuchipudi tradition. The masters of Kuchipudi themselves thought of this new type and it evolved through women -artistes of courtesan families (Kalavantula) who were proficient in the solo dance -art of the Nautch. The Kuchipudi tradition did not permit women to play female roles in its Bhagavata stories and the Nautch had its own repertoire of detached pieces and love songs. By crossing the features of these two, the form named Veethi Bhagavata or Gollakalapa was developed. The Veethi Bhagavata is performed during temple festivals, on occasions of marriage and other happy celebrations in the houses of rich patrons.

The Veethi Bhagavata has a single female artists, the main dancer, she supported by a secondary female artistes. The role of Vidhushaka is used to entertain and put across humour effectively in the play. He also add vehicle of wisdom. He is versatile and multi purpose character, the constant companion of the lady and also her chorist. It is its dialogue or argument in which the chief lady, representing a milkmaid (Golla), carries on with the Brahmin, that provides the Kalapam. She cross- examines the Brahmin as to his real Brahmin hood and expatiates on what a real Brahmin is according to the Sastras and under the torrent of her questions and Sanskrit quotation from the sastras, the poor Brahmin is left breathless.

Veg Kolhapuri : Veg Kolhapuri is a vegetarian dish from Kolhapur, Maharashtra in India. It can be described as a mixed vegetable dry gravy dish. It is frequently eaten as a main course. It is accompanied by a chapati in the rural areas and from its native land. However, it is accompanied by roti, paratha, naan or kulcha as the bread, in other areas, especially at fast food outlets in India.

Vegetable Sandwich : Vegetable sandwich is the most common type of sandwich in India. It is a purely vegetarian item (though not vegan if butter is used), and is often seen prepared and served fresh by roadside vendors as well as in many restaurants. It consists of vegetable filling between two slices of white bread. The most commonly used vegetables for this sandwich are the tomato, the cucumber and the potato. Other vegetables used include beetroot and onion.

Potatoes are boiled well in advance, and peeled prior to assembly. The tomatoes, cucumbers, potatoes and other ingredient vegetables are cut into thin slices and stacked between two slices of white bread that have been spread with butter and spicy green chutney on the inner sides. This sandwich is then toasted in a sandwich toaster (or in the case of roadside vendors, in toasting tongs over a portable gas stove). After toasting, the sandwich is cut into six rectangular pieces, and its top side is slathered once more with butter and chutney. Finally, tomato ketchup is squirted onto the top of the sandwich.

Vehari District : Vehari District was created in 1976 out of the two tehsils of Multan District namely Vehari and Mailsi and Sub-tehsil Gaggo of Sahiwal District. Its boundaries meet with Khanewal District on North West, with Lodhran District on West, with Bahawalpur District on South and Bahawalnagar District on the South East across the river Sutlej, which passes from East to West. The Sahiwal District lies on its North East.

Velankanni : Velankanni is located 12 km south of Nagapattinam on the Coromandel Coast, in Tamil Nadu. The shrine here is dedicated to Our Lady of Health, the Madonna of Velankanni and is popularly known as 'Sacred Arogya Matha Church'.

Virgin Mary is believed to have miraculous healing powers. Thousands of pilgrims belonging to various castes and communities flock daily to this 'Lourdes of the East'. The church has an imposing facade with tall spires and the wings present the shape of a cross. In a niche in the alter is enshrined the statue of Our Lady of Health.

In 1560, Virgin Mary is said to have appeared to a shepherd, asking him for milk to quench the thirst of baby

Jesus. When the shepherd returned to his master, after performing the good deed, his pitcher kept filling up with milk. Consequently, a small thatched chapel was built at the site. At the end of the 16th century, Virgin Mary appeared again in front of a lame boy, who regained the use of his limbs. The actual church was constructed after the incident.

The tradition is to offer Our Lady of Health, a candle in the shape of the respective ailment- a heart in case of cardiac complications, a liver in case of jaundice, lungs in case of tuberculosis and so on. In case of the ailment getting cured, many bring with them small gold and silver replicas of parts of the body that has been cured to donate to the church.

Some times offering are sent in sealed bottles or big hollow bamboos duly closed and thrown in to the sea with the address of the shrine written on them. Such offerings are believed to reach the holy spot. There is a small church museum which has a display of the offerings made by those whose prayers were conceded.

A festival is celebrated for ten days from August 28 to September 10 every year and pilgrims from all over the country and even abroad flock to the site, bathe religiously in the sea, have their heads shaved and then walk on their knees or roll up to the shrine as rituals.

Velavadar Black Buck National Park : Velavadar National Park, the only tropical grassland in India recognized as a National park is located in Bhavnagar district, in the Bhal region of Saurashtra, Gujarat. The park, now spread over an area of 34.08 Sq.kms used to be a private grassland of the ex- princely state of Bhavnagar with an area of about 1788.88 ha which was subsequently declared as a reserve forest and later notified as a National Park in 1976. An area of 1622.23 ha was further added in

1980. The main attraction of the park located seventy-two km away from the city of Bhavnagar is the massive population of Black Buck, Antelope, Wolf and other endangered species of birds.

Velha Goa : Velha Goa was founded in the 15th century as a port for the Vijayanagar and Bahamni kings. Old Goa was the second capitol of Bijapur under the rule of Adil Shah. The city was surrounded by a moat and contained the Shah's palace, and his mosques and temples. The city of Goa in south-western India was under Portuguese rule from 1510 and became the capital of Portuguese India until its incorporation in the Republic of India in 1961. At its peak it was as large as London or Paris. Malaria and cholera epidemics ravaged the city in the 17th century and it was largely abandoned only having a remaining population of 1,500 in 1775. The viceroy then moved the palace of Adil Shah to Panaji. In 1835 after religious suppression the city was virtually deserted. The population was roughly 200,000 by 1543. It was the administrative seat of Portuguese India until 1843, although the Viceroy's residence was transferred in 1759 to the future capital, Panaji. Old Goa contains churches affiliated to various congregations, including the Se Cathedral (the seat of the Archbishop of Goa), the church of St Francis of Assisi, the church of S. Caetano, and notably, the Basilica of Bom Jesus which contains the incorruptible body of Saint Francis Xavier.

Vembanad Lake : Vembanad Lake (Vembanad Kayal or Vembanad Kol) is the largest lake in Kerala, India. It covers an area of 200 km^2, and bordered by Alappuzha, Kottayam, and Ernakulam districts. The lake lies at sea level, and is separated from the Arabian Sea by a narrow barrier island. Canals link the lake to coastal lakes to the north and south. Several rivers flow into the lake, including the Achenkovil, Manimala, Meenachil,

Muvattupuzha, Pamba and Periyar. The lake surrounds the islands of Pathiramanal, Perumbalam and Pallippuram.

The port of Kochi (Cochin) is located at the lake's outlet to the Arabian Sea. The town of Alapuzha (also known as Allepey), is sometimes called the "Venice of the East" for its large network of canals that meander through the town. The Vallam Kali (the Snake Boat Race) held every year in August is a major attraction. Vembanad Lake is designated a wetland of international importance under the Ramsar Convention.

Vemulavada : Vemulavada (alternatively spelt Vemulawada) is a town 38 km from Karimnagar, in the Andhra Pradesh state, India. It is chiefly notable for the Sri Raja Rajeshwara Swamy Temple complex, a site of pilgrimage for both Hindu (particularly devotees of Vishnu and Shiva) and Muslim worshippers.

Built by Chaluka Kings between AD 750 and 975, the complex is named for its presiding deity Sri Raja Rajeswara Swamy, an incarnation of Shiva. It houses several temples dedicated to other deities including Sri Rama, Lakshmana, Lakshmi, Ganapathy, Lord Padmanabha Swamy and Lord Bhimeshwara. The complex also contains a 400 year old mosque.

Architectural features include its open galleries (such as the Mirror Gallery Addala Mantapa and a corridor with a number of Shiva idols) and a Dhrama Kundam, a holy tank where pilgrims bathe then proceed for darshan and whose water is believed to have curative properties.

Venkatagiri Kota : Venkatagiri Kota (also known as V-Kota) is a small town in the Chittoor district of Andhra Pradesh. The National Highway 4 between Bangalore and Chennai runs through V-Kota. The road leading to Gudiyattam and Vellore in Tamil Nadu is a beautiful stretch, the road descends from the Deccan Plateau to the plains of Tamil Nadu. One can actually feel the difference in temperatures as one descends it becomes hotter and hotter.

Venkateshwara : In Hinduism, Venkateshwara (also spelled as Venkateswara, Venkateshwer or Venkatachalapathi) is a much-worshipped form of Vishnu. He is also known as Balaji or Lord Venkateswara. He is also worshiped with the name Tirupati Thimmappa all over Karnataka by traditionally Shiva worshipping communities.

Vishnu, in the form of Venkateshwara, is much worshipped at Tirupati temple. Venkateshwara is the presiding deity at the Tirumala temple complex, believed to be the richest of all the Hindu shrines in the world. The temple is situated in southern Andhra Pradesh in Chittoor district. It is around 120 km away from Chennai. The presence of seven hills influenced alternate names for the diety: Edu kondala vadu in Telugu and as Elumalaiyan in Tamil both of which mean Lord of the Seven Hills.

Vesara : Vesara is a type of Indian architecture primarily used in temples. The two other prominent styles are Dravida and Nagara. Etymologically, the term Vesara is believed to have been derived from the Sanskrit word Mishra, which means a blend or a mixture. This is also in conformity with the prevalence of Vesara style of architecture in the Deccan and central parts of South Asia vis-à-vis Nagara style prevalent in North India and Dravida style prevalent in South India. Accordingly, the Vesara style contain elements of both Dravida and Nagara styles. The Vesara style is also described in some texts as the 'Central Indian temple architecture style' or 'Deccan architecture'. However many historian agree that the vesara style originated in the what is today Karnataka. The trend was started by the Chalukyas of Badami (500-

753AD) who built temples in a style that was essentially a mixture of the nagara and the dravida styles, further refined by the Rashtrakutas of Manyakheta (750-983AD) in Ellora, Chalukyas of Kalyani (983-1195AD) in Lakkundi, Dambal, Gadag etc. and epitomized by the Hoysalas (1000-1330AD).

The Hoysalas temples at Belur, Halebidu and Somnathpura are supreme examples of this style. These temples are now proposed as a UNESCO world heritage site. It is understood that the Virupaksha temple at Aihole and Pattadakal in northern Karnataka served as an inspiration for the design of the famous Khajuraho temples at Madhya Pradesh. Early temples constructed in this style include temples at Sirpur, Baijnath, Baroli and Amarkantak. The temple complex at Khajuraho, a World Heritage Site, is a typical example of the Vesara style.

Victoria Memorial : This is one of India's most beautiful monument built between 1906 and 1921 on the lines of white marble in West Bengal. It stands on the southern side of the maidan (ground) near Jawaharlal Nehru Road. All monuments of this memorial were designed in Italian Renaissance-Mughal style and build of white marble from Rajasthan. The memorial was the inspiration of Lord Curzon, who in 1901, felt that his lately departed Queen Empress, required a suitable monument to her memory. It took 20 years to build at a cost of 10 million rupees.

The Prince of Wales formally inaugurated it in 1921. Set in beautiful garden grounds, the Victoria Memorial houses a large bronze statue of the Queen Empress Topped with a moving angel this memorial faces the Calcutta Maidan. The statues of Motherhood, Prudence, Learning, Art, Justice, Architecture and Charity are brought from Italy. It also has a 5 meter tall bronze winged figure of

Victory, weighing 3 tons. It houses paintings, manuscripts, and other objects of historic value in its Museum and Art Gallery. Two regular sound and light shows are held in the evening.

Vidarbha : Vidarbha is the north-eastern region of Maharashtra state, now forming two divisions (Nagpur and Amravati). It is comparatively backward, and is one of several aspirant states of India. The main crop is cotton. Nagpur was the capital of the Bhonsle dynasty of Marathas, who in the mid eighteenth century created a state that covered much of east-central India. After their defeat in the Third Anglo-Maratha War in 1818, the Bhonsle dominions were reduced to Nagpur division, which was taken over by the British in 1853 when the last Maharaja of Nagpur died without a male heir. The Nagpur division became a part of the British Raj's Central Provinces in 1861. Amravati division, formerly known as Berar, was administered by the Nizam of Hyderabad until 1853, when the British took over governance of the province under the charge of misgovernance by the Nizam. Berar was added to the Central Provinces in 1903. After Indian Independence, the Central Provinces and Berar became the Indian state of Madhya Pradesh. Vidarbha was transferred to Bombay state in 1956 to unify all Marathi-speaking areas, and became part of Maharashtra state in 1960, when Bombay state was split into the linguistic states of Maharashtra and Gujarat. Ramayana has the reference of Vidarbha as one on the Janapadas at that time.

Videsh Sanchar Nigam Ltd (VSNL) : Videsh Sanchar Nigam Ltd (VSNL) was India's sole telecom carrier for international calls until 2002. While domestic calls are carried by Mahanagar Telephone Nigam Limited (MTNL), Bharat Sanchar Nigam Limited (BSNL), and private companies, international calls were routed through VSNL. It also provided bandwidth for Internet service providers.

VSNL was incorporated on April 1, 1986 as a wholly owned government entity. In 2002 the Indian Government privatized VSNL. The Tata Group group acquired a controlling stake in VSNL and the government holds a minority stake. The company is now branded as VSNL TataIndicom. The company stock is now traded on the Bombay Stock Exchange and also trades in the United States as an American Depository Receipt (ADR) under the ticker symbol VSL. Revenues for the financial year 2004 stood at approximately 780 Million USD

Vidhan Soudha : It is at Dr.Ambedkar Veddi Road, Banglore. It is a beautiful building, built between 1954 and 1958. It houses the state legislature and secretariat. Opposite side of the Vidhan soudha there is another attractive public building, red brick High court of Karnataka, built in 1885.

Vidisha : Vidisha or Besnagar is a city in Madhya Pradesh state of central India. It is the administrative headquarters of Vidisha District. The town is situated east of the Betwa River, in the fork of the Betwa and Bes rivers, 10 km from Sanchi. The town of Besnagar, 3 km from present-day Vidisha on the west side of the river, became an important trade center in the sixth and fifth centuries BCE, under the Sungas, Nagas, Satavahanas, and Guptas, and was mentioned in the Pali scriptures. The Emperor Ashoka was the governor of Vidisha and it finds mention in Kalidasa's immortal Meghdoot. Besnagar was abandoned in the sixth century, it came into prominance again as Bhilsa during the medieval period. Vidisha was established in the ninth century by Muslims. The Bija Mandal mosque in Vidisha was constructed after demolishing the Vijayamandir Hindu temple during the time of Mughal emperor Aurangzeb. It thus, passed on to the Malwa Sultans, the Mugals and the Scindias.

The ruins of a Brahmanical shrine at Vidisha dedicated to Vishnu reveal that the foundation bricks were cemented together with lime mortar, the first known example of the use of cement in India. The ruins are of period prior to 2nd century BC. Close to the ruins are the remains of votive pillars with palm-leaf capitals; the only one that still stands is the Heliodorus pillar, also known as Khamba Baba. A monolithic free-standing column, the pillar bears an inscription which states that it was Garuda Pillar, raised in honour of Vasudeva by Heliodorous, a rsident of Taxila, who had been sent to the court of Bhagabhadra as an envoy of Indo-Bactrian monarch, Antialkidas. This inscription is a valuable historical record, revealing both the relations that existed between the region and the Greek kingdoms of the Punjab, and the remarkable fact that a Greek had become a follower of Hindu god Vishnu. The inclusion of the name of Antialkidas dates the erection of the pillar to approximately 140 BC.

Vidyarambham : This is done either when the child attains three or five years in Kerala. On the tongue of the child the letters "Hari Sri Ganapataye Namah Avignamastu "and all the alphabets are written with a piece of gold. The child is made to write the same letters from "Hari Sri" onwards with its ring finger on raw rice in a bell metal vessel and the child is made to utter each word when it is written.

Vidyasagar Setu : Vidyasagar Setu (commonly known as the Second Howrah Bridge or Second Hooghly Bridge) is a bridge over the Hooghly River in West Bengal, India. It links the city of Howrah to its twin city of Kolkata. The bridge is a toll bridge for vehicles. The bridge is named for the great son of Bengal Ishwar Chandra Vidyasagar. The bridge also has sister bridges over the river at different points, namely the Howrah Bridge (Rabindra Setu) and the Vivekananda Setu. It is a cable-stayed bridge, with a main span of a little over 457 metres, and a deck 35 metres wide. Construction started in 1978 and the bridge was finally inaguarated in October, 1992. The commissioning agency was the Hooghly River Bridge Commission (HRBC) and the contractors for the construction was the consortium of Braithwaite, Burn and Jessop also called BBJ.

Vijay Amritraj : Vijay Amritraj (born December 14, 1953) in Madras, India, is a former tennis champion and actor. Amritraj and his brother, Anand Amritraj, were among the first Indians to play in top-flight international tour tennis. In 1976, the brothers were semi-finalists in the Wimbledon men's doubles.

Playing his first grand prix event in 1970, Amritraj achieved his first significant success in singles in 1973 when he reached the quarter-final stage at two Grand Slam events. At Wimbledon he lost 5-7 in the fifth set to the eventual champion Jan Kodes and later that summer at the U.S. Open lost to tennis great Ken Rosewall after having beaten another legend, Rod Laver, two rounds earlier.

Amritraj was the captain of the Indian Davis Cup for much of the late 1970's and 1980's, helping India reach the finals in 1974 and 1987. He compiled a career singles win-lose record 384-296, winning 16 singles titles to go along with 13 in doubles. He beat the best, including McEnroe at his peak in 1984 (in the first round in Cincinnati) and had five career wins over Connors in their 11 matches. He reached his career high ranking in singles of World No. 16 in July, 1980.

Vijay also had a brief acting career, appearing with Roger Moore in the James Bond film, Octopussy and in Star Trek IV: The Voyage Home. He has since gone on to become a sports commentator, and has developed a successful multimedia business.

Vijay Diwas: Vijay Diwas (Victory Day) is celebrated in India on 16 December every year to mark the Indian victory in the Indo-Pakistani War of 1971. Bangladesh also commemorates the victory over Pakistan on the same day in 1971 on Victory Day.

Vijayanagara Empire : The Vijayanagara empire was based in the Deccan, in peninsular and southern India, from 1336 onwards. It was founded by Harihara, also known as Hakka, and his brother Bukka Raya. It is named after its capital city Vijayanagara, whose impressive ruins surround Hampi in modern Karnataka, India. It lasted from about 1336 to perhaps about 1660, though throughout its last century it was in a slow decline due to a massive and catastrophic defeat at the hands of an alliance of the sultanates, and the capital was taken and brutally razed and looted. Its foundation, and even great part of its history, is obscure; but its power and wealth are attested by more than one European traveller, such as the Portuguese travelers Domingo Paes and Nuniz, and the Venetian Niccolò Da Conti.

The founding of the original kingdom was based on the principality of Anegondi, based on a fortified town on the Tungabhadra river in the Deccan. In the century preceding the founding of the empire, the old kingdoms of the Deccan had been overrun by Muslim invaders from the north. From 1309, Malik Kafur reached and captured Warangal, later on reaching the Malabar kingdoms. Mubarak of Delhi reached Warangal again in 1323. Between 1334 and 1336, Muhammad Tughlaq of Delhi again overran the region, capturing Anegondi.

In the following two centuries, the Vijayanagar empire dominated all of southern India, and was probably stronger than any other power in the subcontinent. The empire during that period served as a bulwark against invasion from the Turkic Sultanates of the Indo-Gangetic

Plain; and remained in constant competition and conflict with the five Deccan Sultanates that established themselves in the Deccan to the north of it. It remained a land power.

The empire is generally considered to have reached its peak during the rule of Krishna Deva Raya. hE conquered or subjugated territories on the east of the Deccan that belonged previously to Orissa. Many of the great monuments of the empire date from his time. Among these are the Hazara Rama temple, the Krishna temple and the Ugra Narasimha idol, all at Vijayanagara.

While the empire still continued to have some power, and commanded respect, it went into a considerable decline. The rulers of this period are difficult to place clearly. It is known however that they continued to trade with the Portuguese, and that they gave the British the land grant that enabled the establishment of Madras.

Vijayawada : Vijayawada literally translates to "The Place of Victory". It is also known as Bezawada or Blazewada because of its heat. It is the third largest city in Andhra Pradesh, India and is located on the banks of the Krishna River, bounded by the lndrakeeladri Hills on the west and the Budameru canal on the north. It is situated along the Madras-Howrah, and Madras-Delhi rail route, this is the largest railway junction of the South Central Railways. The city is in the Krishna District, about 275 km from the state capital Hyderabad and is known as the business capital of Andhra Pradesh. It is spread over an area of 58 km^2 (urban area) with a population of 825,436 (agglomeration 1,011,152) (2001 census) and 1,025,436 (agglomeration 1,411,152) (2006 census).

Vijayawada is an important link in connecting the three regions of Andhra Pradesh and is a major transit point. Two National Highways, No. 5 from Chennai to Kolkata and the No. 9 from Machilipatnam to Pune pass through the City connecting it to other parts of the country. It is connected to other areas of the state by state highways and district roads. Vijayawada is also one of the busiest railway junctions in India. The domestic airport located at Gannavaram, is about 20 km from the city and connects Vijayawada to Hyderabad by air.

Vijaykanth : Vijaykanth is a famous Tamil film actor (veteran of 147 films), and budding Politician. He is famously known as "Captain" by his fans and colleagues in Kollywood, Vijaykanth became famous with his film "Captain Prabhakaran" and is still known in the industry as Captain. He has the biggest fan club in Tamil Nadu among all heroes in Kollywood.

He is the President of South Indian Film Artistes Association, also recently led a tour of South Indian artistes including matinee idols Kamal Haasan and Rajnikanth to Singapore and Malaysia and conducted star nites and the collection was used to wipe out the debts incurred by the Association.

Vikas Khanna : Vikas Khanna (born November 14, 1971) is an Indian chef, who has also become famous as food writer and a humanitarian. Born in Amritsar, India to Davinder and Bindu Khanna. Starting as a helper in his grandmother's kitchen, he learnt most the secrets and correct use of spices from her. His first job, at the age of 12, was that of supplying glassware to Amritsar Club.

He had started developing recipes at a very young age and at 16, opened his own banquets called Lawrence Gardens banquets to host weddings and family functions. Graduated from Welcomgroup Graduate School of Hotel Administration in 1994. Started "SAANCH"—The cultural festival at the college which brought together foods and traditions of different regions of India, which is an integral part of the college even now. Learnt the art of sculpting stone and wood from Jaipur, Mysore, Udipi and Sagar in Karnataka, which was exhibited in the college.

He has worked for the Taj, Oberoi, Welcomgroup, and Leela Group of Hotels, with some of the most influential chefs of India. Moved to the New York in December, 2000 and has studied at Cornell University, Culinary Institute of America, New York University and many more while starting as a dishwasher and working his way up to becoming the Executive Chef of Salaam Bombay Restaurant in New York. He frequently lectures at many Univerisities around the country.

Vikram : "Chiyaan" Vikram (born on [April 17,1966], Paramakkudi), is an Indian born actor who has starred in a number of top-grossing Tamil films and is currently one of the reigning heroes of Tamil Film Industry (Kollywood). With numerous blockbusters to his credit, Vikram has carefully niched a place for himself on the silver screen.

He won the prestigious National Award of India for his breathtaking performance as an undertaker in Pithamagan, 2003.

Vikram Ambalal Sarabhai : Vikram Ambalal Sarabhai (August 12, 1919 – December 31, 1971) was an Indian physicist. He is considered the Father of the Indian space program. Many Indians consider him to be a national hero Vikram Sarabhai was born in Ahmedabad, India to an affluent, business family. He was one of eight children of Ambalal and Sarla Devi.

He was educated at St. John's College, Cambridge University where he received his undergraduate degree in 1940 and a Ph.D in 1947. He studied cosmic rays under the Nobel laureate Dr.C. V. Raman at the Indian Institute of Science (IISc), Bangalore from 1941 to 1945. His interest in solar physics and cosmic ray led him to set up many observation stations around the country. He was instrumental in establishing the Physical Research Laboratory (PRL) in Ahmedabad in November 1947.

After Dr. Homi Bhabha 's demise, Dr. Sarabhai became the director of Atomic Energy Commission of India in 1966 where he continued his work. Dr. A P J Abdul Kalam, the current President of India has described it as his good fortune to work with Dr. Sarabhai. Along with his work on the science front, he took utmost interest and managed family business of Textiles and Pharmaceuticals.

The establishment of the Indian Space Research Organization (ISRO) was one of his greatest achievements. He successfully convinced the government of the importance of a space programme for a developing country like India after the Russian, Sputnik launch. Dr. Bhabha supported Dr. Sarabhai in setting up the first rocket launching station in the India. This center was established at Thumba near Thiruvananthapuram on the coast of Arabian Sea, primarily because of its proximity to the equator. After a monstrous effort in infrastructure, personnel, communication links, and launch pads, on November 21, 1963 the inaugural flight was launched with sodium vapour payload.

Vikram Sarabhai Space Centre (VSSC) : The Vikram Sarabhai Space Centre (VSSC) is located at Thumba near Trivandrum, a city of the Kerala state in India. It is a major space research centre of the Indian Space Research Organisation (ISRO),where space vehicles are developed for the Indian satellite programme.

The Vikram Sarabhai Space Center is ISRO's one of the main Research & Development establishment. Its facilities were built near the Thumba Equatorial Rocket Launching Station (TERLS), on the west coast of India, about 10 miles

(16km) north of Thiruvananthapuram in Kerala State. Named after the late Professor Vikram Sarabhai (1919-1971), founder of the Indian Space Program. VSSC is an entirely national facility working on the development of sounding rockets; Rohini and Menaka, launchers; ASLV, PSLV and GSLV, along with the solid motor program.

"There are some who question the relevance of space activities in a developing nation. To us, there is no ambiguity of purpose. We do not have the fantasy of competing with the economically advanced nations in the exploration of the moon or the planets or manned space-flight. But we are convinced that if we are to play a meaningful role nationally, and in the community of nations, we must be second to none in the application of advanced technologies to the real problems of man and society. " ISRO's Launch Vehicle programme started with development of SLV-3, first successfully launched on July 18, 1980 followed by two more flights. The second launch vehicle was Augmented Satellite Launch Vehicle which had two successful flights. The development of Polar Satellite Launch Vehicle has been completed with two successful flights and is now available for operational use. Geosynchronous Satellite Launch Vehicle (GSLV) is under development.

Vikram Seth : Vikram Seth was born in Calcutta in 1952. He earned degrees in Philosophy, Politics and Economics from Oxford University. He has published 6 books of poetry and 3 novels since 1980. His novel "A suitable boy" won the W.H.Smith prize in 1993. The latest novel written by Vikram Seth is 'An Equal music' and it is about the troubled love life of a violinist. Vikram Seth received one of Britain top honours for his services to literature. The award of the commander of the order3 of the British Empire was announced earlier in the year by Queen Elizabeth II and given to Seth on 14 February 2001.

Vikram Seth creates a living, breathing world that enchants and grips the reader in all his novels.

Vikramshila University : Vikramshila University was one of the two most important centers of Buddhist learning in India, along with Nalanda University. Vikramashila was established by King Dharampal of Bengal (783 to 820) in response to a supposed decline in the quality of scholarship at Nalanda. Atisha, the renowned pandita, is sometimes listed as a notable abbot. Vikramashila was destroyed by Muslim invaders along with the other major centers of Buddhism in India around 1200. Remains have been partially excavated at village Antichak in the Bhagalpur district, Bihar state, India, and the process is still underway.

Vikramuurvashiiya : This play by Kalidasa is about the love story between Pururava and Urvashi. The story centers on Urvashi's abduction by demons and Pururava rescue efforts. Subsequently Urvashi falls in love with him. But Pururuva is already married. The play revolves around the dilemma that pururuva faces due to his love for Urvashi and love and commitment to his wife.

Vilasrao Deshmukh : Vilasrao Dadoji Deshmukh (born May 25, 1945) is an Indian politician from the economically backward Marathwada region of the state of Maharashtra. He is the Chief Minister of Maharashtra (Term: October 2004 - October 2009). He is from the Congress party.

He has been a minister in various governments in Maharashtra from 1982 to 1995 holding portfolios of revenue, cooperation, agriculture, home, industries and education. He became the Chief Minister of Maharashtra in 1999 but had to step down in January 2003 and make way for Sushilkumar Shinde, a prominent Dalit face of Congress, following factionalism in the state unit of the party.

Viluppuram : Viluppuram (also Villupuram) is one of thirty districts which make up Tamil Nadu State situated on the southern tip of India. Viluppuram District came into existence on 30 September 1993 when it was created out of South Arcot District. The district headquarters are located at Viluppuram. The district occupies an area of 7217 km^2 and has a population of 2,943,917 (as of 2001)

Vinayak Damodar Savarkar : Vinayak Damodar Savarkar (May 28, 1883-1966), sometimes called Veer Savarkar or Vir Savarkar, was an Indian freedom fighter and a Hindu nationalist leader. The Vir Savarkar Airport in Port Blair, Andaman Islands is named after him. Vinayak Savarkar was a great orator, prolific writer, historian, poet, philosopher and social worker who devoted his entire life to the cause of the Indian Independence movement. He is regarded by some as one of the greatest revolutionaries in the Indian freedom struggle, while others consider him a communalist and Machiavellian manipulator. He was also one of the most controversial figures of the independence movement.

Being a descendant of a line of Sanskrit scholars, Vinayak Damodar Savarkar took great interest in History, Politics, Literature and Indian culture. His book, First war of Indian Independence Movement: 1857, served as an inspiration for many freedom fighters.

Vindaloo : Vindaloo is a popular Indian food dish. It was first brought to Goa by the Portuguese and soon became a pleasing Goan meal often served during special occasions. Historically this was a pork dish cooked with plenty of wine vinegar and garlic, known as "Vinha d'Alho", however it soon received the Goanese treatment of adding plentiful amounts of spice and chili. Restaurants often serve this dish with chicken or lamb sometimes mixed with potatoes. Traditional vindaloos do not include potatoes, the discrepancy arising because the word "aloo" means "potato" in Hindi.

The dish gained added popularity in Britain, and became a common fixture at Indian restaurants and curry houses there. In colloquial English it is often referred to as "A Vindy" and is well known for its heat, being one of the hotter curries available.

Vindhya Pradesh : Vindhya Pradesh is a former state of India. It was created in 1948, shortly after Indian independence, from the territories of the princely states in the eastern portion of the former Central India Agency. The eastern part of the state included the large princely state of Rewa, formerly part of Bagelkhand agency, and the western part of the state was made up of the numerous states of the former Bundelkhand agency of Central India. It was named for the Vindhya Range, which runs through the center of the province. The capital of the state was Rewa. It lay between Uttar Pradesh to the north and Madhya Pradesh to the south, and the enclave of Datia, which lay a short distance to the west, was surrounded by the state of Madhya Bharat.

Vindhya Pradesh, together with the states of Madhya Bharat and Bhopal, was merged into Madhya Pradesh on November 1, 1956. In 2000, Srinivas Tiwari, speaker of the Madhya Pradesh assembly, advocated that nine districts be separated from Madhya Pradesh to create a new state of Vindhya Pradesh.

Vindhya Range : The Vindhya Range is a range of hills in central India, which geographically separates The Indian subcontinent into northern India (the Indo-Gangetic plain) and Southern India.

The western end of the range rises in eastern Gujarat state, near the border with Madhya Pradesh, and the range runs east and north nearly to the Ganges River at Mirzapur. The southern slopes of the range are drained by the Narmada River, which drains westward to the Arabian Sea in the depression between the Vindhya Range and the parallel Satpura Range to the south. The northern slopes of the range are drained by tributaries of the Ganges, including the Kali Sindh, Parbati, Betwa, and Ken. The Son, a tributary of the Ganges, drains the southern slopes of the range at its eastern end. The Vindhyan tableland is a plateau that lies to the north of the central part of the range. The cities of Bhopal, the capital of Madhya Pradesh, and Indore lie on the tableland, which rises higher than the Indo-Gangetic plain to its north.

Vinoba Bhave : Vinoba Bhave, born Vinayak Narahari Bhave and often called Acharya (In Sanskrit and Hindi means teacher), is considered as a National Teacher of India and the spiritual successor of Mahatma Gandhi.

He was associated with Mahatma Gandhi in the Indian independence movement. In 1932 he was sent to jail by the British colonial government because of his fight against British rule. There he gave a series of talks on the Gita, in his native language Marathi, to his fellow prisoners.

These highly inspiring talks were later published as the book "Talks on the Gita", and it has been translated to many languages both in India and elsewhere. Vinoba felt that the source of these talks was something above and he believed that its influence will endure even if his other works were forgotten. In 1940 he was chosen by Gandhi to be the first Individual Satyagrahi (an Individual standing up for Truth instead of a collective action) against the British rule. Bhave also participated in the Quit India Movement.

Vinoba's religious outlook was very broad and it synthesized the truths of many religions. This can be seen in one of his hymns "Om Tat" which contains symbols of many religions. He was also a scholar of many languages. Vinoba observed the life of the average Indian living in a village and tried to find solutions for the problems he faced with a firm spiritual foundation. This formed the core of his Sarvodaya (Awakening of all potentials) movement. Another example of this is the Bhoodhan (land gift) movement. He walked all across India asking people with land to consider him as one of their sons and so give him a portion of their land which he then distributed to landless poor. Nonviolence and compassion being a hallmark of his philosophy, he also campaigned against the slaughtering of cows.

Violin : Violin is an integral part of Karnatic music. It is one of the foreign instruments adopted by Indian music. Though it is a Western instrument, in Southern India it is tuned in the Indian style. The violin is remarkable for its smooth sweeps from one end of the string to the other.

It is held in a position between the right heel and chest. The left hand moves freely and the fingers of the player have a range of two and a half octaves. Tone of the strings and the facility to play the embellishments peculiar to Indian music have made violin irrevocably Indian. In recent times, north Indian musicians have also started using violin.

Vir Chakra : Vir Chakra is an Indian gallantry award presented for acts of bravery in the battle field. To denote this award, the awardees can append the letters Vr.C. to their name. It is third in precedence in the war time gallantry awards and comes after the Param Vir Chakra and Maha Vir Chakra.

Virachand Gandhi : Virachand Gandhi (1864 - 1901) was the first Jain to arrive in USA and is thus considered to the father of American Jainism. He was a great Jain scholar and a barrister by training. He participated in the World Religions Conference held in Chicago in 1893. His statue today stands in the Jain temple of Chicago. During his travels Virchand Gandhi delivered 535 lectures. He spoke fourteen languages including Gujarati, Hindi, Bengali, English, Sanskrit and French.

Gandhi was the first honorary secretary of the Jain Association of India in 1885 at the age of 21. He worked for the abolition of poll-tax levied on pilgrims to Mt. Shatrunjay, Gujarat. India. In 1891, Mr. Boddam, an English man, started a factory for slaughtering animals near Mt. Sametshikhar, a holy place of Jain pilgrimage. Virchand Gandhi stayed in Calcutta for six months, learned Bengali, prepared his case against the factory, and was successful in getting the factory to close.

Viranatyam : Viranatyam also known as Virabhadra Natyam is a community or the traditional ceremonial dance in Andhra Pradesh, that used to be presented in the Siva and Virabhadra temples when Virasaivism was at its Zenith. Veerabhadra, the destroyer of Daksha's sacrifice is said to be the originator of this dance. Holding a sword in one hand and a shield in another hand the devotee dances and plays steps according to the beat of Viramam. It is a big percussion instrument which produces sharp and piercing sounds. Viramam sounds resembles the sounds of war drums and trumpets and Viranatyam resembles Tandavanrityam in its force and vigour. Dhole, Tashamarpa and Sonmayi are also played during the Viranatyam. At the time of Lingodbhava on the sacred day of Sivaratri, these artistes present Urdhava Tandavam, a special type of dance.

Viranatyam is performed by Viramushti, Jangam, Balija and Devanga communities of Virasaiva cult. In Telangana, Viranatyam is presented by Viramushti and Jangam communities during the festivals in Virabhadreswara temple at Kovari and Kottakonda while offering Virabhadra Palleram to the deity. A big plate with burning oil or camphor flames is held in both the hands from palms up to elbows and shown before the deity as an offering.

The dancers also recite poems called Khadgalu in praise of Virabhadra and his exploits. The artistes wield swords while singing these panegyrics. It is a vigorous and awful dance with long steps and upward movements of legs and hands. In devotional frenzy and fervor, the artistes also pierce their tongues, cheeks, eyelids, throats and lips with spears and spikes of different denominations called Ekanarasam, Kantimarasam, Kanthanarasam and Sulanarasam. They bleed and dance in frenzy. This ceremonial dance has now gained wide popularity as a folk art due to the many nuances introduced in the dance styles.

Virender Singh Sehwag : Virender Singh Sehwag (born 20 October 1978, in Delhi) is an Indian cricketer (batsman) and member of the Indian national cricket team since 1998 (one-dayers) and 2001 (Tests). He was given the vice-captaincy of the Indian team on July 18, 2005.

He has scored over 4,000 ODI runs at a strike rate of 96.98 runs per 100 balls which makes him one of the fastest batsmen in the world. He has also scored over 7,000 runs in first-class cricket at an average of more than 50 with 23 first class centuries.

Visakhapatnam : Visakhapatnam (also Vishakhapatnam, shortened and Anglicized: Vizag or Vizagapatnam) is a Port city in the Indian state of Andhra Pradesh. It is located on the eastern shore of India nestled among the Eastern Ghats Hill Ranges and facing the Bay of Bengal on the East. City is about 650 KM on North-East from Hyderabad.

Alternatively, it sometimes goes by its British colonial name- Waltair. During the colonial era, the city had at its hub the Waltair railway station, and that part of the city still goes by the name of Waltair. The City is home to several state owned heavy industries, has one of the country's largest ports, and its oldest shipyard. It has the only natural harbour on the eastern coast of India. Andhra University, a prominent seat of education in Andhra Pradesh, is located here.

Vizag is primarily an industrial city, apart from being a Tourist Destination. It draws tourists to its unspoilt beaches, nearby scenic Araku valley and Borra caves, the 11th century Simhachalam temple, and ancient Buddhist sites spread across the area. The city boasts a submarine museum, the first of its kind in South East Asia, at Rama Krishna Beach. Visakhapatnam is also the headquarters of the Eastern Naval Command of the Indian Navy.

Vishnu : Vishnu is also known as Mahavishnu, represents Sattvaguna and is the centripetal force as it were responsible for sustenance, protection and maintenance of the created Universe. Another name of Vishnu is Narayana. Vishnu is always described as Nialamegahasyana, of a dark blue hue like than of the rain-bearing cloud.The icon of Vishnu has one face and four arms each one holding Sankha (conch), Chakra (discus), Gada (mace), Padma (lotus) and wears a necklace with the famous gem Kaustubha dangling on the lock of hair Srivatsa, on the left chest. He also wears a garland (of gems or fragrant flowers) Vaijayanti by name. The Sankha represents the five elements like the earth, water etc; chakra stands for the cosmic mind, Gada indicates the cosmic intellect and the Padma points to the evolving world. The curl of hair, Srivatsa, represents all objects of enjoyment, the products of nature. The gem Kaustubha, resting on it, stands for the enjoyer. The garland Vaijayanti is symbolical of the subtle elements.

Vishnu's consort is the beautiful Lakshmi, who came from the sea and is the goddess of wealth, prosperity, honour and love. Vishnu's vehicle is the half man, half-eagle known as the Garuda. Vishnu is supposed to have 10 incarnations (Dasavatara). The incarnations of Vishnu is countless. His complete incarnations are ten in number. They are called Dasavataras (the ten incarnations)

1. In the Matsyavatara, (fish incarnation) the Lord is said to have saved Manu (the progenitor of mankind) and the Saptarsis (the seven sages, mind-born sons of Brahma) along with their wives during the deluge. Once, while Brahma was reciting the Vedas (the scriptures), an asura named Hayagriva stole the Vedas from the side of Brahma and with them he went under water to the bottom of the ocean and hid himself there. So Mahavishnu decided to take the form of a fish to recover the stolen Vedas.

2. Lord Vishnu incarnated himself as the Kurma (the tortoise) is order to support the mount Mandara which started sinking during the churning of the ocean (samudramathana).

3. In Varahavatara (boar incarnation) the Lord killed the demon Hiranyaksa and lifted the earth out of the flood waters in which it had been Submerged. This may be a symbolic representation of the extrication of the world from the deluge of sin by the power of the supreme being.

4. A combination of man and lion, Narasimha represents another form of Vishnu. Narasimha is especially the embodiment of valour which is a divine attribute and hence worshipped by rulers and warriors. When Prahlada, the great devotee of Vishnu was being severely tortured by his father, the demon Hiranyakasipu, Vishnu appeared as Narasimha (man-lion) emerging out of the pillar shown by Hiranyakasipu and killed him.

5. The next incarnation of Vishnu is Vamana (the dwarf). Bali, a demon, achieved supernatural power by asceticism. To protect the world, Vishnu appeared before him in the form of a dwarf and asked him a favour. Bali granted Vishnu as much land as he could cover in three steps. Vishnu then became a giant. With the first and the second steps he covered the earth and heaven and with the third, he pushed down Bali to the pathala (underworld). Hence he is also known as Trivikrama, one who encompassed the world with three big steps.

6. Parasurama is the sixth Avatara born as the son of the sage-couple, Jamadagni and Renuka. He exterminated the tyrannical among the Kshatriyas led by Kartavirya, who were oppressing the people.

7. Sri Rama, one of the two most popular incarnations of the Lord Vishnu, comes next in the series. As told in the Ramayana, Vishnu came in the form of Rama to rescue the world from the demon, Ravana.

8. Balarama, the elder brother of Sri Krishna, is the eighth incarnation. His adventures include the slaying of the ape Dvivida and the demon Dhenuka, shaking the ramparts of Hastinapura (the capital city of the Pandavas) and dragging the river Yamuna out of its course.

9. Sri Krishna, the ninth incarnation of Lord Vishnu, is the most popular. He was the charioteer of Arjuna in the battle of Kurukshetra in Mahabharata. To the Hindus, Sri Krishna is the supreme statesman, warrior, hero, philosopher and teacher. He is the great expounder of the 'song celestial', the Bhagavad Gita.

10. The tenth Avatara is Kalki. It is believed that he will descend upon the earth at the end of the present age (Kali Yuga). Riding on the back of a white horse, with

a drawn sword, he will destroy the enemies of Dharma and re-establish it in all its glory.

The list of incarnations of Vishnu sometimes include Buddha instead of Sri Krishna or Balarama.

Vishnu Prabhakar : Vishnu Prabhakar is a Hindi writer. He has written several short stories, novels, plays and travelogues to his credit. He was born in Mirapur village of Muzaffarnagar district in Uttar Pradesh. He completed his metric from Hisar in 1929 and joined government service. Even with his work he pursued his interest in literature. He also joined a Natak company in Hissar. He wrote in 1939, Hatya Ke Baad, his first play. For some time he took writing as his full time career. After independence he worked as a drama director in Aakashvani, New Delhi. He came into news when in 2005 he threatened to return his Padma Bhushan award after he allegedly had to face misconduct at Rashtrapati Bhavan.

Vishnu Sarma : Vishnu Sarma was the author of the anthropomorphic political treatise called Panchatantra. He lived in Benares at around 200 BC. He was a scholar in Sanskrit and the official Guru of the then princes of Kasi. He started writing down Panchatantra to teach political science to his royal young disciples. The Panchatantra is the oldest collection of Indian fables surviving today.

Vishnu Vaman Shirwadkar : Vishnu Vaman Shirwadkar, popularly known in Maharashtra, India, and in the larger Marathi community as "Kusumagraj", was a well-known and renowned Marathi poet. He belonged to Nashik, loved the city, and so was known as tatyasaheb in the city. He is also good writer. His drama "Natsamrat" is very popular. He is also a honoured by best awards in Literature "Gyanpeeth" for his poetry album "Vishakha".

Vishnukundina : The Vishnukundina dynasty ruled over the eastern Deccan in South India comprising of the area covered by modern day Andhra Pradesh and Kalinga (Orissa. It played an important role in the history of the Deccan during the 5th and 6th centuries C.E.). They are believed to be one of the ancestors of the Raju community.

By 514 C.E., the Vakataka empire was reduced to areas of present day Telangana area. The area north of the Godavari, (Kalinga), became independent. The area south of the Krishna River fell to the Pallavas. The Vishnukundin reign came to an end with the conquest of the eastern Deccan by the Chalukya, Pulakesi II. Pulakesei appointed his brother Kubja Vishnuvardhana as Viceroy to rule over the conquered lands. Vishnuvardhana eventually started the Eastern Chalukya dynasty.

Vishnupad Temple : It is in the center of the town, built over Lord Vishnu's footprint. This footprint imprinted on a rock inside the temple is set in a silver basin. It has a height of 30 meters. The temple is supported by eight rows of beautiful carved pillars which support the pavilion. This pavilion was refurnished in 1787 by Rani Ahalyabai of Indore. The banyan tree under which Buddha meditated for 6 years is still seen here.

Vishnupur : Vishnupur (the distance from Kolkata is 132 km), now the headquarters of the subdivision of the same name in Bankura district, is a seat of crafts and culture. For almost a thousand years it was the capital of the Malla kings of Mallabhum, of which Bankura was a part, till their power waned during the times when Mughal rule weakened under the last monarchs of the dynasty.

The patronage of Malla king Veer Hambir and his successors Raja Raghunath Singha and Veer Singha made Vishnupur one of the principal centres of culture in Bengal. Most of the exquisite terracotta temples for which town is justly famous were built during this period. Apart from the unique architecture of the period, Vishnupur is also famous for its terracotta craft and its own Baluchari sarees made of tussar silk. Royal patronage also gave rise to Vishnupuri gharana (school) of Hindustani classical music and the Vishnupur school of painting.

Vishu : Vishu is a festival held in the state of Kerala (and adjoining areas of Tamil Nadu) in India around the first day in the Malayalam month of Medam (April – May). This occasion signifies the Sun's transit to the zodiac Mesha Mesha Raasi as per Indian astrological calculations. This day always falls on April 14 of every year. It is also known as the malayalam new year day and thus the importance of this day to all malayalees regardless of any religion or sect. Similarly this day is celebrated in almost all places in India by the Hindus albeit by different names. In Assam this day is called Bihu, in Punjab Baisakhi and in Tamil Nadu Puthandu.

The festival is marked with offerings to the divine called Vishukkani. The offerings consist of a ritual arrangement in the puja room of auspicious articles like raw rice, fresh linen, golden cucumber, betel leaves, arecanut, metal mirror, the yellow flowers konna (Cassia fistula), and a holy text and coins, in a bell metal vessel called uruli. A lighted bell metal lamp called nilavilakku is also placed alongside. This arrangement is completed by women the previous night. On the day of Vishu, the custom is to wake up at dawn and go to the puja room with the eyes closed so that the Vishukanni is the first thing one sees. The Vishukani is later taken and distributed among the poor people. It is not uncommon for children to burst fireworks after the Vishukanni. The people wear new clothes (kodi vastram) for the occasion and the elders of the family distribute tokens of money to the children, servants and tenants. These tokens are called the Vishukaineetam and are usually in form of coins. People carry on this custom believing that in this way, their children will be blessed with prosperity in future.

Vishu is also a day of feasting, wherein the edibles consist of roughly equal proportions of salty, sweet, sour and bitter items. Feast items include 'Veppampoorasam' (a bitter preparation of neem) and 'Mampazhapachadi' (a sour mango soup). 'Vishu' is equivalent to the harbinger of spring season that ushers in good agricultural produce, symbolizing prosperity and abundance.

Vishva Hindu Parishad (VHP) : The Vishva Hindu Parishad (VHP; "World Hindu Council" in Hindi), is a Hindu nationalist organisation in India, an offshoot of the Rashtriya Swayamsevak Sangh. It was founded in 1964. Its slogan is "Dharmo rakshiti rakshitah", or "By defending what is righteous, you will be protected." Its symbol is a banyan tree.

Vishvanath Temple (Golden Temple) : The most sacred temple in Varanasi is the Vishwanath temple, located at Vishvanath Gali dedicated to Lord Shiva. Hindus believe Shiva lives here, so it's far too holy a place for non-Hindus to view, the followers of other religions are permitted a view from the Naubat Khana (seat of temple choir). The shivalinga at the Vishwanath temple is among one of the 12 Jyotrilingas. The current temple was built in 1776 by Ahalya Bai of Indore with about 800 kg of gold plating on the towers, which gives the temple its colloquial name, Golden Temple. The gold plated spire, was the gift of the Sikh Maharaja Ranjit Singh of Lahore in 1835, more than 50 years later. The well of wisdom or 'Gyan Vapi' which is nearby is believed to have been built by Lord Shiva himself to cool the 'linga' of Vishwanath with water.

Vishwa Karma Puja : This festival takes place on 17th September every year in Sikkim and honour Vishwa Karma—the God of Machines, statues of this deity are put up in temporary sheds called pandals and worshipped especially by those who are involved in handling machines like drivers and mechanics.

Vishwanath Temple : Vishwanath temple, Varanasi, the most famous temple of the city of Varanasi, India, is dedicated to Lord Shiva. The original was supposed to have been built in 1490. In the ensuring years, the temple has been destroyed and rebuilt several times due to demolitions by invaders. The Mughal emperor Akbar allowed the temple to be constructed at Gyan Vapi in 1585 but Aurangzeb ordered its demolition in 1669 and constructed a mosque, which still exists. This mosque has minarets towering 71 metres above the Ganges. The traces of the old temple can be seen behind the mosque. The modern-day temple was built across the road by Ahilya Bai of Indore in 1776.

Visva-Bharati University : Established by Rabindranath Tagore in 1921, the Visva-Bharati University, located at Santiniketan, West Bengal in India is a central university and an institution of national importance. It has several institutes within itself for undergraduate, postgraduate and doctoral studies: Vidya Bhavana (Institute of Humanities), Shiksha Bhavana (Institute of Sciences), Palli-Shiksha Bhavana (Institute of Agricultural Sciences), Binay Bhavana (Institute of Education) and Kala Bhavana (Institute of Fine Arts). In addition, Patha-Bhavana, Shiksha Satra (two elementary and secondary schools) and Uttar Shiksha Sadana (a higher secondary school) also confer certificates of the university.

Viswanathan Anand : Viswanathan Anand is the first Asian to win the World Chess Championship title. He won the title on 24th December 2000, defeating Spain's Alexei Shirovyoungest at Teheran.

Born in Chennai in December 1969, he started playing chess at the age of 6. He learnt chess from his mother Susheela. His parents encouraged him and used to take him to the Tal Chess club. Young Anand had an exceptional memory power and an ability to grasp things fast which made him excel in Chess. Anand got his B.Com degree from Loyola College.

He has won many titles even from a young age. He was the youngest Asian to win the International Master's Title at the age of fifteen. At sixteen he became the National Champion; At eighteen India's First Grandmaster. In 1987, he became the first Asian to win the World Junior Chess Championship. In 1992, he won the formidable Reggio Emilia Tournament. He was the runner up to Kasparov in World Championship final in 1995. He beat Kasparov in the rapid chess tournament in September 96 and Karpov in June 97 in Hamburg Rapid Chess. Anand outplayed the most popular chess software programme, Fritz in July, 99.

Anand has also received many awards; Arjuna Award for Outstanding Indian Sportsman in 1985, Padmashree, National Citizens Award and Soviet Land Nehru Award in 1987, Rajiv Gandhi Khel Ratna Award, Chess Oscar and so on. Anand's wife Aruna supports him in his preparations for the tournaments. This genius, although he has achieved so much still remains simple in character. He wrote a book 'My Best Games of Chess' for which he got the British Chess Federation 'Book of the Year' Award in 1998.

Viswantha Satyanarayana : Viswantha Satyanarayana (1895–1976), popularly known as the Kavi Samraat or the emperor of poetry, was a modern Telugu poet. Born in the village of Nandamuru in the Indian state of Andhra Pradesh, Viswanatha was a disciple of the "Tirupati Venkata Kavulu" duo. Viswanatha's style of poetry was classical in nature and his popular works include Ramayana Kalpa Vrikshamu (A resourceful tree called Ramayana), Kinnersani patalau (Mermaid songs) and Veyipadagalu (A thousand hooded snake). He was awarded the Jnanpith Award and Padma Bhushan in 1970.

Vivekananda Setu : Vivekananda Setu (also known as Bally Bridge) is a bridge over the Hoogli River in West Bengal, India. It links the city of Howrah, at Bally, to its twin city of Kolkata, at Dakhineshwar. The bridge serves both road and rail. The bridge also has sister bridges over the river at different points, namely the Howrah Bridge (Rabindra Setu) and the Vidyasagar Setu.

Vizianagaram : Vizianagaram, sometimes seen as Vizianagram is the main city of the Vizianagaram District of North Eastern Andhra Pradesh in Southern India. Vizianagaram district was formed on the 1st of June 1979, with some parts carved from the neighbouring districts of Srikakulam and Visakhapatnam. The population of the city is 174,324 (agglomeration 195,462) (2001 census). It is located about 18 km inland from the Bay of Bengal, and 40 km northeast of Visakhapatnam. It is also sometimes referred to as the city of education in these parts as there are many colleges and schools here.

V K Gokak : V. K. Gokak (Vinayak Krishna Gokak) (1909-1992) was an author and scholar of Kannada literature. He was awarded the Jnanpith award for his epic Bharatha Sindhu Rashmi.

Bharatha Sindhu Rashmi is perhaps the longest epic written in any language in the 20th Century. It deals with the vedic age. Surprisingly, Gokak was a Professor of English Literature.

V K Krishna Menon : Vengalil Krishnan (V.K.) Krishna Menon (May 3, 1897 - October 6, 1974) was an Indian nationalist and politician. Menon was born at Panniyankara in Calicut, Kerala, into the powerful Vengalil family of South India. He was the grandson of the Raja of Kartanad and the first son of a successful lawyer of the Calicut bar, Komath Krishna Kurup, one of Kerala's richest men at the time. Menon had his early education in

Tellicherry and he took his B.A. degree from Presidency College, Chennai.

While in college, he started taking an active interest in the national movement. While studying in the Law College of Madras, he became involved in Theosophy and actively associated with Annie Besant and the Home Rule Movement. He was a leading member of the 'Brothers of Service', founded by Annie Besant who spotted his gifts and helped him travel to England in 1924.

In London, Menon pursued further education at the London School of Economics and University College London, and at the same time he became a passionate proponent of India's freedom.

In England, he worked hard for Indian independence as a journalist and secretary (1929 - 1947) of the India League, and became associated with fellow Indian nationalist leader Jawaharlal Nehru. After India was granted independence in 1947, Menon was appointed high commissioner to the United Kingd

om, a post in which he remained until 1952. Subsequently, he led the Indian delegation to the United Nations (1952 - 1962), where he adopted a policy of non-alignment, loudly criticizing the United States and voicing support for the People's Republic of China.Even till date Krishna Menon's speech is the longest ever delivered in the Unites Nations Security Council(UNSC). On 23 January 1975 he delivered an unpresidented 8 hour speech on defending india's stand on Kashmir.

Krishna Menon became a member of the Rajya Sabha in 1953. On February 3, 1956, he joined the Union Cabinet as Minister without Portfolio. In 1957 he was elected to the Lok Sabha from Bombay, and in April of that year he was named minister of defence under Prime Minister

Nehru. However, after India's staggering defeat in the Sino-Indian War of 1962, he was removed from office for the country's apparent lack of military preparedness. In 1967 he lost his parliamentary seat but was re-elected in 1969. He died on October 6, 1974 in New Delhi.

V P Menon : Vapal Pangunni Menon was an Indian civil servant who played a vital role in the partition of India and the integration of independent India, during the period 1945-1950. Coming of a background stepped in poverty, Menon had begun as a clerk in the Indian Civil Service, but working assiduously hard, Menon rose through the ranks to become the highest serving Indian officer in British India. In 1946, he was appointed Political Reforms Commissioner to the British Viceroy.

Menon was the political advisor of the last Viceroy of India, Lord Louis Mountbatten. When the interim Government had collapsed due to the rivalry between the Indian National Congress and the Muslim League, Menon had proposed to Mountbatten, Jawaharlal Nehru and Sardar Vallabhbhai Patel, the Indian leaders, the plan to partition India into two independent nations—India and Pakistan. Menon's resourcefulness during this period caught the eye of Sardar Patel, who would become the Deputy Prime Minister of India in 1947.

After the independence of India, Menon became the secretary of the Ministry of the States, headed by Sardar Vallabhbhai Patel, with whom he had developed a bond of trust. Patel respected Menon's political genius and work ethic, while Menon obtained the respect for his work that a civil servant needs from his political superior. Menon worked closely with Patel over the integration of over 500 princely states into the union of India, managing the diplomacy between the States Ministry and the various Indian princes, acting as Patel's envoy and striking deals with reluctant princes and rulers. Patel respected Menon's ingenuity in diplomacy, and often did not question if Menon exceeded any instructions. Menon also worked with Patel over the military action against the hostile states of Junagadh and Hyderabad, as well as advising Nehru and Patel on relations with Pakistan and the Kashmir conflict. The Cabinet had dispatched Menon to obtain the accession of Kashmir into India in 1947.

V P Singh : Born on June 25, 1931 at Allahabad, Shri V.P. Singh is the son of Raja Bahadur Ram Gopal Singh. He was educated at Allahabad and Poona Universities. He was married to Smt. Sita Kumari on June 25, 1955 and has two sons.

A scholarly man, he was the proud founder of Gopal Vidyalaya, Intermediate College, Koraon, Allahabad. He was the President of the Students Union at Udai Pratap College, Varanasi in 1947-48 and was the Vice-President, Allahabad University Students Union. He actively participated in Bhoodan movement in 1957 and donated a well-established farm in village Pasna, District Allahabad.

He was the member of All India Congress Committee; Executive Body, Allahabad University, 1969-71 and Legislative Assembly, Uttar Pradesh 1969-71. He was the Whip, Congress Legislative Party, 1970-71; Member of Parliament (Lok Sabha), 1971-74; Union Deputy Minister of Commerce, October 1974-November 1976; Union State Minister of Commerce, November 1976-March 1977; Member of Parliament (Lok Sabha), January 3-July 26,1980. He was the Chief Minister of Uttar Pradesh, June 9, 1980-June 28, 1982; Member, Legislative Council, Uttar Pradesh, November 21, 1980-June 14,1981; Member Legislative Assembly, Uttar Pradesh, June 15, 1981-July 16, 1983.

As a Union Minister of Commerce in January 29,1983, he also held additional charge of the Department of Supply in February 15,1983. He was the Member of Parliament

(Rajya Sabha) in July 16, 1983; on September 1, 1984 he was elected President, Uttar Pradesh Congress Committee and on December 31, 1984 he became the Union Finance Minister.

Vrindavan: Vrindavan, in Mathura district, Uttar Pradesh is a town on the site of the original forest of Vrindavana. It is about 15km away from Mathura city, near the Agra-Delhi highway. Also known by the name Vrindaban, Brindavan, or Brindavana, or Brindaban it is the site of the original mythic forest or forested region, in which the Hindu deity Krishna spent his childhood. He was raised there in the cowherding village of Gokula by foster parents.

Two major categories of the stories of Krishna are placed in this forest. First, there are the stories of him as a child, killing demons, stealing butter and indulging in childhood pranks. Secondly, there are the stories of him as a young man, playing with the girls and young women of the village. These inspired the works of the Gita Govinda.

In later times the name of the forest has often been used within Hindu India, to represent an idyllic place or garden. It is the location of many ancient and several modern temples and religious institutions based on the connections with Krishna's childhood. It is the most important Vaishnava place of pilgrimage and is the theological center for many forms of Vaishnava Theology, including Gaudiya Vaishnava Theology.

V Shanta: Dr.V. Shanta's medical life which spans over 50 years has been dedicated to organising care for cancer patients, the study of the disease, its prevention and control, and intensive research. In her association with the Cancer Institute (WIA), Adyar, Chennai, since 1955, she has played a pioneering role in all of its achievements. She was responsible for the recognition and practice of Medical Oncology as a speciality, and the creation of a separate medical oncology division in the institute, the first of its kind in the country. Key positions, as director of WIA from 1980-1997, and innumerable awards including the Padma Shri in 1986, besides 95 papers published in national and international journals, and many prestigious orations worldwide comprise her illustrious career. Dr.V. Shanta, honorary chairperson, WIA

She is a member of the World Health Organisation's Advisory Committee on Health and has been on several national and international committees on health and medicine. But for her the real reward is the joy of those who return home cured.

Vyasa : Vyasa or Veda Vyasa is an important and much revered figure in the Hindu tradition and its literature. He is considered to be an ideal Brahmarishi- omniscient, truthful, purest of the pure and possessor of knowledge of the essence of Brahman.

Vykathu Ashtami : The festival is celebrated in the month of Vrischigam (Nov-Dec) in the well known Siva shrine at Vykam in Kerala. Though the Malayalis take part in it, the majority of pilgrims come from Madura, Tanjore, Trichinopoly, Tirunelvelly. The chief part of the festival consists in the pilgrims worshipping Siva early in the morning before day break. This worship goes on till morning. The Brahmans among the pilgrims is given a grand feast and in the night the God is carried in procession round the temple on richly caparisoned elephant with all the temple paraphernalia. It is considered highly meritorious to worship the god before the sun's rays fall on the copper plate roofing of the temple, so devotees rush to the temple at early dawn.

W

Waghai : Waghai is a town in the Dang District of the southern part of Gujarat state in India. It is about 32 km north from the district headquarter of Ahwa, and about 52 km south of the hill station of Saputara. It is linked by state highway to the town of Chikhali (where the road meets National highway 8), and by a narrow gauge to the town of Billimora.

Wah : Wah is a small town in Punjab, Pakistan. the population of Wah is estimated to be over 500,000. Amenities include a garden said to have been built by the Mughal emperor Akbar in the 16th century. It is connected by road with Peshawar, Islamabad and Rawalpindi and is a growing industrial centre. Wah's industries include one of the largest cement factories in the South Asia, ordnance and tractor plants, and agricultural implements and spare-parts manufacturing.

Wah Cantt : Wah Cantt is located approximately 50 km northwest of Islamabad City. Wah Cantt is located in a valley which is surrounded by hills from all directions. Wah Cantonment is a multicultural city including people from every corner of the Pakistan that are serving here. Most of these are away from their home with one mission and that is to serve the country by strengthening its defense capability. This has been the case since 1951, when the Prime Minster at the time, Khawaja Nazam-u-Din, unveiled the stone of Pakistan Ordnance Factories (POF), a military complex of 14 factories

Waheed Murad : Pakistan film personality Waheed Murad was the producer, writer, and protagonist of many film musicals. The only son of well-off film distributor Mr. Nisar Murad, born on October 2, 1938 at Karachi. He got early education from Karachi Grammar School and did B.A. from S.M. Science College Karachi.

He is best known for the romantic film Armaan. The successful combination of actor Waheed Murad, director Pervaiz Malik, poet Masroor Anwar, musician Sohail Rana and singer Ahmad Rushdi combined to create a number of Pakistan's most successful films during the 1960s and 1970s. He was the first Rock n' Roll dancing star in South Asia.He was also famously known as the "chocolate hero".

Waheguru : Waheguru means "The Wonderful Lord" in the Punjabi language. God has many names in Sikhism and Waheguru is the most important. Others words used by Sikhs for God are: Ek Onkar, Onkar, Satguru, Satnaam (true name), Akal-Purkh, Rabh, Hari, Raam, Pritam and numerous more.

Waheguru (and its variant, Wahguru) is used only 16 times in the Guru Granth Sahib. Of these, Waheguru occurs 9 times on page 1402 and 4 times on page 1403. Wahguru occurs 2 times on page 1403 and 1 time on page 1404. Bhai Gurdas, the first writer of Sikh Guru Granth Sahib, explains in his writings the definition of the word. The V stands for Vishnu, H stands for Hari, R stands for Ram and G stands for Govind. The use of the name of a Hindu avatar does not refer to the avatar itself, but instead is a reference to God.

Wahid Kakar : Wahid Kakar was Chief of Army Staff, Pakistan. President Ghulam Ishaq Khan and Prime Minister

Nawaz Sharif came into public on the appointment of the Chief of Army staff after the sudden death of General Asif Nawaz in January 1993. Nawaz Sharif wanted to place his own candidate in the vacant position, against the wishes of both the army and the President.

Considering Sharif's intentions a direct threat to his political authority, President Ghulam Ishaq Khan used his constitutional privilege effectively to place his candidate, General Abdul Wahid Kakar Commander XII corps in Quetta, as commander-in-chief superseding many seniors. Nawaz Sharif reportedly threatened "not to let the new COAS work". Within 24 hours of a statement by Prime Minister Nawaz Sharif that the appointment of the new COAS would take some time, President Ghulam Ishaq Khan had named General Abdul Waheed as the COAS on January 11. What is more, Nawaz Sharif was told about the new appointment just a few minutes before the ceremony. It was the first public setback to the Prime Minister.

General Wahid Kakar is remembered for starting the Shaheen Nuclear Missile Project. It was Kakar who forced Ghulam Ishaq Khan and Nawaz Sharif to hand over their resignations at the height of the crisis in 1993. In September 1995, General Abdul Waheed Kakar discovered a plot by a group of army officers headed by Major-General Zaheer-ul-Islam Abbasi, acting in complicity with the HUJI an Extremist Group, to assassinate him and Benazir Bhutto, the then prime minister, and capture power.This plan was foiled and those involved captured and arrested.General Abbasi was however released after a few years.

Wai Wai : Wai Wai is a popular snack in Nepal, Sikkim and parts of northern West Bengal in India. Wai Wais are a kind of noodles which are eaten straight from the package or in soup form. Unlike ordinary noodles, wai

wai is pre-cooked, flavoured, seasoned and fried before packaging. On opening, chilli powder, masala (mixed spices) and onion oil which are included in the package are added to give it an additional taste. This is eaten raw or with water in soup form. Wai wais are rich in carbohydrates, minerals and proteins. Chicken and vegetarian flavoured wai wai are the most popular flavours. Wai Wai has gained popularity in about thirty countries around Asia and Europe, with most foreign tourists taking a liking to it and importing it into their respective countries.

Wainganga : The Wainganga is a river of India, which originates in the southern slopes of the Satpura Range, and flows south through Madhya Pradesh and Maharashtra in a very winding course of approximatedly 360 miles. After joining the Wardha, the united stream, known as the Pranhita, ultimately falls into the Godavari. In Rudyard Kipling's Jungle Book the Wainganga is a major landmark for all the people of the jungle. It is the primary source of water, the location of the Peace Rock, the final battleground in "Red Dog", and the place where Shere Khan vows to place Mowgli's bones once he has killed him.

Wakhi Tajiki Language : The Wakhi Tajiki language is an Iranian language in the subbranch of Southeastern Iranian languages. Wakhi Tajiks are also known as Pamiri Tajiks or Mountain Tajiks. The origin of this language is Wakhan in the extreme northeast of Afghanistan. A very rough estimate of the population of Wakhi Tajiks is 50,000 worldwide. Wakhi people live in four different countries. In the northern areas of Pakistan the Wakhi people mainly live in Gojal, Ishkoman, Darkut, and Broghol. They also live in many parts of Tajikistan, Afghanistan, and China. The religion of the Wakhi Tajiks is Shia Ismaili Islam; they are followers of Prince Karim Aga Khan.

Walled City of Lahore : The Walled City of Lahore, also known as the Old City, or Anderoon Shehr, is the section of Lahore, Pakistan that was fortified by a city wall during the Mughal era. Much of the wall remains intact today.

Walluvanad : Walluvanad was a princely state in Kerala state (south India) extending from the Nilá River (Bharathapuzha) in the south to the Panthaloor Mala in the North. On the west, it was bounded by the Sea at Ponnani and on the east by Attapadi Hills. There is a belief that Walluvanad Kings are descendants of a Pallava prince "Sreevallabha". He moved the entire family from Srevilliputhur in north Tamilnadu to the area around the Nila River (Bharathapuzha) about the year AD 300. The eldest person in the family is called Sree Vallabhan or Valluokonathiri. The capital of the easrtwhile Waluvanad was at the present day town of Angadipuram, which is now famous for its Thirumandhamkunnu Temple. During the British period, the capital was moved to Perinthalmanna, a few km from Angadipuram.

Walong : Walong is a small cantonment and administative town in the Lohit District of the state of Arunachal Pradesh in northeastern India. Its approximate position is 28 degrees 06 minutes North, 97 degrees East. It lies on the west bank of the Lohit River (a tributary of the Brahmaputra), approximately 20 kilometres south of the Chinese border. Just north of the border lies the Tibetan trading town of Rima. It is approximately 180 km. by road from the district headquarter town of Tezu. Walong had an Advanced Landing Ground (ALG) capable of taking Otters and Caribous which has now been abandoned. There is an operational helipad. The town is connected to Tezu by a thrice-weekly bus.

In autumn of 1962 Walong was the scene of the Battle of Walong when the outnumbered Indian Army 11th

Infantry Brigade blocked the thrust of the invading Chinese. The Brigade put up a valiant and tenacious defence between 22 October and 16 November 1962 until it was reduced to pitiful remnants, and then withdrew down the valley to Hayuliang. The Chinese, who had suffered large casualties, did not follow up beyond Changwinty.

Wana : Wana is a town in South Waziristan in Pakistan's FATA. It is currently in the eye of a storm because of ongoing joint operations by Pakistan and U.S. forces against alleged Al-Qaeda militant groups hiding in the region. The Pakistan Armed forces have been conducting armed operation against these Al qaeda members since August 2003 off and on. In this respect the armed forces have been quite successful in gradually evicting these embedded elements from their strong holds. These operations are being conducted under enormous pressure from the left hand fundamentalist religious groups, which had earlier been supporting these elements.

Wancho : The Wancho are a tribal people inhabiting the Patkoi Hills of Tirap. They have a population of 35,000. A Naga sub-tribe, they are ethnically related to the Nocte and the Konyak Naga of the Mon and Tirap district. Their language belongs to the Tibeto-Burman family.

Unlike the other Naga, the Wancho are an exception, together with the Nocte and a small minority of the Konyak, still loyally retained the belief of Animism, although small and scattered communities of Baptist Christians are found. Hinduism has little influence on the Wancho tribe, because they live on higher elevations than the Nocte.

Tatooing plays a major role among the Wancho tribe. According to tradition, a man is tatooed on his four limbs and his entire face, with the exception of certain regions around the eyes and the lips. The women adorn themselves with necklaces and bangles, along with some light tatooing as well.

The Wancho are traditionally governed by a council of elderly chieftans, known as Wangchu-Wangcha. Like most neighbouring tribes, the Wancho construct houses made out of wood and bamboo, and roofs were thatched with dry leaves. Dormitories, known as Murung, where the boys are trained to be men by their fathers. Although the girls do not have dormitories like the boys, they sleep in one big, single house, with the care of an old lady.

Wancho Dances : The Wancho tribes in Arunachal perform dances during appropriate occasions like festivals, ceremonies etc. Ozele festival of Wanchos is celebrated in February-March after the sowing of millet. It lasts for four days and was observed in Longkhau village. The dance is performed from about 9 p.m. to 11 p.m. inside the chief's house. Among the male-folk, boys, youths and adults take part while among women, only girls and those young married women who have not joined the husband's family, take part in the dance. The dancers, dressed in their fineries, stand in a circle surrounding a bonfire. The girls stand on one side of the circle holding each other's hands. The male dancers hold a sword in the right hand and most of them place the left hand over the shoulder of the dancer to the left. The male dancers start singing when all take a short step with the right foot to the right, flex the knees with an accompanying forward swing of the sword and gently bring the left foot up to the heel of the right one.

Wangala Dance : In Tripura, after the happy harvest 'Wangala'(1st rice eating ceremony) is performed in every houses. The Sangnakma, head of the communities visits every house and cuts a pumpkin as a part of worship. This pumpkin is sacrificed on this occasion. After that the women dance to the beat of 'Dama' and 'Aaduri' made of buffalo horn. The dance projects the rehearsal for war.

Wankaner Palace : Half way up the hill, overlooking the township of Wankaner on the river Machchhu is the palace of Wankaner, built by Maharana Raj saheb at the beginning of Twentieth century. A few palaces in India equal it on the ground of the scenic beauty, architecture, climate, communication, accommodation & recreation. It is open for exclusive invites to stay as princely house guests receiving personal attention & reliving a bygone era of splendour. The attractions at the palace are the museum of ensigns, relics & antique weapons, beautifully carved beds, chairs of silver, old chariots, Vintage cars etc.

Waqar Younis : Waqar Younis Maitla (born November 16, 1971) is a famous Pakistani cricketer from Burewala, Punjab, one of the greatest fast bowlers the game has ever known and the master of reverse swing. He attended Pakistani College, Sharjah and Government College, Vehari. Playing as a fast bowler, he took 373 Test wickets and 416 wickets in One-day Internationals.

Waraich : Waraich or varaich is a one of the jatt tribes. Mass population of Waraich is found in Majha region in Punjab. Waraich (Warraich) is derivative name from an estate that existed as Bharoch, near Agra. Formerly Bharhaich which then changed over the years to Warraich. They link their origins to Suraj Bansi (Suryavanshi) clan of Aryan Rajput families. Presently they are considered part of the Jatt nations. Settled in areas on the banks of river Chennab in Gujrat, Gujranwala and Sargodha in Pakistan. All the Waraich in Punjab are progeny of three brothers, Hariya, Gunia and Kurtal, rulers of Bharoch.

Warangal : Warangal is a city in Andhra Pradesh state of southeastern India. Warangal is 157 km northeast of the state capital of Hyderabad. Warangal is the administrative seat of Warangal District. It is the fourth-largest city in Andhra Pradesh with a population is 528,570 (agglomeration 577,190) (2001 census).

The city is home to Kakatiya Medical College, Kakatiya University, Kakatiya Institute of Technology and Sciences(KITS-Wgl) and the National Institute of Technology, Warangal (NITW), formerly known as Regional Engineering College, Warangal (REC).

Warangal District has an area of 12,846 km², and a population of 2,818,832 (1991 census). The district is bounded by Karimnagar District to the north, Khammam District to the east and southeast, Nalgonda District to the southwest, and Medak District to the west. Warangal is well known for granite quarries (notably the black and brown varieties), grain market for rice, chillies, cotton, and tobacco

Wardha : Wardha is a city in Maharashtra, India. Wardha gets its name from the Wardha River which flows at the North, West and South boundaries of district. Founded in 1866, it is now an important centre for the cotton trade. It is the administrative center of Wardha District.

Wardha is a sister city for Sevagram, and both were used as major centers for the Indian Independence Movement, especially as headquarters for an annual meet of the Indian National Congress in 1934, and Mahatma Gandhi's Ashram.

The existing Wardha district was part of Nagpur district till 1862. Further it was separated for convenient administrative purpose and Kawatha near Pulgaon was the district Head quarter. In the year 1866, the district head quarter moved at Palakwadi village which is the existing place and then Wardha city is habited there

Wari-Bateshwar : Wari-Bateshwar a significant archaeological site in Bangladesh. Located three kilometres west of Belabo thana of Narshingdi district, Wari (Wari) and Bateshwar (Bateshvar) are two contiguous villages long known for being the find-spot of silver punch-marked coins in Bengal. The villages are situated on the Pleistocene flat surface of the eastern Madhupur tract. A small dried-up river, called Kayra, flows in an east west direction on the northern side of the villages. The landscape of the area suggests that during an early historic period the old Brahmaputra river used to flow near the village. The river has now shifted a few kilometres eastward. The Meghna flows only a few kms to the south of this area and the Arial Khan flows into it. The location of the two villages on a comparatively high, flood-free ground; their proximity to the old Brahmaputra, and access to the Meghna add significance to the site.

Waris Shah : Waris Shah (1719 or 1730–1790) was a Punjabi poet from the Punjab, most well-known for his seminal work Heer Ranjha, based on the traditional folk tale of Heer and her lover Ranjha. Heer is considered one of the quintessential works of classical Punjabi literature. The story of Heer was also put to paper by several other writers, including Damodar Daas, Mukbal, Ahmed Gujjar, but Waris Shah's version is by far the most popular today.

Wasif Ali Wasif : Wasif Ali Wasif (15 Jan 1929 - 18 Jan 1993), was a writer, poet and sufi from Pakistan who was famous for his unique literary style.

He used to write short pieces of prose on topics like life, fear, expectations, happiness, and so on. Probably no contemporary Urdu writer is more cited in quotations then him. Later years he used to answer questions in specially arranged gatherings at Lahore attended by the notable community. Some of these sessions were recorded in audio and were later published as Guftago (talk) series.

Wasim Akram : Wasim Akram (born June 3, 1966 in Lahore) is a former fast bowler for the Pakistani cricket team. At his best, Wasim Akram was one of the finest fast bowlers of his generation.

There were few skills of the fast bowlers armory which he did not have at his disposal: in addition to his genuine pace, pin point control of line and length and seam position he had complete control over both outswing and inswing.

Wasim Sajjad : Wasim Sajjad (b. March 30, 1941) was President of Pakistan on two occasions, serving as interim President prior to elections. Sajjad was born on March 30, 1941 in Jalandhar, Punjab. His father was a justice, and he would follow in his footsteps, becoming a lawyer, and attending Oxford University on a Rhodes Scholarship.

He secured Honors in Jurisprudence in 1966, and a Degree of Bachelor of Civil Law from Oxford University in 1967. He also did a M. A. from Oxford University in 1967. He obtained first position in Administrative Law at Oxford and his Barrister of Law from the Inner Temple, London. At London, Wasim Sajjad was also the President of the Oxford University Islamic Society in 1966, and President of the Oxford University Pakistan Society from 1965 to 1966. He was elected President Oxford University Birkenhead Society 1965-1967, and as Secretary of Wadham College, Oxford, in 1966. He later graduated in 1964.

His political career began in the 1980s when he was elected to the Pakistani Senate. He moved up to Chairman of the Senate, and served his first term as President in 1993, following the resignation of Ghulam Ishaq Khan. As interim president, Sajjad was essentially a placeholder for the office until elections were completed. He would run in the election for President, but was defeated by Farooq Leghari. In 1997, Sajjad was again made interim President and stepped down upon the election of Muhammad Rafiq Tarar. Sajjad continues to serve in the Pakistani government, and is known for his conciliatory nature among parties.

Wayanad : Wayanad is a district, in the north-east of Kerala, India, was formed on November 1, 1980 as the 12th district, carved out of Kozhikode and Kannur districts. Though the etymology of the word Wayanad is popularly known to be Vayal (paddy) Naad (land); 'Land of Paddy Fields', the scholars disagree. The region was known as Mayakshetra (Maya's land) in the earliest records. Mayakshetra evolved into Mayanad and finally to Wayanad. There are many indigenous tribals in this area. It is set high on the majestic Western Ghats with altitudes ranging from 700 to 2100 m. The district is going through its worst agrarian crisis.

Wazirabad : Wazirabad is a town situated on the banks of the Chenab River, in the Gujranwala district of the Punjab, Pakistan. Lying 100km north of Lahore, Wazirabad is an important railway junction on the main line of the North-Western railway. Local industry includes ship-building and steel and iron manufacturing.

Waziri Language : Waziri language is a Southeastern Iranian language spoken in the Waziristan district of Sarhad province of Pakistan and some of the neighboring provinces in Pakistan and Afghanistan. The language can be considered a dialect of the Pushtu language but has some distinctive features and vocabulary.

Waziristan : Waziristan is a mountainous region of northwest Pakistan, bordering Afghanistan and covering some 11 585 km^2 (4,473 mi^2). It comprises the area west and southwest of Peshawar between the Tochi river to the north and the Gomal river to the south, forming part of Pakistan's Federally Administered Tribal Areas. The North-West Frontier Province lies immediately to the east. The region was an independent tribal territory from 1893, remaining outside of British-ruled empire and Afghanistan. Tribal raiding into British-ruled territory was a constant problem for the British, requiring frequent punitive expeditions between 1860 and 1945. The region became part of Pakistan in 1947.

Waziristan is divided into two "agencies", North Waziristan and South Waziristan, with estimated populations (as of 1998) of 361,246 and 429,841 respectively. The two parts have quite distinct characteristics, though both tribes are subgroups of the Waziris and speak a common Waziri language. They have a formidable reputation as warriors and are known for their frequent blood feuds. Traditionally, feuding local Waziri religious leaders have enlisted outsiders in the Pakistani government, and U.S. forces hunting al-Qaeda fugitives, in attempts at score-settling. The tribes are divided into sub-tribes governed by male village elders who meet in a tribal jirga. Socially and religiously Waziristan is an extremely conservative area. Women are carefully guarded, and every household must be headed by a male figure. Tribal cohesiveness is so strong through so-called Collective Responsibility Acts in the Frontier Crimes Regulation.

Waziristan War : The Waziristan War is an armed conflict that began in 2004 when the Pakistani Army began its search for al-Qaeda members in Pakistan's mountainous Waziristan area (or the Federally Administered Tribal Areas). Clashes erupted between the Pakistani troops who are frequently assisted by frequent US precision strikes, and al-Qaeda militants joined by local armed rebels. The struggle there is seen as a part of the US-led War on

Terrorism. In July 2002, Pakistani troops entered the Tirah Valley in Khyber tribal agency, for the first time in 55 years. They preceded to move into the Shawal valley of North Waziristan, and later South Waziristan. This was made possible after long negotiations with various tribes, who reluctantly agreed to allow the military's presence on the assurance that it would bring in funds and development work.

But once the military action started in South Waziristan a number of Waziri sub-tribes took it as an attempt to subjugate them. Attempts to persuade them into handing over the foreign militants failed, and with an apparently mishandling by the authorities, the security campaign against suspected al-Qaeda militants turned into an undeclared war in 2004 between the Pakistani military and the rebel tribesmen.

In March 2004, heavy fighting broke out at Azam Warsak, near the South Waziristan town of Wana, between Pakistani troops and an estimated 400 militants holed up in several fortified settlements. It was speculated that bin Laden's deputy Ayman al-Zawahiri was among those trapped by the Pakistani Army.

The latest turn of events was an U.S. airstrike on the village of Damadola, on January 13, 2006. The attack occurred in the Bajaur tribal area, about 7 km from the Afghan border, and killed at least 18 people. The attack targeted Ayman al-Zawahiri, but he was most probably not there. DNA evidence showed that at least five high-ranking Al Qaeda foreigners were killed, including Midhat Mirsi, a bomb buiding expert, for whom a $5 million award was offered.

West Bengal : West Bengal is a state in the eastern region of India. Neighbouring regions are Nepal to the northwest, Sikkim and Bhutan to the north, Assam to the northeast, Bangladesh to the east, the Bay of Bengal to the south, Orissa to the southwest and Jharkhand and Bihar to the west. Bengal was ruled by the Buddhist Pala dynasty from 750 to 1161. The Palas were eclipsed by the Hindu Sena dynasty, who ruled Bengal from 1095 to 1260. Bengal came under Islamic rule starting in the 13th century, and developed into a wealthy centre of trade and industry under the Mughal Empire during the 16th century. European traders had arrived in the late 15th century and eventually the British East India Company controlled the region by the late 18th century, from which the British extended their rule over all of India.

When Indian independence was achieved in 1947, Bengal was partitioned into predominantly Hindu West Bengal and predominantly Muslim East Bengal. East Bengal later became known as East Pakistan, and became the independent nation of Bangladesh in 1971. On 2 October 1955, Chandannagar, a former enclave of French India which had passed into Indian control after 1950, was integrated into West Bengal state.

West Garo Hills : West Garo Hills is an administrative district in the state of Meghalaya in India. The district headquarters are located at Tura. The district occupies an area of 3714 km^2 and has a population of 515,813 (as of 2001). The name Tura is a British colonialist distortion of Dura or Durama, the guardian goddess of the range of hills by which this town is bounded. In our time the town became famous as the parliamentary constituency from which Purno Agitok Sangma, former Union minister and Lok Sabha (House of the People) Speaker had been repeatedly reelected from 1975. Tura is also the centre of one of the oldest American Baptist missions in India. The church established by this mission in 1868 still occupies pride of place in the middle of the town. Tura has a mixed population of Garos or Achiks (as they prefer to call themselves), Bengalis, Nepalis, Assamese, members of other ethnic groups such as the Hajongs, Rabhas and Koches, Mizos and a fair sprinkling of South Indians in the Catholic Church, the teaching profession and the paramilitary forces.

West Godavari : West Godavari is a district in Andhra Pradesh in India. The headquarters is the town of Eluru. Other important places in the district are Bhimavaram and Tadepalligudem. The district is located in delta region of the Krishna and Godavari rivers. Khammam District lies to the north, East Godavari District to the east, the Bay of Bengal to the south, and Krishna District to the west.

The region is extremely fertile and the local economy is heavily dependent on agriculture. Farmers and estate owners in the area have profited immensely from their paddy crops. Further, the region is well known for its seafood exports. Kolleru lake, one of the largest fresh water lakes in Asia and habitat for up to 50,000 resident and migratory birds, is located partially within the district. The temples in Bhimavaram (Bhimarama) and Palakol (KsheeraRama), part of Pancharama temples, are piligrim centres in West Godavari.

Antarvedi is famous for the temple of Sri Laxmi Narasimha Swamy, built during the 15th -16th centuries. Antarvedi is located 10 km from Narsapur, at the confluence of the Bay of Bengal and Godavari River. The experience of the trip from Narsapur to Antarvedi by a steamer boat during rainy season when the river is flodded with water is memorable.

West India : West India is a region of India consisting of the states of Maharashtra, Gujarat, and Goa, along with the Union Territories of Daman and Diu and Dadra and Nagar Haveli. Maharashtra, in particular, is in many respects intermediate between North India and South India;

but the region has definite particularities of its own. Much of this area was formerly part of the Bombay Presidency. Ganesha is a particularly believed deity in this region. Mumbai is the great metropolis of the region; but there are many other important cities, including Ahmedabad, Surat, and Pune.

West Kameng : West Kameng is a district of Arunachal Pradesh in India. It accounts for 8.86% of the total area of the state. The name is derived from the Kameng river, a tributary of the Brahmaputra, that flows through the district. West Kameng lies approximately between 91° 30' to 92° 40' East longitudes and 26° 54' to 28° 01' North latitudes. The district shares an international border with Tibet in the north, Bhutan in the west, Tawang district in the northwest, and East Kameng district in the east. The southern border is shared with Sonitpur district and Darrang district of Assam.

West Pakistan : West Pakistan was the popular and sometimes official name of the western wing of Pakistan until 1971, when the eastern wing (East Pakistan) became independent as Bangladesh. The politically dominant western wing was composed of three Governor's provinces (North-West Frontier Province, Punjab and Sindh), one Chief Commissioner's province (Balochistan), the Baluchistan States Union, several other princely states (notably Bahawalpur, Chitral, Dir, Hunza, Khairpur and Swat), the Federal Capital Territory (around Karachi) and the tribal areas. The eastern wing formed the single province of East Bengal (including the former Assam district of Sylhet), which despite having half of the population had a disproportionately small number of seats in the Constituent Assembly. This inequality of the two wings and the geographical distance between them was believed to be holding up the adoption of a new constitution.

West Punjab : West Punjab was a former province of Pakistan which existed from 1947 to 1955. The province covered an area of 160,622 km² including much of the current Punjab province and the Islamabad Capital Territory but excluding the former princely state of Bahawalpur. The capital was the city of Lahore and the province was composed of four divisions (Lahore, Sargodha, Multan and Rawalpindi). The province was bordered by the Indian states of Punjab and Jammu and Kashmir to the east, the princely state of Bahawalpur to the south, the provinces of Balochistan and Sindh to the southwest, the Northwest Frontier Province to the northwest, and Azad Kashmir to the northeast.

West Sikkim : West Sikkim is a district of the Indian state of Sikkim. Its capital is Geyzing, also known as Gyalshing. The district is a favourite with trekkers due to the high elevations. Other important towns include Pelling and Jorethang. The district has a wide variety of fauna and flora to offer. Since most of the district is hilly it enjoys a temperate climate. Above 3,800 m (12,000 feet) the slopes are full of rhododendron forests.

West Sikkim also has the ancient capital of the state Yuksom. It served as the capital beginning in 1642 for almost 50 years till it was shifted to Rabtense. The district was under the occupation of the Nepalese for many decades in the eighteenth and nineteenth centuries. After the Gorkha War, the district was returned to Sikkim. The economy is mainly agrarian, despite most of the land being unfit for cultivation owing to the precipitous and rocky slopes. Attractions include the Khecheoperi lake which as legend has it, not a leaf is allowed to fall on the surface of the lake and the Pemyangtse monastery, the first monastery of the state.

Western Ghats : The Western Ghats (or Sahyadri mountains (as they are known in Maharashtra) run along the western edge of India's Deccan Plateau, and separate the plateau from a narrow coastal plain along the Arabian Sea. The range starts south of the Tapti River near the border of Gujarat and Maharashtra, and runs approximately 1600 km through the states of Maharashtra, Goa, Karnataka, Kerala, and Tamil Nadu, to the southern tip of the Indian peninsula. The average elevation is around 900 meters. Higher peaks occur in the northern section of the range in Maharashtra, notably Kalsubai 1646 m (5427 ft), Mahabaleshwar 1438 m (4710 ft) and Harishchandragarh 1424 m (4691 ft); in southwest Karnataka, notably Kudremukh at 1862 m (6,109 ft); and in the southern part of the range, with Anai Mudi in Kerala at 2695 meters (8,842 ft) height the highest peak in the Western Ghats, Chembra Peak in Kerala at 2100m, Banasura Peak in Kerala at 2073m and Vellarimala in Kerala at 2200 meters. The only major gaps in the range are the Goa gap and the Palghat Gap that joins Tamil Nadu to Kerala. Smaller ranges, including the Nilgiri Hills (with Doddabetta being the highest peak at 2623 meters) of northwestern Tamil Nadu and Biligirirangans southeast of Mysore in Karnataka, meet the Shevaroys (Servarayan range) and Tirumala range farther east, linking the Western Ghats to the Eastern Ghats. These ranges of hills serve as important wildlife corridors, allowing species like elephants to move between the ranges.

Western Kshatrapas : The Western Kshatrapas, or Western Satraps, (35-405 CE) were Saka rulers of the western and central part of India (Saurashtra and Malwa : modern Gujarat, Maharashtra, Rajasthan and Madhya Pradesh states). They were contemporaneous with the Kushans who ruled the northern part of the Indian subcontinent, and the Satavahana (Andhra) who ruled in Central India. Altogether, there were 27 independent Kshatrapa rulers during a period of about 350 years. The word Kshatrapa stands for satrap, and its equivalent in

Persian Ksatrapavan, which means viceroy or governor of a province.

White-bellied Sea Eagle : The White-bellied Sea Eagle (Haliaeetus leucogaster) is a large bird of prey in the family Accipitridae which also includes many other diurnal raptors such as kites, buzzards and harriers. It is resident from India through southeast Asia to Australia on coasts and major waterways. This large eagle is very distinctive. The adult has white head, breast underwing coverts and tail.

The upperparts are grey and the black underwing flight feathers contrast with the white coverts. The tail is short and wedge-shaped as with its relatives, the Bald Eagle and White-tailed Eagle.

Wildlife Sanctuaries : Arunachal Pradesh is home to a very rich mammalian wildlife population as the wide variety of altitudinal and climatic conditions have given rise to different forest types which create corresponding natural shelter, food etc. to varieties of wildlife. It has two National Parks and four Wildlife Sanctuaries. It is home to many rare and highly endangered species of Wild life like Mishmi, Takin, Hoolock Gibbon, Musk Deer, Bharal, Hisbid Hare, Flying Squirrel and more than 500 species of birds. In Arunachal Pradesh orchids occur naturally in diverse habitats. In the rich tropical forests of the Tirap district, clusters of the beautiful blue Vanda (Vanda Coerulea) adorn the trees. Their large blue—violet blooms are delicately veined. The bamboo orchid, Arundina Graminifolia, a pretty evergreen species attractive pink—purple flowers is common in open sunny areas near Tipi where an Orchid Research Centre boasts of a good collection of orchids.

William Carey : William Carey (August 17, 1761 – June 9, 1834) was an English missionary and Baptist minister, known as the "father of modern missions." Carey was one of the founders of the Baptist Missionary Society.

As a missionary in Serampore, India, he translated the Bible into Bengali, Sanskrit, and numerous other languages and dialects.

William Stephen Atkinson : William Stephen Atkinson (1820 - 1876) was an Indian lepidopterist. Atkinson lived for many years in Calcutta collecting and painting specimens. His collection was purchased on his death by William Chapman Hewitson and deposited with the Natural History Museum in London. Frederic Moore (1830-1907) published many of the new species found by him.

Willington Island : Willington Island is a man made Island created from the materials dredged while deepening Cochin Port, its in Ernakulam district of Kerala in south India. Its named after the former Viceroy and Governor-General of India, Lord Willington. It is a major artificial port in India, a landmark in the city of Kochi, Kerala. It serves as a link between the other sea ports of the world. Willington Island is connected to the mainland by the road and railway Venduruthy Bridge. Navy headquarters is located in this charming island. Cochin shipyard is also located near this island. It is also a major tourist center. Willington Island today plays an important role in the city of Kochi and houses some of the district's best hotels, commercial and industrial offices.

An artificial lake that was made by the dumping of the materials that were dug out while Cochin Port was being deepened. Willington Island sites some of the district's best hotels. Apart from these, it is here that the airport used to be positioned (till it was moved to present location in Nedumbassery near Kochi) along with the shipbuilding yard, wharf, the Southern Naval Command

Head Quarters and the customs house. Cochin Chamber of Commerce and Industries has been strategically placed here, as is the Government of India Tourist Information Office in the vicinity of the airport. This island is a hub of activity with a number of offices, branches of national and international banks, travel agencies and souvenir shop warehouses and one cannot possibly miss visiting the place while being in the city of Kochi.

Wipro Technologies : Wipro Technologies is the global technology services division of Wipro established in 1980. It has 30 offices worldwide, 50,100 employees and over 300 customers across USA, Europe and Japan including 50 of the Fortune 500 companies. Some of its customers are Boeing, Cisco, Ericsson, IBM, Microsoft, Prudential, Seagate, Sony, and Toshiba. It is listed at New York Stock Exchange and is part of the TMT (technology-media-telecom) index of it.

Wodeyar : The Wodeyar dynasty was an Indian royal dynasty that ruled the Kingdom of Mysore from 1399 to 1947, until the independence of India from British rule and the subsequent unification of British dominions and princely states into the Republic of India. The dynasty was established by Vijaya, who by some accounts came to Mysore from Dwaraka. Vijaya took on the name Yaduraya and ruled Mysore, then a small town, from 1399 to 1423. The Mysore kingdom was ruled by a succession of rulers of the Wodeyar dynasty for the next couple of centuries. However, the kingdom remained fairly small during this period and was not independent, being a subsidiary of the Vijayanagara Empire.

Wokha : Wokha is an important district and urban agglomeration in the state of Nagaland, India. It has a population of around 37,000 people

Wood Inlay : Woodinlay is one of Bihar's ancient industries. The inlay continues to be done with different materials, metal, ivory and, stage horn chips of woods in other grains or tints are used to get varied effects to great advantage. Apart from decorative pieces like wall hanging, tabletops, trays, a number of utility articles are also ornamented with inlay work. Patna also manufactures articles in deaper work utilising waste pieces of wood. The old skill, the experienced eye, the innate taste of the vetran craftsman is seen here in the marvellous objects that are turned out in the way of trays, boxes and other articles far the household. The designs are mostly geometrical but very fine and colourful.

Workers Party of Bangladesh : The Workers Party of Bangladesh is a Communist party in Bangladesh. It is the fraternal party of CPI(M) in the country. WPB was founded in 1980 by the Bangladesh Communist Party (Leninist), Revolutionary Communist League, Majdur Party and another group. Amal Sen was the founding general secretary. In 1984 the party split in two factions, both using the name WPB. One group was led by Amal Sen and Nazrul Islam. They other was led by Rashid Khan Menon In 1992 they reunited. The current president of the party is Rashed Khan Menon.

X

Xuanzang : Xuanzang (602-644/664) was a famous Chinese Buddhist monk. Xuanzang was born near Luoyang, Henan in 602 as Chen Yi. He came from a scholarly family, and had three elder brothers.

He became famous for his seventeen year-long trip to India, during which he studied with many famous Buddhist masters, especially at the famous center of Buddhist learning in Nalanda. When he returned, he brought with him some 657 Sanskrit texts. With the emperor's support, he set up a large translation bureau in Chang'an, drawing students and collaborators from all over East Asia. He is credited with the translation of some 1,330 fascicles of scriptures into Chinese.

The force of his own study, translation and commentary of the texts of these traditions initiated the development of the Faxiang school in East Asia. Although the school itself did not thrive for a long time, its theories regarding perception, consciousness, karma, rebirth, etc. found their way into the doctrines of other more successful schools. Xuanzang's closest and most eminent student was Kuiji who became recognized as the first patriarch of the Faxiang school.

Y

Yadava Dynasty : The Yadava Dynasty ruled a kingdom in what is now Maharashtra, India from the 12th century to the 14th century. The Yadavas were feudatories of the Chalukyas until the late 12th century, when Bhillam (also spelled Bhilama) revolted successfully against the Chalukyas. He established Devagiri as his capital. In 1292 Ramachandra annexed Gujarat. In 1294 the armies of Ala ud din Khilji, Sultan of Delhi surrounded Devagiri, and Ramachandra was forced to pay tribute. Ala ud din captured Gujarat in 1297–98. Ramachandra's successor Shankaragana refused to pay tribute, and the Sultanate captured the kingdom in 1311. The Yadava kingdom was revived briefly by Ramachandra II, before being finally captured by the Sultanate in 1318.

Yahya Khan : Agha Muhammad Yahya Khan (February 4, 1917 – August 10, 1980) was the President of Pakistan and Chief of Army Staff from 1969 to 1971, following the resignation of Ayub Khan. His rule was characterized by tensions in East Pakistan in the early 1970s that finally led to its secession following the Bangladesh Liberation War. The twin failures, the dismemberment of the nation and the military defeat at the hands of arch rival India, forced him to resign and hand over power to Zulfiqar Ali Bhutto.

Yahya Khan was born in Chakwal in 1917 to a family of Persian speaking soldiers. He attended Punjab University and finished first in his class. He then joined the British Army, and served in World War II as an officer in the British Indian 4th Division. He served in Iraq, Italy, and North Africa.

Later anger over its humiliating defeat by India boiled into street demonstrations throughout Pakistan, rumors of an impending coup d'état by younger army officers against the government of President Mohammed Agha Yahya Khan swept the country. Yahya became the highest-ranking casualty of the war: to forestall further unrest, he hastily surrendered his powers to Zulfikar Ali Bhutto, age 43, the ambitious leader of West Pakistan's powerful People's Party. Yahya Khan died in August 1980, in Rawalpindi.

Yajurveda : The Yajurveda (Sanskrit yajurveda, a tatpurusha compound of yajus "sacrifice" + veda "knowledge") is one of the four Hindu Vedas; it contains religious texts focussing on liturgy and ritual. The Yajurveda was written sometime during the Vedic period between 1500 BC and 500 BC, along with the other Vedas.

Yakshagana : Yakshagana is believed to have a history of one thousand years. Yakshagana is believed to have represented a specific type of music of the 'yakhas'. Yaksha is the name of certain demi-gods attending on 'Kubera'- the god of wealth in the Hindu mythology. 'Gaana' means song. By combining the meaning, the term Yakshagana might mean the 'song of Yakshas'.

Of the 20 districts in Karnataka, Yakshagana has established its firm roots in the districts of Dakshina Kannada, Uttara Kannada, Dharwad, Mysore and Hassan. Based on its technique of presentation, Yakshagana has been broadly classified into 'Mudalapaya' (the custom of the east) and 'Paduvalapaya' (the custom of the west). Popularly known as 'Bayalata' or 'Aata', Mudalapaya is widely practiced in places like Tumkur, Bangalore, Kolar, Mandya, Mysore, Hassan, Chitradurga, Bellary, Dharwad, Bijapur, Gulbarga, Raichur, Bidar and Belgaum.

While Yakshagana of North Karnataka has assumed varied forms like 'Sannata', 'Doddata', 'Krishna Parijatha' and 'Dasarata'. The form of Paduvalapaya' popular extensively in Uttara and Dakshina Kannad districts has been further divided into 'Thenku Tittu' (south) and 'Badagu Tittu' *(north).* Paduvalapaya is practiced in places like Karki, Keladi, Ikkeri, Sagar, Kolluru, Maranakatt, Sankuru, Coondapur, Kotesvara, Kota, Udupi, Dharmasthala, Mangalore, Brahmavara, Suratkal and Saligrama.

Yamini Krishnamurthy : Yamini Krishnamurthy (b. 1940, Chidambaram, Tamilnadu in a Telgu family, is an eminent Indian dancer of Bharatnatyam and Kuchipudi styles of dancing. She was born on a full moon night, and her grandfather named her Yamini Poornatilaka, which means "a beautiful mark on the brow of light." Beginning her dancing debut in 1957 in Chennai, then called Madras, Yamini had led an eventful dancing career. She has the honor of being Asthana Nartaki (resident dancer) of the Tirumala Tirupati Devasthanam. Her dancing career brought her many awards, including the Padma Shree (1968) and the Padma Bhushan (2001), which are among the highest civilian awards of the Republic of India.

Yamuna : Yamuna (sometimes called Jamuna) is a major river of northern India, with a total length of around 1370 km. It is the largest tributary of the Ganga. Its source is at Yamunotri, in the Uttaranchal Himalaya. It flows through the states of Delhi, Haryana and Uttar Pradesh, before merging with the Ganges at Allahabad. The cities of Delhi, Mathura and Agra lie on its banks. The major tributaries of this river are the Tons, Chambal, Betwa, Sindh and Ken; with the Tons being the largest.

There is some evidence indicating Yamuna was a tributary of the Sarasvati river in the ancient past. It chaged its course to east following a tectonic event in north India and became a tributary of the Ganges instead. According to legend the goddess of the river is the sister of the Hindu god of death, Yama and the daughter of Surya, the Sun god. The river Yamuna is also connected to the mythology surrounding the Hindu god Krishna. A little known fact about the Yamuna is that it is the frontier of the Indian elephant. West of the Yamuna, there are no elephants to be found over 900 km of the western Himalayas and their foothills. The forests of the lower Yamuna offer ideal corridors for elephant movement. The principal forests to be found here are of Sal, Khair (Acacia), and Sissoo (Rosewood) trees, and the Chir Pine forests of the Shivalik Hills.

Yamuna Nagar : Yamuna Nagar is an industrial city in the Haryana state of India. It is situated in Yamuna Nagar District The main industries are stainless steel utensil making, Plywood board, Paper, Sugar, Industrial boilers etc. The city has a large paper industry owned by Thapar group of India. Prior to Indian independence the paper factory was owned by British. The city is one of the better developed cities of Haryana and has good educational and medical facilities. It has highest Literacy rate in Haryana as far as education is concerned. A canal of the river Yamuna flows on one side of the city. The river itself marks the boundary of the district with the state of Uttar Pradesh which borders the city on the eastern side of river Yamuna. The neighbouring city being Saharanpur in the state of Uttar Pradesh. In the north the district borders the state of Himachal Pradesh, Sirmaur being the district and the towns of Nahan and Paonta Sahib being the towns nearby. Tajewala headworks from where the Yamuna canal is diverted is also north of the city.

Yamunotri : Yamunotri, the source of the Yamuna River and the seat of the goddess Yamuna, is one of the four sites in India's Char Dham pilgrimage. The Yamunotri temple is located in Uttaranchal, India, a full day's journey from Uttaranchal's main towns — Rishikesh, Haridwar or Dehradun. The actual temple is only accessible by a six kilometer walk from the town of Hanuman Chatti (horses or palanquins are available for rent). The current temple is of recent origin, as past iterations have been destroyed by the weather and elements. Lodging at the temple itself is limited to a few small ashrams and guesthouses. Ritual duties such as the making and distribution of prasad (sanctified offerings) and the supervision of pujas (ritual venerations) are performed by the Uniyal family of pujaris (priests). Unique aspects of ritual practice at the site include hot springs where raw rice is cooked and made into prasad.

Yamunotri Temple : Yamunotri Temple lies in the western region of Garhwal Himalayas. It is situated at a height of 3235m. Goddess Yamuna the river goddess is worshipped here and has special significance in Hindu scriptures. The idol is made of black marble. The river Yamuna emerges from Yamunotri glacier which is at a height of 4420 m near the Kalind mountain. This place was the home of Sage Asit. The temple was constructed by Maharaja Pratap Shah of Tehri Garhwal. A hot sulphur spring pond is situated at Yamunotri close to the temple. Devotees cook potato and rice at this pond and offer to the Goddess.

Yanam : Yanam or Yanaon is a district of the Union territory of Pondicherry and a town in that district. It forms a 30 km2 enclave in the district of East Godavari in Andhra Pradesh. It has a population of 32 000, most of whom speak Telugu and to a meagre extent Tamil. Apart from the town of Yanam itself, the following villages fall under the district's jurisdiction: Agraharam, Darialatippa, Farampeta, Guerempeta, Jambavanpeta, Kanakalapeta, Kurasampeta and Mettakur.

In 1723 Yanam was the third French colony established in India. The colony was abandoned in 1727 because of lack of commercial interest. In 1742 it was re-occupied, and the Mughal emperor issued a decree (firman}, confirming the concessions granted by Salabathjung, the local leader. In 1750 Musaffar Yung, Nizam of Hyderabad, accepted the French claims. The name Yanam is a distorted form of the persian word inam (a granted piece of a land).The town is close to the village of Neelapalli which was under English control. This led to conflicts between the two nations, and during the 18th century Yanam now and then shortly came under English control. It was previously also called as kalyanapuram.Because many andhra people come and do marriages(mainly child marriages)here since french government doenot oppose child marriages. After the British Raj became independent in 1947 Yanam remained under French control till June 13, 1954, when it joined the Republic of India

Yandabu Accord : Yandabu Accord or the Treaty of Yandaboo between the British East India Company and the Burmese King of Ava, signed on February 24, 1826 marked the end of the First Burmese War. By the terms of the treaty, the British took posession of the former independent kingdom of Arakan and the former Siamese (then Burmese) territories of Ye, Tavoy and Mergui typically known as Tennasserim. Financial penalties were implosed on the Burmese kingdom by the treaty and the

Burmese were compelled to accept the presence of the British in their capital. Starting in the later 1700s, the Burmese Kingdom began a period of military expansion in all directions. By the 1820s, the Burmese had reached the borders of British India. Disputes over the affairs of border kingdoms and the activities of anti-Burmese exiles in Indian territory led eventually to war. The signing of Yandaboo treaty effectively ended the war.

Yaosang : In Manipur, Yaosang, the Holi festival is celebrated on the full moon of Lamda (Feb/March). It lasts for six days. One and all in the valley celebrate it. The young boys and girls take active part in this festival. The bamboo huts, 'Yaosangs', are constructed on the roadside. An idol of Chaitanya is placed in the hut by a Brahmin. Puja is offered to the idol. Kirtans and recitations from the holy books are chanted. The idol is removed from the hut and the hut is set on fire. The shouts of 'Hari-Bola' and 'He Hari' are exchanged while the hut is burning. The burnt embers are considered to be very auspicious. Therefore, the ash is collected and used to mark the foreheads of the worshippers and the entrance of the houses. The same thing is performed in the Mandapas of some temples. The entire valley reflects a festive look during the days of Holi.

The real festive show of Holi is celebrated in Govindajee temple. In the Mandapa portion of the temple there are two wells which are kept covered with wooden planks on other days. During the days of Holi these wells are filled with water and the colour powder is mixed, then it is sprayed in playing Holi. Men and women visit the temple Mandapa and play Holi. The music is also played. Songs are sung in praise of Lord Krishna.

Yasin Valley : Yasin Valley is a high mountain valley in the Hindu Kush mountains, in the northwest region of Gilgit in northern Pakistan. Yasin is separated from the

Ishkoman Valley by a high mountain pass. Yasin was originally ruled by the Khushwakhte Dynasty, a collateral line of the Katur Dynasty of Chitral. The Rajas of Yasin were great warriors and fought against the Sikhs and the Dogras of Kashmir, but this house eventually lost power and the ownership of Yasin changed hands several times between the rule of the Mehtar of Chitral, and the Maharaja of Kashmir. Although sparsely populated, Yasin was important because it leads to a high mountain pass, to Yarkhun in Chitral, and then to Broghol Pass, the Wakhan Corridor of Afghanistan, and into Tajikistan. Thus, Yasin could have formed an invasion route from Czarist Russia into India.

Yaska Acharya : Yaska Acharya is a celebrated Sanskrit scholar and grammarian of ancient India. He is believed to have flourished, according to one school as early as during eighth BCE, while according to other, as late as during third century BCE. Acharya Yaska is the author of a well known ancient work on etymology of Sanskrit words, known as Nirukta. He is thought to have succeeded Sakatayana, an old grammarian and expositor of the Vedas, as the latter has mentioned the former in his Nirukta. The Nirukta (etymology) of Yaska is in the form of explanations of words and it formed the basis for later lexicons and dictionaries. It is, in fact, a Vedic glossary of difficult words. The work tells of various attempts to interpret difficult Vedic mythologies. Nirukta (etymology) of Yaska consists of three parts, viz. :(i) Naighantuka, a collection of synonyms; (ii) Naigama, a collection of words peculiar to the Vedas, and (iii) Daivata, words relating to deities and sacrifices.

Yasodharman : Yasodharman was the king of Malwa, in central India, during the early part of the 6th century. The Gupta empire had been weakened by the attacks of the Indo-Hephthalites, known in India as the Hunas, towards the end of the 5th century, which caused it to break up into smaller states. Yasodharman defeated a Huna army in 528, which checked the Huna expansion in India. Twin monolithic pillars at Sondani in Mandsaur District were erected by Yasodharman as a record of his victory.

Yatee : The Yatee, the Apatani rain shield from Arunachal, is made in two parts, held together by long loops of twisted bamboo rope. The top part is rectangular. The second part is a flat rectangular piece that shields the back. Both parts have braided bamboo straps that rest on the forehead. When the top part is not required, it is pushed back to hang suspended from the back shield by two long loops of twisted bamboo rope. Both parts are made with two layers of an open-hexagonal weave, sandwiching a layer of leaves between them. All the edges are held between two half splits of cane tightly bound together.

Yaum-e-azadi : Pakistan Day is observed on 14 Augest. The day on which Pakistan got indepedence from British rule in 1947.

Yavanajataka : The Yavanajataka (Sanskrit for "Saying (Jataka) of the Greeks (Yavanas)") is the earliest writing of Indian astrology. It is a translation from Greek to Sanskrit made by "Yavanesvara" ("Lord of the Greeks") in 149–150 CE, under the rule of the Western Kshatrapa king Rudrakarman I, and then versified 120 years later by Sphujidhwaja.

Yellaramma Jatara : Yellaramma temple is situated in Madapaka in Tanuku Taluk of West Godavari district. Yellaramma Jatara is celebrated on the full moon day in the month of chaitra. Yellaramma is companion of Kakatamma, the famous goddess of Kaktiya monarch. She has four hands, holding a Damaruka and a sword in the two right hands and a trident and a drinking vessel in the two left hands. Below the feet of the deity is the image of an animal identified as a fox by some and a bandicoot by others. Goddess Yellamma (Yellaramma) is worshipped all over Andhra. The Garaga procession of this place is very famous and a fair is also organised. Other temples in the Madapaka like Someswaraswami, Kesavaswami and Srirama Ganapati also celebrate Kalyanotsavams. Someswaraswami Kalyanotswavam is celebrated for five days in the month of Magha. Kesavaswami Kalyanotsavam is celebrated for seven days in the month of phalguna.

Yellu Amavasya : Yellu Amavasya is observed on new moon day in the month of December and it marks the culmination of the Kharif season in Karnataka. On this day the villagers visit the Maruto temple and in the noon the members of the households go to their respective fields taking along with them a variety of dishes like Holige, bread from bajra flour, a vegetable curry, butter, etc. They pick up five smooth stones from their fields and worship them. Later, a small quantity of the various dishes brought by them is thrown in various directions in the field as a symbol of offerings. The members of the family then sit together in their field along with their guests and partake of the food.

Yoga : Yoga is a family of ancient spiritual practices that originated in India, where it remains a vibrant living tradition and is seen as a means to enlightenment. Karma Yoga, Bhakti Yoga, Jnana Yoga, and Raja Yoga are considered the four main yogas, but there are many other types. In other parts of the world where yoga is popular, notably the United States, yoga has become associated with the asanas (postures) of Hatha Yoga, which are popular as fitness exercises. Yoga as a means to enlightenment is central to Hinduism, Buddhism, Sikhism, and Jainism, and has influenced other religious and spiritual practices throughout the world. Important Hindu texts establishing the basis for yoga include the Yoga Sutras of Patanjali, the Bhagavad Gita, and the Hatha Yoga Pradipika.

Yoga Sutras : The Yoga Sutras of Patanjali are one of the six Darshanas of Hindu or Vedic schools and, alongside the Bhagavad Gita and Hatha Yoga Pradipika, are a milestone in the history of Yoga. The book is a set of 195 Aphorisms (sutras), which are short, terse phrases designed to be easy to memorize. Though brief, the Yoga Sutras are an enormously influential work that is just as relevant for yoga philosophy and practice today as it was when it was written. To understand the work's title, it is necessary to consider the meanings of its two component words. The Sanskrit word Yoga, as used by Patanjali, refers to a state of mind where thoughts and feelings are held in check. Sutra means "thread". This is a reference to the thread of a mala, upon which (figuratively speaking) the yoga aphorisms that make up the work's content are strung like beads. For that reason the title is sometimes rendered in English as the Yoga Aphorisms.

The Padma Purana defines a sutra as "A sutra should have few alphabets (alpa-akshara), an unambiguous meaning, be full of essence (sara-yukta), said only after considering all arguments for and against it, infallible and without blemish." Traditionally, the most prominent commentary is that of Vyasa, to whose work Vachaspati Misra has contributed an explanation of Vyasa's commentary.

Yogoda Satsanga Society of India (YSS) : Yogoda Satsanga Society of India (YSS) is a non-profit religious organisation founded by Paramahansa Yogananda in 1917. Its headquarters, Yogoda Satsanga Math, is situated on the banks of the Ganges at Dakshineswar, near Kolkata, with a branch math at Ranchi, Jharkhand and many branch centres. In addition to meditation centres throughout India, there are twenty-three educational institutions, from primary through college level. "Yogoda," a word coined by Paramahansa Yogananda, is derived from Yoga, union, harmony, equilibrium; and da, "that which imparts". "Satsanga" is composed of Sat, truth and Sanga, fellowship. For the west, Paramahansaji translated the Indian name as Self-Realization Fellowship (SRF).

In 1920, he carried India's sacred soul liberating science of Raja Yoga to the West where, in Los Angeles, California, U.S.A., he established the international headquarters of Self-Realization Fellowship (SRF). YSS/SRF is devoted to the spiritual upliftment of mankind. Paramahansa Yogananda dedicated his life to awakening in the hearts of all a deep love for God. He opened the door of his teachings to all persons regardless of race, caste, or religion, and showed them the way, through scientific Raja Yoga techniques of meditation, to realise the Divine and live an ideal balanced life.

Y S Rajasekhara Reddy : Dr. Yeduguri Sandinti Rajasekhara Reddy (born 1949), popularly known as Y.S.R., is the present Chief Minister of the Indian state of Andhra Pradesh. He is known for his forthright speech and frank approach. Dr. Y.S. Rajasekhara Reddy hails from Pulivendula, a small town from Cuddapah district of the Rayalaseema region of Andhra Pradesh.

Dr.Reddy belongs to the Indian National Congress party and was elected to the Andhra Pradesh Legislative Assembly from the Pulivendula Assembly Constituency of Cuddapah District. He has been Chief Minister since May 14, 2004. He served as the leader of the Opposition in the House for the previous term during which N. Chandrababu Naidu was the Chief Minister.

Y.S.R. had an active political career over a quarter of a century and has been representing his party on different fora. He was elected to the Lok Sabha from the Cuddapah constituency four times, and a similar number of times to the Andhra Pradesh State Assembly, from the Pulivendula constituency. He twice served as the APCC President. He remains one of the very few national politicians who have never lost an election.

Younis Khan : Mohammad Younis Khan, (born November 29, 1977 in Mardan, Pakistan) popularly known as Younis Khan is a Pakistani cricketer and member of the Pakistani cricket team since February 2000.

Younis Khan made his international debut in the One-day international (ODI) against Sri Lanka at Karachi in February 2000, and has since played over 120 ODIs for Pakistan. His highest score in Test innings (as of January 2006) came in the third Test against India in March 2005 when he scored 267 off 504 balls in the first innings, to set up a famous series levelling victory in Bangalore. As well as being an accomplished batsman, Younis is also an athletic fielder and occasional leg-spin bowler.

Yuga Purana : The Yuga Purana ("Story of the Ages") is an ancient Indian text, part of the larger Puranas litterature. It is considered as one of the oldest Purana, written before around 250 CE. The Yuga Purana consist in two chapter, within the larger text of the Gargi Samhita (Narrations of Garga), also called Vriddha Gargiya Jyotisha (Astrology of the Sage Garga). It is the most extensive Indian text to describe the invasion of the country by foreign rulers (Indo-Greeks and Indo-Scythians) during the 2nd and 1st century BCE.

Yukta Mookhey : Yukta Mookhey, the 5 feet 11 inches tall Miss World 1999, belongs to a middle class family in Mumbai. The twenty year old lady won the title from among 94 talented contestants in a keenly competitive pageant.

Born in 1979 to parents Inder Lal and Aruna, Yukta's earlier education was in the Gulf because her father's work took the family there. Later settled in Mumbai, she graduated in zoology from Kelkar College, Mumbai. The talented Yukta has won a number of essay and public speaking competitions and wanted to pursue a career in mass communications and computer graphics. On the personal front, Yukta has a passion for music and has studied Hindustani classical music for three years. She likes to go out with friends for a movie or check out on good food in the latest eating joints in town. Interested in modelling she did a few ramp shows for Avon cosmetics, L'oreal and the likes. It was her mother Aruna who runs a grooming workshop at Santa Cruz, who encouraged her to enter the Femina Miss India contest. Yukta firmly believes that it is not just beauty but intelligence that made her what she is today and that anybody can achieve whatever he/she really sets their mind on. This straight forward, serene girl thinks inner beauty is what matters most. She won $ 100,000 and a year of travel around the world in the pageant. Two years after she won the title, Yukta is made her debut in Bollywood, in the Hindi film 'Pyaasa' directed by editor-turned-director A. Muthu, but the movie bombed and no other films are in sight.

Yulo : The Nishis perform a number of religious ceremonies of which one called 'yulo' is important. Yulo is performed for the welfare of the society. The ceremony is marked by a sacrifice of 'mithuns' in which the priest collects the blood of animals in a bamboo tube and hangs it in front of his house as a mark of distinction.

Yuvraj Singh : Yuvraj Singh (born 12 December 1981 in Chandigarh, India) is a cricketer from India, and the son of former Indian fast bowler Yograj Singh. He has been a member of the Indian cricket team since 2000.

Yuvraj made his one-day international debut against Kenya at Nairobi, at the ICC Knock-Out Trophy, and Test debut against New Zealand at Mohali. He showed his potential in his second ODI which was against the Australians where he scored a quickfire 84 off 82 balls against a quality pace attack consisting of bowlers like Glenn McGrath, Brett Lee and Jason Gillespie.

Yuvraj is primarily a left-handed batsman but can bowl part-time left-arm spin. He is one of the better fielders in the Indian team, fielding primarily at point. One of his most memorable innings was a partnership with Mohammad Kaif in the Natwest Series final against England which led India to victory. He scored his first century in his fourth season with the Indian team against Bangladesh. After that he also scored hundreds against Zimbabwe and Australia. In the Indian Oil Cup 2005, he made 110 (of 114 balls) (his third century) and an important partnership worth 165 runs with Mohammad Kaif, to become the man of the match against West Indies in the last match of the round robin league. He scored his first Test century against Pakistan in his second Test at Lahore.

Z

Zafar Iqbal : Zafar Iqbal, is a famous poet of Urdu language, based in Okara, Pakistan. He is known for his innovative style of poetry, in the genre of ghazal. The diction of his ghazal is entirely different from the traditions of Urdu poetry. Which is why he is considered as one of the most controversial poets of sub-continent, being highly popular and unpopular at the same time. He also writes columns in an Urdu newspaper, Daily Jinnah. Zafar is a lawyer by profession.

Zaheer Abbas : Syed Zaheer Abbas Kirmani (born 24 July 1947) is a former Pakistani cricketer. He is rated one of the best batsmen to come from Pakistan. Abbas played his first Test in 1969, and in only his second Test he played an innings of 274 against England, still the fourth highest score by a Pakistani. This was the first of four double-centuries Abbas made; only six men have made more.

He also had great success in first-class cricket, and is the only Asian batsman to have scored one hundred centuries.He also had a long stint playing with Gloucestershire.Zaheer's connection with Gloucestershire began in 1972 when he opted to join the county's cricket team. Gloucestershire life and cricket must have agreed with him because he decided to stay with the club for thirteen years.

Zahir Raihan : Zahir Raihan (1935-1972) was a Bangladeshi novelist, writer and filmmaker. He is perhaps most wellknown for his documentary Stop Genocide made during the Bangladesh Liberation War. He disappeared on December 30, 1971 trying to locate his brother, the famous writer Shahidullah Kaiser, who was captured and killed by the Pakistan army and/or local collaborators during the last days of the war.

Zaib-un-Nissa : Begum Zaib-un-Nissa Hamidullah (December 25, 1921 - September 10, 2000) was a pioneer of Pakistani literature and journalism in English, and also a pioneer of feminism in Pakistan.

She was Pakistan's first female journalist and the founder and editor-publisher of 'The Mirror', a popular Pakistani magazine. Zaibunnisa Street in Karachi was named in her honour.

Zainul Abedin : Zainul Abedin (1914-1976) an artist of exceptional talent and international repute. He played a pioneering role in the modern art movement in Bangladesh that began, by all accounts, with the setting up of the Government Institute of Arts and Crafts (now Institute of Fine Arts) in 1948 in Dhaka of which he was the founding principal. He was well known for his leadership qualities in organising artists and art activities in a place that had practically no recent history of institutional or professional art. It was through the efforts of Zainul Abedin and a few of his colleagues that a tradition of modern art took shape in Bangladesh just within a decade. For his artistic and visionary qualities the title of Shilpacharya has been bestowed on him.

Zainul Abedin's works throughout the fifties and sixties reflected his preference for realism, his aesthetic discipline, his predilection for folk forms and primary colours. Increasingly, however, he came to realise the limitations of folk art its lack of dimensionality, its flat surface, an absence of the intricate relationship between light and shade, and their lack of dynamism. As a way of transcending these limitations, Zainul went back to nature, to rural life, and the daily struggles of man, and to a combination of styles that would be realistic in essence, but modernist in appearance. Zainul's idea of modernism was not confined to merely abstracted, non-representational styles, but to a deeper understanding of the term 'modernity' itself in which social progress and individual dynamism are two leading components.

In 1975, Zainul Abedin set up a folk museum at sonargaon, and a gallery in Mymensingh (Shilpacharya Zainul Abedin Museum) to house some of his works. He became actively involved in a movement to preserve the heritage of Bengal, and reorient Bengal art to the roots of Bengali culture, as he felt the futility of unimaginative copying of western techniques and styles that modern art somehow inspired in a section of the local artists. His health began to deteriorate however, as he developed lung cancer. He died on 28 May 1976 in Dhaka.

Zakat and Ushr Ordinance : The Zakat and Ushr Ordinance was promulgated on June 20, 1980 to empower the government to deduct 2.5% Zakat annually from mainly interest-bearing savings and shares held in the National Investment Trust, the Investment Corporation of Pakistan and other companies of which the majority of shares are owned by the Muslims. Foreign Exchange Bearer Certificate scheme that offered fixed interest was exempted from the compulsory Zakat deduction. This ordinance drew sharp criticism from the Shia sect which was later exempted from the compulsory deduction of Zakat. Even Sunnis were critical of the compulsory deduction and the way Zakat was distributed.

Zakhir Hussain : Zakhir Hussain Alla Rakha Qureishi, one of the most accomplished Tabla player in the world was born in Mumbai on 9 March, 1951.The style and mastery over the Tabla seen in his brilliant performances have established him as a genius in the world of percussion both in India and abroad. This innovator has helped in bridging both the Hindustani and Carnatic traditions as well as the East and the West by performing with North and South Indian masters as well as with western musicians.

Zakir Hussain, son of renowned tabla maestro Ustad Alla Rakha, showed unusual talent on tabla drums as a child. He began his musical career at the age of seven and was touring by the age of twelve. At the age of 19, he accompanied the legendary sitar player, Pandit Ravi Shankar to the United States to perform at the Fillmore East. Three years later, he became the leader of the Tal Vadya Rhythm Band. The group subsequently evolved into the Diga Rhythm Band. In 1976, the band collaborated on a self-titled album with Mickey Hart of Grateful Dead. In 1975, Hussain joined with British guitarist John McLaughlin, Indian violinist L. Shankar and ghatam drummer Vikku Vinayakram to form the east-meets-west super group, 'Shakti'. Although the group disbanded in 1978, they reunited to tour as Remember Shakti in 1998. He founded Moment Records in 1992 which releases recordings and live concerts albums of great masters in Classical music.

In 1987, Zakir's first solo release, 'Making Music', was acclaimed as 'one of the most inspired East-West fusion albums ever recorded'. He has also composed and released many albums with the likes of George Harrison, Van Morrison, Joe Henderson etc and soundtracks of films like 'Apocalyse Now', 'In Custody', 'Little Buddha', 'Heat and Dust' etc for which he was nominated for the best music Director at the 1983 Cannes Film Festival. He arranged the opening music for the 1996 Summer Olympics in Atlanta.

Zakir has received many awards for his contributions to the world of music. In 1988, he became the youngest percussionist to be awarded the title 'Padma Shri' by the Indian government. In 1990, he was awarded the Indo-American Award, in recognition for his outstanding contribution to relations between the United States and India. In 1991, the President of India honoured him with the Sangeet Natak Akademi Award. In 1992, one of the projects 'Planet Drum' that Zakir Hussian did with Mickey Hart, received a Grammy for 'Best World Music Album', the Downbeat Critics Poll for 'Best World Beat Album' and the NARM India Best Seller Award for World Music Recording. This musical maestro continues to tour the world tirelessly in various live concerts. Zakir married to Antonia Minnecola,an Italian American, Kathak dancer and they have two grown daughters, Anisa Qureshi and Isabella Qureshi.

Zakir Husain : Dr. Zakir Husain (February 8, 1897—May 3, 1969) was the third President of India from May 13, 1967 until his death. Hussain was born in Hyderabad, India, where his father had migrated from Uttar Pradesh. He went for higher education to Anglo-Muhammadan Oriental College (now Aligarh Muslim University). He was known even in those days for his love of knowledge, his wit and eloquence and his readiness to help his fellow students.

Zakir Husain, then only 23 and a student of the M.A., was among the small group of students and teachers who decided to establish a National Muslim University and named it Jamia Millia Islamia. Recounting, years later, the impact of Mahatma Gandhi, he said: "I began my public career at the feet of Gandhiji, and he has been my guide and inspirer."

Zakir Husain's unceasing quest for knowledge also took him to Germany in the 1920's. During his three year stay there, he acquired a deep love for European art and literature on music and he also got a Doctorate from the University of Berlin in Economics. In 1963, he was awarded the highest honour of the land, the Bharat Ratna for his great service to the nation. After serving as the Governor of Bihar from 1957 to 1962, and as the Vice President of India for a term of five years, from 1962 to 1967, Dr. Zakir Husain was elected President of India on May 13, 1967. In his deeply moving inaugural speech he said that the whole of India was his home and all its people were his family. He died in office.

Zamindari : Also known as Zamindari, or the Zamindari System were employed by the Mughals to collect taxes from peasants. The practice was continued under British rule. After independence, however, the system was abolished in India and East Pakistan (present day Bangladesh), but is still current in Pakistan.

In the Mughal Era, the Zamindari system was begun to ensure proper collection of taxes during a period when the power and influence of the Mughal emperors was in decline. With the Mughal conquest of Bengal, "zamindar" became a generic title embracing people with different kinds of landholdings and rights that ranged from the autonomous or semi-independent chieftains to the peasant-proprietors. All categories of zamindars under the Mughals were required to perform certain police, judicial and military duties. Zamindars under the Mughals were, in fact, more the public functionaries than revenue collecting agents. Although zamindaris were allowed to be held hereditarily, the holders were not considered to be the proprietors of their estates.

The territorial zamindars had judicial powers. Naturally, judge-magistracy, as an element of state authority conferred status with attendant power, which really made them the lords of their domains. They held regular courts, called zamindari adalat. The courts fetched them not only power and status but some income as well by way of fines, presents and perquisites. The petty zamindars also had some share in the dispensation of civil and criminal justice. The Chowdhurys, who were zamindars in most cases, had authority to deal with the complaints of debts, thefts and petty quarrels and to impose paltry fines.

The Zamindari system was a way of collecting taxes from peasants. The zamindar was considered a lord, and would collect all taxes on his lands and then hand over the collected taxes to the British authorities. The similarities to medieval feudalism are evident. Under the British, they resembled landed gentry and sometimes styled themselves as little kings, or rajas. Some new Zamindars were old Rajas. Many descended from eighteenth century revenue speculators and military adventurers. Several families are of very ancient lineage and had been independent rulers at earlier periods of history. They frequently intermarried with the ruling families of the princely states. Their tenants numbered from dozens to many thousands, and under imperial law, had to pay rent to Zamindars to retain rights to their land.

Zamindari mansions were generally large, spacious homes built of stone and teak wood, with a wraparound porch and rooms leading off from a large central courtyard, although this varied with the region. The mansion was a part of a vast estate. The Zamindari system was mostly abolished in India soon after its independence. The term is usually associated with the aristocracy as zamindars are still considered to be of the landed gentry . Zamindars tend to marry into families of the same social class; however, there have been cases of impoverished nobles marrying into rich families with no titles.

The abolition of the Zamindari system (which divided the society into lords, owners of property, and commoners, users of property) in East Pakistan was a major landmark in Bangladesh's movement to a "people's state". In present day Pakistan the Zamindari System is still present, especially in the provinces of Sindh and Punjab. Zamindars are known by different terms in different provinces. In Sindh, for example, zamindars are known as 'Wadara', while in Punjab, different terms such as 'Chauhdari' and 'Malik' are used.

Zamorin : Zamorin is the anglicised version of Samoothirippadu or Samoothiri, a title of the rulers of the erstwhile Hindu state of Kozhikode (previously known as Calicut), located in the present day state of Kerala, India, between the 14th and 18th century AD. Manavikraman Raja, the Samoothiri of Kozhikode is famous for being the ruler that received the Portuguese explorer Vasco da Gama on May 18, 1498.

The Samoothiri were previously known as the Eradis (rulers of Eranad). Eranad was a small state next to Polanad state, of which Kozhikode was the capital. It is said that during the 14th century, the Samoothiris killed Porlathiri the ruler of Polanad by treachery, and usurped that state. All of this may have been precipitated by the great flood of the Periyar river in about 1341AD. This flood resulted in the silting of the harbour of Kodungallur (anglicised as Cranganore), a town known to be frequented by Arab and Roman and Chinese traders. The silting led to the rise in prosperity of other ports like Kochi (also known as Cochin), and Kozhikode. After acquiring the Polanad state, the Samoothiri turned his attention to other states (nadus) around him. He next annexed the state of Nedunganad. Between 1353-1361 AD, the Samoothiri Raja fought a series of small battles with smaller states called the Thirunavaya War.

The two larger states were Walluvanad and Perumpadappu (also known as Perumpadapu Swaroopam). Walluvanad was the prime producer of rice and agricultural products in Malabar region. As a result of the feud, the Perumpadappu Rajas were forced to move their capital from Thirunavaya to Thiruvanchikkulam, when the Samoothiri captured Thirunavaya. After Thirunavaya was captured, the Samoothiri proclaimed himself as the Rakshapurusha (Malayalam for chief protector) and announced that from then on, he had the sole right of conducting the Mamankam festival - a major Hindu festival of the Bhagvati deity held at Thirunavaya. The Raja then turned to the prospering port state of Kochi. The Perumpadappu Rajas, or rulers of Kochi were forced again to shift their capital from Thiruvanchikkulam to Kochi during 1405 A.D.

The Samoothiri Raja's army then landed via the sea at Ponnani where they built a fort during 1498. Samoothiri continued to battle the Walluvanad Raja without much success. The Kochi Rajas eventually succumbed to the Samoothiri around 1500, and becames his vassals. During December, 1500 the Samoothiri expelled the Portuguese from Kozhikode due to their demand for a monopoly, and they moved to a trading post at the city of Kochi.

The Samoothiris had an interesting tradition which dictated that every Samoothiri who ruled over twelve years would have to publicly cut his throat. In the 17th century, this tradition was modified and led to an annual event where the Samoothiri declared that after an annual 12-day festival (Mamankam festival), it was lawful for anyone wishing, to try to assassinate him. The Samoothiri would be seated in a national assembly, surrounded by guards. This revised tradition led to the development of suicide squads, called chaver, by neighbouring states with the objective of killing the Samoothiri. Although the

Samoothiri received the Portuguese warmly, relations between the two soured soon. This may have begun because the Portuguese at the outset demanded a trade monopoly to be granted to them, and the Arabs to be expelled from Kozhikode.

Vasco da Gama, who was a swordsman by trade had been sent by King Manuel I of Portugal with a fleet of four ships to find the fabled land of India. However, Vasco's fleet was equipped by Captain Bartolomeu Dias, who had previously sailed to the tip of South Africa in 1488, but had to turn back from going onwards to India due to a mutiny on his ship. Diaz, who was used to dealing with African tribes that inhabited the West coast of Africa at that time, equipped the fleet with goods like glass beads, copper bowls, tin bells, tin rings, striped cotton cloth, olive oil, and sugar that had proved useful to him in trade with the tribes. Vasco was not equipped to deal with a sophisticated culture like India at that time, which was used to providing luxury material like cotton calico cloth, spices, pepper to the West.

Hence, Vasco could not offer the Samoothiri any substantial gift, and not having anything worthwhile to trade, he could not purchase the fabulous spices and other luxury goods that were offered to him. This may have led to his frustration with the Samoothiri, which was also reciprocated. However soon afterwards, the Portuguese turned against the Samoothiri. The Samoothiri joined a coalition led by the Muslim Sultan of Gujarat, Mahmud Begara in the Battle of Diu in 1509 to try and defeat the Portuguese. A struggle by the Raja's navy led by his famous admiral, Kunjali Marakkar ensued and lasted several years. Finally the Raja had to allow the first European post in his realm to be established at Chaliyam during 1530. The subsequent Rajas collaborated with the Dutch East India Company to defeat the Portuguese/Kochi coalition during 1661, ensuring the rise of the Dutch in Kerala. The Rajas finally succumbed to the rising power of the state of Mysore, led by Hyder Ali in 1766.

Zangtalam : Zangtalam is a popular Paihte dance performed by men and women in Mizoram. While dancing, the dancers sing responsive song. A drummer is a leader and director of the dance. The duration of the dance depends on the drummer. *Mizo traditional songs and dances* were the common amusements of the people. A Zu party would always be an occasion for songs and dances. The songs were slow and generally sounded mournful. Songs would be accompanied by beat of drums or gongs. The theme would mostly be narration of some events or praise of some hero or former villages, description of some hunt or simply of love. In a gathering of Zu party or on the occasion of marriage or after a successful hunt, one would start the music by reciting a verse and it would be followed by singing of the verse by all others and this would continue in the same sequence for a long time sometimes even throughout the night.

The young Mizos have, in the recent past, taken up western music and dances with great aplomb. In all the villages, groups of young men and women gather in the evening and sing and dance, sometimes the whole night. The only musical instrument used is the Spanish guitar, called ting tang by the Mizo. The young Mizos, both boys and girls, have a very lilting musical voice and they have a natural flair for music. A very recent development is pop music with a composite band which is popular in towns and big villages.

Zanskar : Zanskar is a region in the Kargil district, part of the north-west Indian state of Jammu and Kashmir. The administrative centre is Padum. Zanskar, together with the neighbouring region of Ladakh, formerly belonged to Guge or Western Tibet.

Zarathushtra : Zarathushtra is said to have been born around 6th century B.C in the town of Amui near Rae, on the salt lake Urumiah renamed Razsieh, in Azarbaijan province. He went up the mountains of that province for meditation and preached his faith for many years among hostile tribes. As a young boy, he was placed under able teachers, but they soon found that he was more advanced. Zarathushtra spent several years in meditation and study, pondering over the fundamentals of life and existence trying to find a rational explanation based upon the Law of nature, Asha. He discovers the perfection which lies in the absolute as possessing perfect power or energy and perfect wisdom, which reality he calls 'Ahura Mazda', Lord of Life and Wisdom.

The religion of the Iranian people of his time was a primitive form of polytheism of Indo-Aryan origin. It is partly based on the Rig-Veda. There were many deities and each family had sacred idols. Each tribe had different rituals, sacred obligations and customs. To this Eastern world, Zarathushtra brought a new universal concept of religion. His religion was not a set of superstitious rituals based on fears, but a universal call for a better life to be achieved with the aid of an invisible god of wisdom, truth, light and goodness.

Zarathushtra was the first man who gave a definitely moral character and direction to religion and at the same time, preached the doctrine of monotheism which offered an eternal foundation of reality to goodness an ideal of perfection. Zarathushtra showed the path of freedom to man, the freedom of moral choice, freedom from blind obedience to meaningless injunctions. He preached that the moral worth of deed comes from the goodness of intention and the value of his religion was upholding man in his life of good thoughts, good words and good deeds. Zarathushtra was the first prophet who emancipated religion from the exclusive narrowness of the tribal god.

At the age of seventy-seven, Zarathushtra was killed by a Turanian soldier during an attack on the city of Bulkh. The active heroic aspects of Zoroastrian religion reflects the character of the people. They had zest in life and confidence in their own, strength. They accepted the world in all seriousness. By force of will and deeds of sacrifice, they tried to achieve Haurvatat, wholeness, well-being, in this world and Ameretatat- immortality.

Zatra : Zatra is the Konkani language term for the pilgrimage festivals celebrated at Hindu temples in Goa; the Hindi and Marathi language equivalents are Yatra and Jatra. During the Zatra, the idol(s) or murtis of the Hindu deity or deities are taken out on special procession either in a "Palkhi" (sort of a Palanquin) or in a large, multi-storied chariot called the Rath. Traditionally, every temple observes this festival once a year on the traditional day. All zatras usually occur after Diwali in October and continues until the Shigmo festival in March.

The most famous Zatra of Goa is that of the temple of the Hindu deiy Damodar at Zambaulim, a place located roughly 40 km away from Margao when people walk on burning coals with bare legs. Also occurring during the Zatra is the phenomenon of possession, usually but not exclusively of women, by the spirit of the deity; this is called Bhar, whereby they act as oracles and claim to predict furture events. Outside of Goa, the most famous Zatra is the Rath Yatra of the Jagannath Temple in Puri, Orissa, India, which contributed the word Juggernaut to the English language.

Zebus : Zebus (Bos taurus indicus), sometimes known as 'humped cattle', are better-adapted to tropical environments than other domestic cattle. Their scientific name was originally Bos indicus, but this name is now deemed invalid by ITIS, who classify the zebu under Bos taurus along with all other domestic cattle, and their aurochs ancestors, domesticated in India about 10,000 years ago. The ancient species of Bos nomadicus cattle or even gaur may have contributed to the development of the zebus.

There are some 75 known breeds, split about evenly between African breeds and South Asian ones. The major Zebu cattle breeds of the world include Gyr, Guzerat, Indu-Brazilian, Nellore, Ongole and Brahman.

Zee TV : Zee TV is an India-based satellite television service, which carries broadcasts in Hindi and Urdu. As well as broadcasting in South Asia it also reaches audiences in Europe, the Middle East, Africa, East Asia, Australasia and North America.

Zekhring : The Zekhring are from the Lohit district of Arunachal Pradesh. They live in the hilly terrain and banks of the Lohit River in the Walong and Kibithoo area. They are also known as Charumba, Meyor, Zaiwa. As of 2002, their tribal population stood at 300.

The Zekhring sustain their livehood through agriculture. They are followers of Tibetan Buddhism, blended with traditional Animist beliefs. The Zekhring are ethnically and linguistically related to the Miju Mishmi and Tibetans.

Zemu Glacier : Zemu Glacier is largest and most well known glacier in the Eastern Himalayas. It is about 26 kilometres in length and found at the base of the Khangchendzonga mountain range in Sikkim, India. It may be one of the sources for the Teesta River.

Zenana Mission : Zenana Mission an evangelical movement conceived and organised in Britain with the objective of proselytizing the Bengalis and Indians. The imperial design was to win over the womenfolk culturally, and finally religiously, by giving them western education at home. It was planned that women missionary teachers ought to visit the 'native' Zenana and give them vernacular and English education so as to enable them to question the validity of heathen belief and social practices.

Zeshan Rehman : Zeshan 'Zesh' Rehman (born October 14, 1983 in Birmingham, England) is an English football defender who is a Fulham Football Club player currently on loan to Norwich City in the The Championship and for the Pakistan national football team. He is often referred to as the first Pakistani to play in the Premiership or the best British Asian footballer around—but such titles are often subjective. He made his international debut for Pakistan, on December 7 2005 at Karachi against Sri Lanka.

Zhob : Zhob is small city in Balochistan, Pakistan. Zhob is located on banks of Zhob River and is the capital of Zhob District. The population of Zhob is estimated to be over 425,000.

Zhob means bubbling water. It refers to the Karez water which pops up everywhere when there is no drought situation. The Zhob district is located in the Balochistan province in the north east of Pakistan. It lies close to the Afghanistan border. Zhob town is just east of Zhob river on an open plain. To the north is a ridge, about 150 ft high, on which is a castle from the time when the British colonized the area. In the winter, the weather is cold and the snow is normal. In the summer, although the temperature can get up to 100 degrees Fahrenheit, there is little moisture, so it is not uncomfortable.

Zhob claims historical significance being the crade of the Pashtuns. Qais Abdul Rashid, who is believed to be the progenitor of Pashtus, is said to have lived around the vicinity of Sulaiman Mountains near Zhob, where he is said to have been born in 575 AD and died somewhere 661

AD, the site is known as Takht-e-Sulaiman or "Kas-Ghar" (the mountain of Qais). He is buried near Takht-e-Sulaiman.

Zhob River : Zhob River is located in Balochistan, Pakistan. The meltwater from the Sulaiman Mountains forms Zhob Rivers and it flows through Balochistan and drains into Gomal River. Zhob city is located on banks of Zhob river. The two principal drainage channels of the Zhob district are the Zhob River and the Kundar River, both flow into the Gomal River. The general direction of the rivers is from Southwest to northeast. The Zhob River rises at Tsari Mehtarazai pass, the watershed a distance of about 400 kilometers. The broad plain of the Zhob River is occupied by the alluvial formation. The Kundar River rises from the central and highest point of the TobaKakar range, a few kilometers northeast of the Sakir. It constitutes boundary between Pakistan and Afghanistan territory for a considerable length. The other subsidiary rivers or streams are the Baskan, Chukhan, Sri Toi, Sawar, Surab, etc.

Zia International Airport : Zia International Airport is the largest airport in Bangladesh located in Uttara, Dhaka. It started operation in 1981, and was named after Bangladesh's former president, Ziaur Rahman. It is the hub of Biman Bangladesh Airlines. It has an area of 1981 acres. Nearly 52% of the country's international and domestic arrivals and departures occur through Zia Airport, while country's second largest international airport at Chittagong handles about 17% of the passengers. About 3.8 million international and 0.8 million domestic passengers and 105,000 tons of freight and mail annually pass through Zia International Airport. Zia Airport has terminal buildings, hangars, technical areas, a freight village (warehouse), and other modern equipment for handling aircraft. It connects almost all the major cities of the world with Bangladesh. From here, Biman Bangladesh goes to 31 cities on 4 continents including the USA and Japan.

Ziarat : Ziarat is a district in the north of Balochistan province of Pakistan. Ziarat district was registered in July, 1986. The district has only one Sub-Division (Ziarat) and one Tehsil (Ziarat). Thus Ziarat town (at an altitude of about 2,400 meters) is headquarters of the district of the Sub division, and also of the tehsil. Khilafat Hills are the highest peak with an altitude of 11.400 feet in Ziarat district. The population of Ziarat district is estimated to be over 100,000 in 2005. Over 99% of the people of the area are Muslims. The major tribes of Ziarat are Bugti, Tareen and Dotani.

Ziaur Rahman : Ziaur Rahman (January 19, 1936 – May 30, 1981) was Bangladesh's President. Born in the northern district of Bogra, he came to prominence when he fought in the Bangladesh Liberation War against Pakistan in 1971. He became President of Bangladesh in 1977 and rose to prominence through his efforts for the country's economic development and self-reliance.

Shahid Ziaur Rahman was commissioned in 1955 as a second lieutenant. He served there for two years, and in 1957, he was transferred to East Bengal Regiment. In 1969, he joined the Second East Bengal Regiment as its second-in-command at Joydevpur. He was sent to West Germany for higher training. On his return home in 1970 Ziaur Rahman, then a major, was transferred to Eighth East Bengal Regiment at Chittagong as its second in command. After the military crackdown since the night of 25 March 1971 sheikh mujibur rahman was arrested and the political leaders dispersed. At this crucial moment when the political leadership failed to give any direction, the Eighth East Bengal Regiment under the leadership of Major Ziaur Rahman revolted against the Pakistan Army and took up the Bangladesh flag as its mainstay on the night between 26 and 27 March 1971. Then he took up the momentous decision of declaring the Independence of Bangladesh. Ziaur

Rahman and his troops were in the forefront of the War of Independence. Major Zia and the armed forces under his command kept the Chittagong and Noakhali areas under control for a few days and went across the border for further preparations. Ziaur Rahman played a brilliant role in the War of Liberation both at the level of planning and execution. As the commander of Sector I up to June 1971, later on as the head of Z-Force, Ziaur Rahman distinguished himself as a brave warrior and was offered the gallantry award of Bir Uttam.

On 7 November 1975, Ziaur Rahman was proclaimed the Chief Martial Law Administrator. In a meeting at the army headquarters on the same day, a new administrative set-up for the running of an interim government was arranged with Justice Sayem as the Chief Martial Law Administrator and the three service chiefs, Major General Zia, Air Vice Marshal MG Tawab and Rear Admiral MH Khan, as Deputy Chief Martial Law Administrators. Ziaur Rahman became Chief Martial Law Administrator on 19 November 1976, when Justice Sayem relinquished his position and ultimately, the President of Bangladesh on 21 April 1977, when President Sayem resigned.

Assuming power, Zia immediately moved to restore law and order in the country and for the purpose strengthened the police force, practically doubling its size from 40,000 to 70,000 and arranging for their proper training. He also restored order in the armed forces. On 1 September 1978, a new political party, Bangladesh Nationalist Party (BNP), was launched with Zia as its chairman. The parliamentary elections were held in February 1979 and BNP won 207 seats out of 300. On 1 April 1979, the first session of the Jatiya Sangsad was convened. On 9 April, martial law was lifted after the enactment of the Fifth Amendment. Zia was assassinated in Chittagong on 30 May 1981 in an abortive army coup. He lies buried at Sher-e-Banglanagar, Dhaka.

Zikirs : Zikirs are songs sung by Assamese Muslims to the accompaniment of dancing in circles and clapping of hands. Mohauhau or Mahkheda It is also considered as a festival. In Kamrup district on a full moon night in Nov-Dec, boys in groups go from house to house and sing and dance, striking the ground with bamboo sticks and taking leaps and turns. The ceremony is believed to be helpful in driving away mosquitoes. Apsara-Sabah This is a ceremony in which the nymphs of the air are invoked during calamities and lean times, women with flowing hair dance in circles. The rhythm is provided by striking bamboo sticks on conch-shells or bangles.

Zina (Adultery) Ordinance : Under the Zina Ordinance the provisions relating to adultery were replaced as that the women and the man guilty will be flogged, each of them, with a hundred stripes, if unmarried. And if they are married they shall be stoned to death. It was argued that the section 497 of the Pakistan Penal Code dealing with the offence of adultery provided certain safeguards to the offender in as much as if the adultery is with the consent or connivance of the husband, no offence of adultery was deemed to have been committed in the eye of law. The wife, under the prevailing law, was also not to be punished as abettor. Islamic law knows no such exception.

The women became the special victims of Zia's so called Islamization and its inconsistencies. The Zina Ordinance carried grave injustices and untold miseries on women in Pakistan and prompted bitter international criticism. Women's rights groups helped in the production of a film titled "Who will cast the first stone?" to highlight the oppression and sufferings of women under the Hudood Ordinances. In September 1981, the first conviction and sentence under the Zina Ordinance, of stoning to death for Fehmida and Allah Bakhsh were set aside under national and international pressure.

In many cases, under the Zina Ordinance, a woman who made an allegation of rape was convicted for adultery whilst the rapist was acquitted. This led to a growing demand by jurists and women activists for repealing the Ordinance. In 1983, Safia Bibi, a 13-year-old blind girl, who alleged rape by her employer and his son was convicted for adultery under the Zina Ordinance whilst, the rapists were acquitted. The decision attracted so much publicity and condemnation from the public and the press that the Federal Shariah Court of its own motion, called for the records of the case and ordered that she should be released from prison on her own bond. Subsequently, on appeal, the finding of the trial court was reversed and the conviction was set aside.

In early 1988, another conviction for stoning to death of Shahida Parveen and Muhammad Sarwar sparked bitter public criticism that led to their retrial and acquittal by the Federal Shariah Court. In this case the trial court took the view that notice of divorce by Shahida's former husband, Khushi Muhammad should have been given to the Chairman of the local council, as stipulated under Section-7(3) of the Muslim Family Laws Ordinance, 1961. This section states that any man who divorces his wife must register it with the Union Council. Otherwise, the court concluded that the divorce stood invalidated and the couple became liable to conviction under the Zina ordinance.

The International Commission of Jurists mission to Pakistan in December 1986 called for repealing of certain sections of the Hudood Ordinances relating to crimes and "Islamic" punishments which discriminate against women and non-Muslims. The commission cited an example that a Muslim woman can be convicted on the evidence of a man, and a non-Muslim can be convicted on the evidence of a Muslim, but not vice versa.

Zoji Pass : The Zoji Pass (also Zojila or Zoji-la Pass) is a pass from Srinagar to Ladakh through the western part of the Himalayan mountains. The pass is at 11,600 feet high.

Zoroastrianism : Zoroastrianism is one of the oldest Religion. It explains man's duties in this life and the high destiny which he can achieve by establishing his conduct in accordance with the eternal and immutable law of nature. Zarathushtra the founder of Zoroastrianism called it the law of Asha. Zoroastrianism is based upon the knowledge and illumination and its emblems are the Fire and the Sun.

Zuari River : The Zuari River is the largest river in the state of Goa, India. The Zuari River, with its cerulean waters, has a total length of 34 kilometres. The Zuari originates at Hemad-Barshem in the Western Ghats. The Zuari is also referred to as the Aghanashani in the interior regions. It flows in the southern-western direction through the talukas of Tiswadi, Ponda, Mormugao, Salcete, Sanguem and Quepem.

The Zuari and Mandovi Rivers form the backbone of Goa's agricultural industry. The Cumbarjuem Canal, linking the two rivers has enabled ships navigate to the interior regions to the iron ore mines. The waters of the Mandovi and Zuari both flush out into the Arabian Sea at Cabo Aguada, a common point forming the Marmogoa harbour. The port city of Vasco da Gama lies on the mouth of the Zuari River.

Zulfikar Ali Bhutto : Zulfikar Ali Bhutto (January 5, 1928 – April 4, 1979) was a Pakistani politician, active in the early years of the Pakistani Government. He was the son of Sir Shah Nawaz Bhutto. Bhutto served in the position of President (from 1971 to 1973) and as Prime Minister, from 1973 to 1977, of Pakistan. He has the rare distinction of being a civilian Chief Martial Law Administrator. Deposed in a coup by General Muhammad Zia-ul-Haq, he was hanged on charges of authorizing the murder of a political opponent in 1974.

Zulfiqar Ali Bhutto was born on January 5, 1928. Before his birth he had two brothers: The first one Sikandar whom Z. A. Bhutto never saw as he fell victim to Pneumonia when he was only seven in 1914 and the second one Imdad Ali who also died of Cirrhosis of the lever at the age of 39 in 1953. Zulfiqar Ali Bhutto completed his early education from Bombay's Cathedral High School. In 1947, he joined the University of Southern California, and later the University of California at Berkeley in June 1949. After completing his degree with honors in Political Science at Berkeley in June 1950, he was admitted to Oxford.

Zulfiqar Ali Bhutto married Nusrat Isphahani on September 8, 1951. He was called to Bar at Lincoln's Inn in 1953, and the same year his first child, Benazir Bhutto, was born on June 21. On his return to Pakistan, Bhutto started practicing Law at Dingomal's. In 1958, he joined President Iskander Mirza's Cabinet as Commerce Minister. He was the youngest Minister in Ayub Khans Cabinet. In 1963, he took over the post of Foreign Minister from Muhammad Ali Bogra. His first major achievement was to conclude the Sino-Pakistan boundary agreement on March 2, 1963. In mid 1964, Bhutto helped convince Ayub of the wisdom of establishing closer economic and diplomatic links with Turkey and Iran. The trio later on formed the R. C. D. In June 1966, Bhutto left Ayub's Cabinet over differences concerning the Tashkent Agreement.

Zulfiqar Ali Bhutto launched Pakistan Peoples Party after leaving Ayub's Cabinet. In the general elections held in December 1970, P. P. P. won a large majority in West

Pakistan but failed to reach an agreement with Sheikh Mujib-ur-Rahman, the majority winner from East Pakistan. Following the 1971 War and the separation of East Pakistan, Yahya Khan resigned and Bhutto took over as President and Chief Martial Law Administrator on December 20, 1971.

In early 1972, Bhutto nationalized ten categories of major industries, and withdrew Pakistan from the Commonwealth of Nations and S. E. A. T. O. when Britain and other western countries recognized the new state of Bangladesh. On March 1, he introduced land reforms, and on July 2, 1972, signed the Simla Agreement with India, which paved the way for the return of occupied lands and the release of Pakistani prisoners captured in East Pakistan in the 1971 war. After the National Assembly passed the 1973 Constitution, Bhutto was sworn-in as the Prime Minister of the country.

On December 30, 1973, Bhutto laid the foundation of Pakistan's first steel mill at Pipri, near Karachi. On January 1, 1974, Bhutto nationalized all banks. On February 22, 1974, the second Islamic Summit was inaugurated in Lahore. Heads of States of most of the 38 Islamic countries attended the Summit. Following a political crisis in the country, Bhutto was imprisoned by General Zia-ul-Haq, who imposed Martial Law on July 5, 1977.

On April 4, 1979, the former Prime Minister was hanged, after the Supreme Court upheld the death sentence passed by the Lahore High Court. The High Court had given him the death sentence on charges of murder of the father of a dissident P. P. P. politician. Zulfiqar Ali Bhutto was buried in his ancestral village at Garhi Khuda Baksh, next to his father's grave.

Zunheboto : Zunheboto is the headquarter of a Zunheboto District in Nagaland, India. It is located at an altitude of 1871 metres above sea level, making it the highest district headquarter in Nagaland. Zunheboto recorded a population of 22,809(2001 census) and is the sixth largest urban centre in Nagaland after Dimapur Chumukedima, Kohima, Mokokchung-Yimyu-Alichen, Wokha and Tuensang.